*...get swamped with people, Bangladesh is a rural wonderland laden with waterways, peppered with villages and bursting with humanity.*

(left) Watering Zareen Tea Estate (p140)
(below) Fishing at sunset

a feature of travel in almost any part of south Asia, but it's sometimes coupled with a sense that your new 'friend' may want something from you. In Bangladesh, though, the fascination with you is genuine, and rarely will you suspect an ulterior motive. The tourism industry is in its infancy and foreign visitors are still an unusual sight outside Dhaka. If you enjoy making friends, mixing with the locals and having the opportunity to travel around a country without bumping into too many other foreign faces, then Bangladesh is probably just the place you've been looking for.

## Slow Down

This isn't a destination to be rushed. Poor infrastructure, an undeveloped tourist industry and the ubiquitous language barrier (not as many people speak English here as you might think) mean that you'll often be left frustrated if you're trying to travel in a hurry. So slow down; don't try to pack too much into your itinerary. Bangladesh isn't a tick-the-sights-off-the-list type of country. It's a place to relax, meet people and discover new ideas and ways of life. And for that you need time.

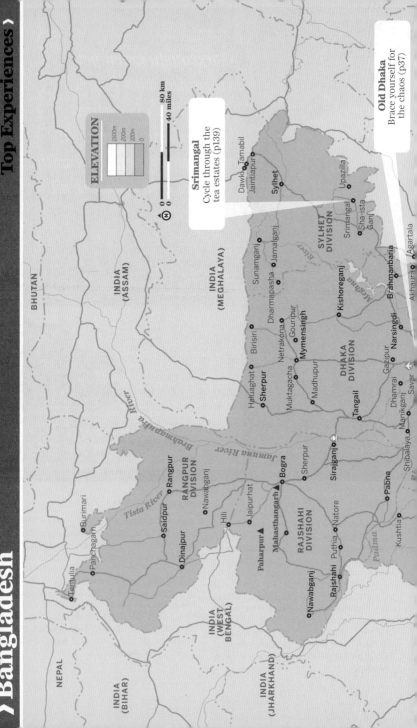

**Srimangal**
Cycle through the tea estates (p139)

**Old Dhaka**
Brace yourself for the chaos (p37)

ELEVATION
1500m
200m
100m
0

80 km
40 miles

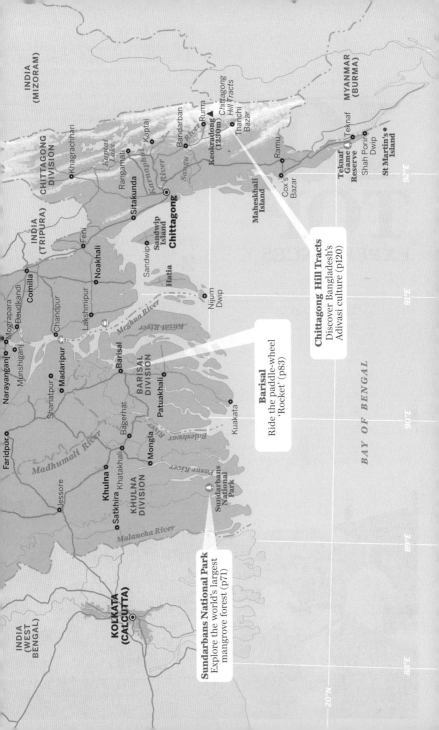

**Sundarbans National Park**
Explore the world's largest mangrove forest (p71)

**Barisal**
Ride the paddle-wheel 'Rocket' (p83)

**Chittagong Hill Tracts**
Discover Bangladesh's Adivasi culture (p120)

INDIA (MIZORAM)

INDIA (TRIPURA)

CHITTAGONG DIVISION

Khagrachhari

Rangamati

Kaptai Lake

Kaptal

Karnaphuli River

Bandarban

Ruma

Sangu River

Keokradong (1230m)

Chittagong Hill Tracts

Thanchi

Bazar

MYANMAR (BURMA)

Teknaf

Teknaf Game Reserve

Shah Porir Dwip

St Martin's Island

92°E

Ramu

Cox's Bazar

Maheskhali Island

Sitakunda

Chittagong

Feni

Noakhali

Sandwip

Sandwip Island

Hatia

Nijum Dwip

INDIA (TRIPURA)

Comilla

Mograpara

Daudkandi

Chandpur

Lakshmipur

Meghna River

Kazal River

Narayanganj

Munshiganj

Madaripur

Shariatpur

Barisal

BARISAL DIVISION

Patuakhali

Kuakata

90°E

Faridpur

Madhumali River

Jessore

Satkhira

Khulna

Khatakhali

KHULNA DIVISION

Bagerhat

Mongla

Balerhwar River

Pasur River

Sundarbans National Park

Malancha River

88°E

INDIA (WEST BENGAL)

KOLKATA (CALCUTTA)

BAY OF BENGAL

91°E

3°E

3°E

20°N

# 10 TOP EXPERIENCES

## River Trips

**1** Rivers are the lifeblood of Bangladesh. Mor than 700 of them criss-cross the country, and travelling along them is an experience not to be missed. From cross-river car ferries or creaking old paddle-wheel steamers to the humble rowboat or traditional wooden yachts, it is said that there are more types of boats in Bangladesh than in any other country. So whether you fancy a multiday adventure deep into the countryside or just a quick jaunt around a city dock, get yourself down to a river ghat, and get involved.

## Tracking Tigers in the Sundarbans

**2** The mangrove forests of the Sundarbans National Park (p71) are home to the larges single population of tigers found anywhere in the world. There are around 400 Royal Bengal tigers roaming the region, and boarding a boat in search of them is an undisputed highlight of a trip to Bangladesh. It's possible to dip into the forest on a self-organised day trip from Mongla but for a true adventure, and to increase your admittedly slim chances of seeing a tiger, book yourself onto a four-day boat tour from Khulna.

## Cycling round Srimangal

**3** Much of Bangladesh is perfect terrain for cycling, but it's only in Srimangal (p139) – the tea-growing capital of Bangladesh – that travellers can easily rent bikes to go exploring. The landscape here is a casual cyclist's dream: hilly enough to be interesting, but not too steep to be exhausting. There are lakes to visit, villages to swing by and forests to free-wheel through – and the gently rolling hills of the surrounding tea estates ensure the scenery is always top notch. Zareen Tea Estate (p140)

## Hiking off the Beaten Track

**4** The country's eastern regions of Sylhet and Chittagong contain forested hills and small, rugged mountains. This is no Himalaya, but the landscape offers plenty of opportunity to stretch your legs with a number of worthwhile hikes on offer. There are relatively simple day hikes you can take from places like Srimangal, but for something more off the beaten track, base yourself in Bandarban, find yourself a good guide and head off in the direction of one of the forested peaks of the Chittagong Hill Tracts. Hills around Bangladesh

## Riding the Rocket

**5** Steeped in almost 100 years of history, Bangladesh's famous paddle-wheel steamer may not be the fastest thing on the waterways these days, but it gets more and more romantic each passing year. There are four remaining Rockets – all built in the early part of the 20th century – and although you can no longer ride them all the way from Dhaka to Khulna, you can still take long overnight trips on them. Book yourself a cabin, put your feet up and watch Bangladesh float by.

## The Locals

**6** Bangladesh isn't the easiest country to travel around. The infrastructure is poor and the travel industry is still in its infancy, but one thing you can be sure of is that whatever difficulties you get into there will always be someone at hand to help you out. Bangladeshis are incredibly warm, welcoming and honest people, and simply meeting the locals and making new friends is one of the highlights of a trip to this part of south Asia.

## Rickshaws

**7** There are cycle-rickshaws all over Asia, but in Bangladesh they're arguably more colourful, more prevalent and more integral to everyday life than anywhere else. Designs are an art form in their own right and riders take great pride in making theirs look best. Almost every town and city has a huge fleet and it's pretty much impossible to avoid travelling on one at some stage. And why would you want to avoid it? They're cheap, fun, environmentally friendly and are often the quickest way to get through the busy streets.

## Hidden Treasures

**8** Modest, unassuming Bangladesh isn't blessed with any of the world-famous, top-draw sights that some of its neighbours are able to boast, but it does contain a number of lesser-known gems, and hunting them down is half the fun. Whether it's a ruined monastery, a tumbledown former mansion, an ancient mosque or a little-visited hilltop temple, plotting a route to these hidden treasures is part of what makes visiting Bangladesh such an adventure. Kantanagar Temple (p98)

## Chittagong Hill Tracts

**9** With most of the country being flat as a paddy field, the forested mountains of the Chittagong Hill Tracts (boxed text p120) dominate the landscape. It's an undoubtedly stunning region, but it also offers a cultural diversity found nowhere else in the country. Around a dozen Adivasi (tribal) groups live here, and more than half the population is Adivasi. Many have closer ties to the people of Myanmar (Burma) than to Bengalis, and visiting their villages to learn about their different ways of life makes a trip out here more than just a chance to gawp at spectacular scenery.

## Old Dhaka

**10** For some, the assault on the senses is too much to handle, but for others, the unrivalled chaos that is squeezed into the narrow streets of Old Dhaka (p37) is the main attraction of a stay in the capital. No matter where you've come from, or what big cities you've visited before, Old Dhaka will knock you for six with its manic streets, its crazy traffic and its nonstop noise and commotion. But the food is fabulous, the historical narrative fascinating and the sheer weight of humanity absolutely unforgettable. Mural, Shankharia Bazar (p38)

# need to know

**Currency**
» Taka (Tk)

**Language**
» Bengali

## When to Go

Bogra
GO Oct–Mar

Sylhet
GO Mar–Nov

Dhaka
GO Oct–Dec

Khulna
GO Oct–Mar

Chittagong
GO Oct–Dec

Tropical climate, wet dry seasons
Warm to hot summers, mild winters

### High Season
(Oct–Mar)

» Cooler temperatures; almost chilly in January and February.

» Dry; the worst of the monsoon has gone; some late rains in October.

» Prices in Cox's Bazar may be inflated.

### Shoulder
(Apr–May)

» Almost unbearably hot temperatures, without the cooling monsoon rains.

» Join honey-harvesters for the honey-collecting season in the Sundarbans.

» Mangos start ripening in May.

### Low Season
(Jun–Sep)

» Monsoon season disrupts plans and sees much of Bangladesh under water.

» Hot, but the rains cool the air.

» Tea-picking season in full swing in Sylhet.

## Your Daily Budget

### Budget less than
# Tk 1000

» Basic accommodation (no air-con, no hot water).

» Eat Bangladeshi food in local restaurants.

» Travel by bus.

### Midrange
# Tk 1000–3000

» Decent rooms with AC and hot water.

» Eat at air-con restaurants serving Chinese, Indian and Bangladeshi food.

» Travel by non-air-con coach.

### Top End over
# Tk 3000

» The best hotel in town, or any half-decent place in Dhaka.

» Eat in your hotel or at restaurants with international cuisine.

» Travel by air-con coach or hire car.

## Money

» Foreign-friendly ATMs in most big towns and cities, but not all. Stock up on *taka* when you can. Take some US dollars for emergencies.

## Visas

» Almost everyone needs them. Maximum stay usually two months, but can extend. Can obtain one-month 'visa on arrival' if arriving at Dhaka airport.

## Mobile Phones

» Easy to use a local SIM as long as your phone is 'unlocked'. No 3G, but can add internet use to SIM-card package.

## Transport

» Cheap and plentiful, buses are the default option, but take trains and boats whenever you can.

## Websites

» **Thorn Tree** (www.lonelyplanet. com/thorntree) The Bangladesh branch has the most current info.

» **Daily Star** (www. thedailystar.net) Bangladesh's best English-language daily.

» **BD News 24** (www. bdnews24.com) Bangladesh's first online newspaper.

» **Bangladesh Railway** (www.railway.gov.bd) Timetables, train fares.

» **Lonely Planet** (www. lonelyplanet.com/ bangladesh) Tips and articles.

» **Radio Dhaka** (www. radiodhaka.net) Live streaming Bangla beats.

## Exchange Rates

| Australia | A$1 | Tk 84 |
|---|---|---|
| Canada | C$1 | Tk 82 |
| Europe | €1 | Tk 106 |
| India | Rs 1 | Tk 1.5 |
| Japan | ¥1 | Tk 1 |
| New Zealand | NZ$1 | Tk 67 |
| UK | £1 | Tk 130 |
| USA | US$ | Tk 82 |

For current exchange rates see www.xe.com

## Important Numbers

To call from outside Bangladesh, dial the Bangladesh country code followed by the city code (minus the leading zero) then the number.

| Country Code | ☏00880 |
|---|---|
| Police | ☏999 |
| Fire | ☏199 |
| Apollo Hospital (Dhaka) | ☏02-8401661 |

## Arriving in Bangladesh

### Hazrat Shahjalal International Airport

» The following prices are estimates for the half-hour journey from Dhaka's airport to Banani in North Dhaka. For more details see p55.

» Local bus – Tk 20

» CNG (auto-rickshaw) – Tk 150

» Taxi from fixed-rate booth – Tk 500

» Taxi from road outside – Tk 300

» Hotel pick-up – Tk 1000

## Don't Leave Home Without...

» A valid visa, if you're staying more than a month or arriving overland

» Loose-fitting, modest clothing

» A hat or headscarf

» Sunscreen and sunglasses

» A torch (flashlight) for power cuts

» A sleeping sheet, for budget hotels

» Mosquito repellent

» Antimalarial drugs, if visiting the Chittagong Hill Tracts

» Some emergency US dollars

# if you like...

## Beaches

Not the first thing you imagine when you think of Bangladesh, but this surprisingly diverse country boasts a handful of decent beaches along its Bay of Bengal coastline, including the world's longest.

**St Martin's Island** Bangladesh's only coral island has much more of a shanty feel to it than flashier Cox's Bazar up the road. You can walk a complete circuit of the island without stepping off sand, and bungalow accommodation adds to the beach-holiday vibe. This is also the only place in the country where you can snorkel and scuba dive. (p128)

**Kuakata** Much less developed than its rivals, Kuakata has a more natural feel to it. You won't find any sun loungers or parasols on the beach here; just wooden fishing boats and washed-up coconuts. (p85)

**Cox's Bazar** The world's longest unbroken natural sand beach (125km) pulls in punters by the beach-bucket load, although it's a bit Costa del Sol for some. (p125)

## Ruins

Kingdoms and religions have come and gone throughout Bengal's long and chequered past, and you'll find ruins scattered across the country, particularly in the northwest.

**Paharpur** Bangladesh's standout archaeological relic, this Unesco-protected site was once the largest Buddhist monastery south of the Himalaya. (p92)

**Puthia** Ancient Hindu temples and crumbling *rajbaris* (mansions) dotted around friendly, tree-shaded villages. (p103)

**Sona Masjid** Discover half the scattered ruins of the lost city of Gaud (the other half is over the border in India). (p102)

**Old Dhaka** Bursting with history, the narrow streets just north of the Buriganga River contain fascinating vestiges of the city's former glories. (p37)

**Painam Nagar** This charmingly decaying street of dilapidated hundred-year-old mansions is the highlight of a trip to Sonargaon, the one-time eastern capital of Bengal. (p59)

## Markets & Bazars

Markets come in all shapes and sizes in Bangladesh, from the huge city-centre clothes bazars of Dhaka to small riverside markets found in pretty much every town.

**New Market** Dhaka's largest market sells absolutely everything. If it's not here, it's not in Bangladesh. (p52)

**Banga Bazar** Dhaka's bargain-bucket clothes market. Don't expect high quality, but do expect some haggling marathons. (p51)

**Bangshal Rd** aka Bicycle St; this Old Dhaka lane is where the capital's multitude of bikes and rickshaws are made, decorated and repaired. (p39)

**Rakhine Market** Just back from the beach at Kuakata, this friendly, colourful market sells clothes and textiles handmade by the descendants of the area's original Buddhist settlers. (p85)

**Rajbari Island Stalls** Just a row of stalls rather than a whole market, this is a great place to buy textiles woven by the Chakma people of the Rangamati region. (p119)

» Strolling around Shiva Temple (p104), Puthia

# Boat Rides

Taking a boat trip is a quintessential Bangladesh experience, but with more than 700 rivers and around 150 different types of boats, where do you begin? Here are some ideas:

**The Rocket** Climb aboard this early 20th-century paddle-wheel steamer and romance your way along the rivers of south Bangladesh. (p26)

**Sundarbans** Don't just dip into the Sundarbans on a day trip from Mongla; explore it properly on a four-day boat ride with a quality tour company. (p71)

**Kaptai Lake** Enjoy the splendid scenery and the awesome expanse of Rangamati's massive artificial lake. (p117)

**Sangu River** For off-the-beaten-track travellers only, just securing a boat ride along this stunning river is a challenge, but the reward for your persever-ance is exceptional natural beauty. (p115)

**City Rivers** For a quick fix of river action, hop on a rowboat at the main ghat of any city and simply cross to the other side. Try Dhaka's Buriganga River. (p43)

# Hiking

Bangladesh isn't all as flat as a rice paddy. The hills to the east, in Sylhet and Chit-tagong, offer some excellent hiking.

**Hum Hum Falls** Remote water-fall, deep inside the monkey-filled Rajkandi Forest Reserve; an adventurous day trip from Srimangal. (p144)

**Boga Lake** Usually possible to do on your own; you'll need two days for a round trip from Bandarban, including the four-hour hike each way to the lake, where you can stay the night. (p115)

**Mt Keokradong** One of Bangladesh's highest peaks, and probably its most climbed; you'll need three days for a round trip from Bandarban. (p122)

**Mowdok Taung** The country's highest peak is right on the border with Myanmar, and you'll need a good guide, a tour operator who can persuade the authorities to give you a permit, and seven days to make the round trip from Bandarban. (p122)

# Wildlife

The man-eating tigers of the Sundarbans steal the head-lines, but Bangladesh has plenty of wildlife besides.

**Royal Bengal tiger** The Sundar-bans National Park has the larg-est single population of tigers in the world. You probably won't see one, of course, but you'll have a lot of fun trying. (p71)

**Hoolock gibbons** Asia's only species of ape, these gibbons are very rare in Bangladesh, but you can sometimes spot them in the forest reserves around Srimangal. (p139)

**Elephants** Most of the wild elephants in Bangladesh are temporary residents, having wandered across the Indian border, but there's a small popu-lation in the forested hills of the Teknaf Game Reserve. (p129)

**Birds** All of Bangladesh is rich in birdlife, but the hard-to-get-to *haors* (wetlands) in northwest-ern Sylhet are like a magnet for bird species, both domestic and migratory. (p138)

# month by month

## January

**Cool and dry, January is one of the more comfortable months, although evenings can get pretty chilly.**

 **Eid Milad un Nabi**
Celebrating the birth of the Prophet Muhammad, mosques around the country hold low-key events. Dates for upcoming years are 24 January 2013; 13 January 2014; and 2 January 2015.

**Bishwa Ijtema** The world's second-largest gathering of Muslims, after the Hajj in Mecca, takes place in two three-day periods in mid- to late January in the north Dhaka suburb of Tongi. Millions line the streets.

 **Chobi Mela** Asia's largest festival of photography is a biennial event organised by DRIK gallery in Dhaka (boxed text p43). The festival usually lasts for two weeks towards the end of January. There are events planned for 2013 and 2015. See www.chobi mela.org for details.

## February

**Similar weather to January; cool and dry. Locals might be wrapping up in hats and scarves, but for most Westerners it's mild rather than cold.**

**Falgun** 13 February marks the beginning of spring for the Bengali calendar. Biggest celebrations are at Dhaka University. Women traditionally wear yellow.

**International Mother Language Day**
Also called National Mourning Day, this solemn occasion on 21 February remembers those killed in 1952 during protests to establish Bengali as an official language of East Pakistan. A large procession moves towards Shaheed Minar, a memorial in Dhaka University.

## March

**The last month before the weather really hots up, March is still an OK time to visit the Sundarbans, the hill tracts and the wetlands.**

 **Holi** Known as Dol Purnima in Bengal, Hinduism's paint-throwing Festival of Colours is best observed in Dhaka's Shankharia Bazar. Will be held on 27 March 2013; 17 March 2014; and 6 March 2015.

**Lalon Utsab** A three-day folk music festival is held in Kushtia during Dol Purnima (Holi) in honour of Lalon Shah, the legendary Baul saint. See p16 for Dol Purnima dates.

**Independence Day**
On 26 March top political leaders and hundreds of visitors go to the National Martyrs' Memorial in Savar, just outside Dhaka, to remember those who lost their lives in the fight for independence.

## April

**It's now too hot for some, although travellers still visit the Sundarbans for honey-collecting trips, and tea picking has begun again in Sylhet.**

### Honey Collecting

The honey-collecting season in the Sundarbans starts on 1 April, and visitors can join special tours that follow bee-sting-hardened honey harvesters into the mangrove forests.

### Boisabi

Celebrated by minority groups in the Chittagong Hill Tracts (who all have different names for it), this three-day festival is held around Bengali New Year in mid-April and sees much eating, drinking (locally brewed rice beers are a favourite tipple) and merriment.

### Bengali New Year

Known locally as Pohela Boishakh. Hundreds of thousands of people gather under the banyan tree in Dhaka's Ramna Park on 14 April to see in the new year before singing, dancing and various processions take place around the city and beyond.

## May

**Really very hot now, with no cooling rains. Best to escape to higher ground in the east of the country if you can.**

### Buddha Purnima

Sometimes called 'Buddha's birthday', this festival actually encompasses the birth, enlightenment and passing away of Gautama Buddha. Good time to be in the Chittagong Hill Tracts, or else at Dharmarajikha Monastery in Dhaka. Upcoming dates

are 25 May 2013; 14 May 2014; and 3 May 2015.

### Nazrul Jayanti

The anniversary of the birth of national poet Kazi Nazrul Islam is celebrated with public readings and songs on 11 May.

### Rabindra Jayanti

The anniversary of the birth of Nobel laureate Rabindranath Tagore is celebrated with public readings and songs on 25 May. It's an interesting time to visit Kushtia.

## June

**Bangladesh breathes a collective sigh of relief with the first rains in June, and the land explodes into life. It doesn't rain all day every day, but sporadic downpours cool the scorching temperatures.**

### Mango Season

May and June is mango season in Bangladesh and markets in west Rajshahi are full of them. The best place to head for is Nawabganj.

## July

**Monsoon rains continue. It's a hit-and-miss time for travel, with unpredictable weather, but the greener-than-green scenery and fabulously moody clouds can be awesome. Tea picking in Sylhet is in full swing.**

### Ramadan

The Muslim month of fasting sees many restaurants either shut

down or change to an *iftar* menu of traditional Ramadan snacks, eaten in the evening. Head to Old Dhaka's Chowk Bazar for evening atmosphere. Starts on 9 July 2013; 28 June 2014; 17 June 2015.

### Rath Jatra

This Hindu festival celebrates Jagannath, lord of the world and a form of Krishna. Images are set upon a jagannath (chariot) and pulled through the streets. Head to Dhamrai, just outside Dhaka. Upcoming dates are 10 July 2013; 29 June 2014; and 18 July 2015.

## August

**The hottest days have now passed, but along with September, this is flood season and huge swathes of Bangladesh disappear underwater, making travel extremely unpredictable.**

### Day of Mourning

15 August, a day to mourn the 1975 assassination of Bangladesh's founder, Sheikh Mujib Rahman. It's a national holiday when the Awami League is in power; at other times flags are flown at half-mast.

### Eid ul Fitr

The Muslim festival that celebrates the end of Ramadan is marked by alms-giving, prayer and feasting. Greet people with 'Eid Mubarrak!'. Upcoming dates: 8 August 2013; 28 July 2014; 17 July 2015.

# September

**Flooding continues, although the worst of the monsoon rains are over. Sylhet's tea estates are lush and active. Temperatures are still hot, but not ridiculously so.**

### Janmasti

Sometimes in August, sometimes in September, this Hindu festival celebrates the birth of Krishna, an avatar of the god Vishnu. Thousands of devotees descend on Dhaka's Dhakeswari Temple.

# October

**The start of the best time to visit. Late rains sometimes spoil plans but generally the weather is dry and comfortable. From now until March is ideal for the wetlands, the hill tracts and the Sundarbans.**

### Eid ul Adha

The Muslim Festival of Sacrifice remembers Abraham's sacrifice of his son Ishmael, and is celebrated with mass morning prayers followed by the slaughter of a cow, sheep or goat. Expect blood-strewn streets. Upcoming dates are 15 October 2013; 4 October 2014; and 23 September 2015.

### Durga Puja

Loud and colourful six-day Hindu festival celebrating the worship of the Hindu goddess Durga. Effigies are built and paraded through Dhaka's Shankharia Bazar before being dumped in the Buriganga River on the final day. Upcoming dates are 9 October 2013; 29 September 2014; and 17 October 2015.

### Lalon Utsab

The second of the two annual, three-day folk-music festivals held in honour of the greatest Baul of them all, Lalon Shah. This one marks the anniversary of his death. Head to Kushtia on 17 October.

# November

**Weather-wise, this is the best single month in which to visit Bangladesh. Temperatures have cooled and the rains have gone, but the landscape is still green and lush.**

### National Revolution Day

7 November commemorates the 1975 uprising that helped Major General Ziaur Rahman, the founder of Bangladesh Nationalist Party (BNP), rise to power. A national holiday when the BNP is in government, but not recognised by the Awami League.

### Maha Raas Leela

This Hindu festival, which celebrates a young Lord Krishna, attracts up to 200,000 pilgrims to the Kantanagar Temple near Dinajpur, and is held at full moon in November. Also celebrated with fervour at Dubla Char, a remote island in the Sundarbans.

# December

**Getting cooler now, but still dry, December is also a very comfortable time to visit, although evenings start getting chilly towards the end of the month.**

### Martyred Intellectuals' Day

Held on 14 December; remembers the murder of hundreds of journalists, doctors and academics that took place just days before the end of the Liberation War. Officials pay their respects at a mass gravesite in the outlying Dhaka neighbourhood of Rayer Bazar.

### Victory Day

A national holiday on 16 December, celebrated to mark the end of the 1971 Liberation War. Expect much flag-waving as well as events at the Liberation War Museum.

# itineraries

*Whether you've got six days or 60, these itineraries provide a starting point for the trip of a lifetime. Want more inspiration? Head online to lonelyplanet .com/thorntree to chat with other travellers.*

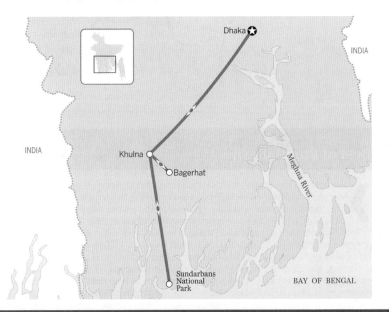

One Week
## Sampling the Sundarbans

One week is just enough time to dip into Dhaka before going on the boat trip of a lifetime through the tiger-filled mangrove swamps of the Sundarbans.

Ease yourself into **Dhaka** by spending your first day in the more upmarket neighbourhood of **Banani** before delving into the chaos with a sightseeing tour of **Old Dhaka** on day two. Don't miss Sadarghat for a rowboat trip on the **Buriganga River**.

You haven't got time to ride the Rocket (you'll need an extra two days for that). Instead, take an overnight bus to **Khulna** to meet up with your Sundarbans tour company, which you'll need in order to properly explore the **Sundarbans National Park**. Then relax on the deck of your boat and enjoy three days of tiger-tinged river adventure before floating back to Khulna.

Consider a day trip to **Bagerhat** before taking the bus back to **Dhaka** for one final day in the capital.

Note that you will need to have booked your Sundarbans trip at least three weeks in advance, so start planning this one from home.

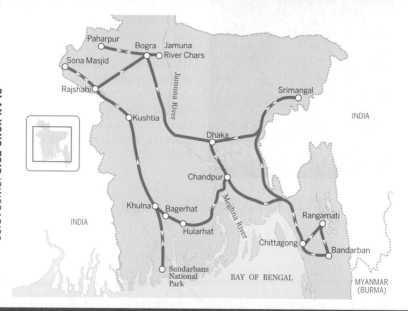

# Best of Bangladesh

Bangladesh is relatively small, so if you have a full month you can see pretty much all the main highlights. This tour takes in Dhaka, the Sundarbans and part of history-rich Rajshahi before whisking you over to the east to sample the tea estates of Srimangal and the forested mountains of the Chittagong Hill Tracts.

Your first job when you arrive in **Dhaka** is to book your cabin on the **Rocket** for your ferry ride the following evening. Tickets in hand, you can spend the rest of that day and the next taking in the sights of Old Dhaka before leaving on the 6pm boat.

Sit back and enjoy the lazy 20-hour river trip to **Hularhat**. Having disembarked mid-morning, grab a rickshaw to the bus stand, then a bus to **Bagerhat**, where you can spend the afternoon admiring the Islamic ruins before hopping on another bus to **Khulna** where you'll meet your Sundarbans tour company. Note: you will have had to have booked your Sundarbans trip at least three weeks in advance.

The next morning, board your boat and enjoy three or four days of unrivalled river adventure as you track tigers in the mangrove forests of the **Sundarbans National Park**.

Back in Khulna, take a bus north, pit-stopping in **Kushtia** – the cultural capital of Bengal – before continuing on to **Rajshahi**.

Take a day trip to **Sona Masjid** to see the scattered ruins of the ancient city of Gaud before catching a bus to **Bogra**.

Not much to see here – although you could consider an unusual day trip to the sand **chars** on the Jamuna River – but Bogra is only a day trip away from the Unesco-protected Buddhist ruins of **Paharpur**.

Catch a bus from Bogra back to **Dhaka**, but don't dally; the next morning you'll be river-bound again, this time a morning ferry from Dhaka's Sadarghat to **Chandpur** before catching the train to **Chittagong**.

Sort out your permit for the hill tracts region while you're in Chittagong, then spend four or five days exploring **Rangamati** and **Bandarban** before heading back to Chittagong.

Take the scenic day train to **Srimangal** where you can rent a bicycle to enjoy the surrounding tea estates, forest reserves and Adivasi villages before catching the train back to **Dhaka**.

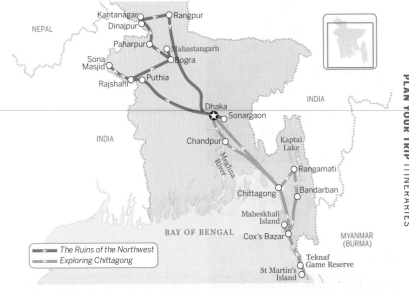

**Legend:**
- The Ruins of the Northwest
- Exploring Chittagong

## Two Weeks
# Ruins of the Northwest

> This tour points you towards the older side of Dhaka before exploring the dusty ruins of history-rich Rajshahi and Rangpur.

Spend your first day visiting the museums and Raj-era architecture of **Central Dhaka** before diving into the living history of **Old Dhaka**. Try to track down the hard-to-find ruins of Bara Katra and Chota Katra in among the chaos of the bazars. A day trip to **Sonargaon** makes an easy day three before you set off by bus to the temple-strewn village of **Puthia**, en route to **Rajshahi**.

Day trip from Rajshahi to **Sona Masjid**, to see the scattered ruins of the lost city of Gaud, before catching the bus to **Bogra**. The ruined settlement of **Mahastangarh** makes a fun half-day trip before you head to the Unesco-protected Buddhist ruins of **Paharpur**, where you can stay the night.

From Paharpur, take a bus to **Dinajpur** (via Jaipurhat and Fulbari) so you can visit the stunning Hindu temple of **Kantanagar** before heading to nearby **Rangpur**, which has a sprinkling of Raj-era architecture, a top-class guesthouse and a daily train to Dhaka.

## Two to Three Weeks
# Exploring Chittagong

> The most diverse region of Bangladesh, Chittagong has mountains, forests, Adivasi villages, elephants and even beaches. This tour has the lot.

After a day visiting the must-see sights of **Dhaka**, hop on a morning ferry to **Chandpur**, from where you can catch a train to **Chittagong**. Sort out your permit for the hill tracts here before taking a bus to laid-back **Rangamati** for a couple of relaxing days by Kaptai Lake. From Rangamati, take a bus to **Bandarban**, the heart of the Chittagong Hill Tracts, and the best place to base yourself for hiking.

After your hill-tracts exertions, take the bus to **Cox's Bazar** where you can rest up by the beach – but don't forget to visit **Maheskhali Island**.

Heading further south, catch a bus to **Teknaf Game Reserve**, home to some of Bangladesh's few remaining wild elephants, before riding the waves to **St Martin's Island** for a more shanty beach experience.

The restrictive ferry schedule means you'll need two days to get back to **Dhaka** from here, via Cox's Bazar (bus) and Chittagong (train), although you could fly back from Cox's Bazar, or take a night bus, if you're pushed for time.

# Border Crossings

## Most Popular Crossings

**Kolkata** The twice-weekly train that connects Kolkata with Dhaka is comfortable and hassle-free. Apart from immigration formalities at the border, it's direct and nonstop.

**Benapole** Main border town on the road route to and from Kolkata. Has direct bus links to Dhaka, Khulna and Jessore.

**Burimari** Bangladesh's gateway to Darjeeling, with transport links via the Indian town of Siliguri. Entering Bangladesh, most people head to Rangpur, but there is a night bus to Dhaka.

**Tamabil** Linking Sylhet with India's northeast tribal states, Tamabil isn't a place to linger, on account of the open mining that goes on around the border (cough! splutter!), but you're only two hours away from Sylhet by bus.

**Akhaura** The other major border for India's northeast tribal states; the Indian side has an airport and a place to process Bangladesh visas. The Bangladesh side has a train station with links to Dhaka, Srimangal and Chittagong.

There are numerous points in Bangladesh where you can cross the border with India, but only six or seven are set up with immigration facilities to service foreigners. At the time of research there was still no border crossing with Myanmar (Burma).

The same system is in place for all of these crossings (apart from the direct train to Kolkata), although differing levels of stringency are applied at each.

If you're leaving Bangladesh and entering India, the most important thing to remember is that you cannot get an Indian visa at any of the border towns, so you must have already sorted this out, preferably in your home country. Foreigners can get an Indian visa in Dhaka (p167) and Chittagong (p112), but it's a bureaucratic nightmare, and many travellers leave the visa office empty handed.

If you're coming into Bangladesh from India, note that you cannot get the same visa-on-arrival that you can get if you fly into Dhaka airport, but you can get Bangladesh visas in Kolkata and Agartala (Akhaura), as well as in New Delhi.

If you're leaving Bangladesh you have to pay a Tk 300 departure tax (see the boxed text p24) and you are supposed to have picked up a change-of-route permit from the Immigration and Passport Office in Dhaka. The departure tax is critical, but the permit isn't asked for these days, so in practice you don't need it.

Be aware that visa regulations for Bangladesh change on a regular basis. For the latest information, check the Bangladesh branch of Lonely Planet's Thorn Tree forum (www.lonelyplanet.com/thorntree).

## SELECTED TRAINS FROM AKHAURA

| DESTINATION | TRAIN NAME | DEPARTS | ARRIVES | FARE (1ST/SHUVON) | OFF DAY |
|---|---|---|---|---|---|
| Chittagong | Mohanagar Provati | 10.45am | 2.45pm | Tk 180/80 | none |
| Chittagong | Paharika Ex | 2.50pm | 7.35am | Tk 180/80 | Sat |
| Chittagong | Mohanagar Godhuli | 6.10pm | 10.10pm | Tk 180/80 | Sun |
| Dhaka | Mohanagar Provati | 11.19am | 2.05pm | Tk 130/75 | Sun |
| Dhaka | Chattala Ex | 1.05pm | 4pm | Tk 130/75 | Tue |
| Dhaka | Upakul Ex | 5.50pm | 8.30pm | Tk 130/75 | Wed |
| Dhaka | Mohanagar Godhuli | 6.45pm | 9.30pm | Tk 130/75 | none |
| Sylhet | Paharika Ex | 12.20pm | 5pm | Tk 155/90 | Mon |

Customs at land borders are fairly lax with foreigners. The same rules regarding what you can bring into the country (in the way of cigarettes and alcohol) apply at border crossings as at airports, though in practice a blind eye is usually turned to your luggage at land crossings.

## Akhaura

This border (open 8am to 6pm) is the closest one to Dhaka and links Bangladesh with India's northeast states. There's a **departure tax payment desk** (⊘10am-3pm Sun-Thu) by immigration where you can pay your Bangladesh departure tax, and unofficial moneychangers operate on both sides of the border.

On the Indian side, the border is 3km from Agartala (rickshaw Rs 50), which has an airport, 12km away, with flights to Kolkata and Guwahati. Agartala's **Bangladesh visa office** (⌂0381 2324807; Airport Rd, Kunjaban; ⊘application 9am-1pm Mon-Thu, 9am-noon Fri, collection same day 4pm) is about 2km north of Ujjayanta Palace.

On the Bangladesh side, the border is 4.5km from the town of Akhaura (shared auto Tk 20, rickshaw Tk 50), which has a train station with direct trains to Dhaka, Chittagong and Sylhet. The Sylhet trains all pass through Srimangal (three hours). The Chittagong trains all pass through Comilla (two hours). If there's no reserved seating left, just buy a standing ticket and pile on. There are plenty of places to eat by the train station.

You can also get to Dhaka, Sylhet and Srimangal by bus via Chandura (shared auto Tk 60), a junction 20km away on the Dhaka–Sylhet Hwy.

There are direct buses to Chandura (Tk 120, three hours) from Dhaka's Sayedabad bus stand.

## Benapole

The Benapole border (open 6.30am to 6.30pm) is on the main road route to and from Kolkata.

On the Bangladesh side, there's a **departure tax payment desk** (⊘Sun-Thu) by immigration. Once over the border you can pick up buses to Kolkata, or trains from nearby Bangaon.

Coming into Bangladesh, Benapole is about 2km from the border (shared auto Tk 5, rickshaw Tk 20). The local bus stand has regular buses to Jessore (Tk 45, one hour) and one to Khulna (Tk 120, 2½ hours, 11.30am). Before you reach the bus stand, you'll see a handful of private coach companies on your left, with regular services to Dhaka (non-air-con/air-con Tk 500/850, 9am to 9pm, eight hours). There's an **AB Bank ATM** opposite the bus stand. Otherwise, you'll see plenty of private moneychangers near the coach offices.

If you get stuck here, the **Parjatan Hotel** (⌂04228 75411; r without/with air-con Tk 1300/2100; ✹), just past the bus stand, away from the border, is decent and has an OK **restaurant** (mains Tk 100-200; ⊘7am-10pm).

## Burimari

This border (open 9am to 6pm) is used by travellers heading for Darjeeling.

Heading to India, most travellers come from Rangpur (p93). First take a bus from Rangpur to Patgram (Tk 140, four hours) then take a tempo (Tk 20, 20 minutes) or bus (Tk 10) the remaining 13km to the border. There's nowhere at immigration to pay the Bangladesh departure tax, although you can do so at the branch of **Janatar Bank** (☉10am-4pm Sun-Thu) in Burimari Bazar, 1km before the border. You can change money on the Indian side of the border in Chengrabandha, from where there are regular buses to Siliguri (Rs 42).

Coming into Bangladesh, there's nowhere to change money; not officially, at least. There's one night bus to Dhaka (Tk 600, 11 hours, 6pm) run by **Shahali Paribahan** (☏01717 756999), 200m past the border. Otherwise you need to catch a tempo to Patgram then a bus to Rangpur (last bus 7pm).

If you get stuck in Burimari, the very basic **Shakhar Plaza** (☏01918 457511; r Tk 200-400), a green two-storey hotel on your left as you walk from the border, is the best you'll get. No English spoken.

## Hili

This little-used border (open 9am to 5.30pm) is the closest to the Unesco-protected ruins of Paharpur (p92). There's nowhere to pay the Bangladesh departure tax.

Coming either from the Paharpur ruins or from Bogra, you need to catch a bus via Jaipurhat, from where it's Tk 25 by bus to Hili. Hili bus stand is a Tk 20 to Tk 30 rickshaw ride from the border.

Coming from Rangpur, you have to catch a bus first to Fulbari (Tk 60, two hours) then to Hili (Tk 30, one hour).

The Indian side of the border is also known as Hili. You may be able to get onward transport to Kolkata (Rs 250, 12 hours) from the border, or else go via Balurghat, 20km away. The nearest train station is Malda.

Coming into Bangladesh, there's nowhere to change money. You need the Hili bus stand for Paharpur and Bogra (via Jaipur-

hat), but you can catch buses to Fulbari (for Rangpur) on the roadside, 200m past the border. **Shyamoli Paribahan** (☏01191 822926), 100m from the border, has four buses to Dhaka (Tk 400, seven to eight hours, 6.30am, 11am, 2.30pm and 10.30pm).

## Kolkata

### Bus

In Kolkata, more than a dozen daily buses leave from Marquis St, bound for Dhaka (Rs 550 to Rs 750, 13 hours), via Benapole, where you'll have to complete immigration formalities. Bus companies running the service include **Shohagh Paribahan** (☏033 22520757) and **Green Line** (☏033 22520571).

For details on buses from Dhaka to Kolkata, see p53.

### Train

The *Maitree Express* (Rs 348 to Rs 869, 12½ hours) to Dhaka departs Kolkata (Chitpore) Station at 7.10am on Saturday and Wednesday. Buy tickets not from the station, but from a **special desk** (☉10am-5pm Mon-Thu, 10am-3pm Fri & Sat) within **Eastern Railways Foreign Tourist Bureau** (☏033 22224206; 6 Fairlie Pl).

For details on the Dhaka to Kolkata train, see p54.

## Sona Masjid (Gaud)

Another infrequently used border post (open 8am to 5pm), Sona Masjid is ideal if you want to explore the ruins of the ancient city of Gaud (p102), which lie scattered on both sides of the border.

Leaving Bangladesh, you'll probably have come from Rajshahi; see p102 for transport details from there. You can pay your Bangladesh departure tax at immigration (Sunday to Thursday only). Once you've had your fill of ruins on the Indian side of border, you'll

---

### BANGLADESH DEPARTURE TAX

You must pay a Tk 300 departure tax (sometimes called a 'travel tax') if you're leaving Bangladesh via a land border. However, it isn't as easy as just handing over your last few taka as you pass through customs. It has to be paid into a branch of **Sonali Bank** (www.sonalibank.com.bd). You will then be given a receipt as proof of payment, and it is this receipt that you hand over as you leave the country. Some border crossings have a small bank desk by immigration (Benapole, Akhaura, Sona Masjid). Otherwise, you need to pay the tax at a proper branch of Sonali Bank, although you can do this at any branch in the country.

Remember, banks in Bangladesh are always closed on Friday, and usually Saturday too.

be able to find onward transport from Gaud to Malda, 15km away, from where there are trains to Kolkata or Siliguri, for Darjeeling.

Entering Bangladesh, there's nowhere to change money. Buses to Rajshahi (Tk 95, three hours, 7.25am to 4.40pm) leave from a small T-junction, 250m past the border.

# Tamabil

The border (open 9am to 6pm) closest to Sylhet (p135) is busy mostly with trucks filled with rocks and coal from the open mines round here, but a few travellers also cross. There's no departure-tax payment desk, but Sylhet has a number of branches of Sonali Bank.

The border is a two-minute walk from where the bus from Sylhet drops you (walk up to your right). Once in India, it's a 1.5km walk to the town of Dawki (taxi Rs 40 to Rs 50), from where buses run to Shillong (Rs 110, three hours).

Entering Bangladesh, buses to Sylhet (Tk 50, two hours) run from the main road just beyond the border post until around 8pm. There's nowhere to change money, but the guys in customs may be able to help you out.

# Boat Trips

## Best for Wildlife

**Sundarbans** Monkeys, wild boars, otters, crocodiles, river dolphins and more than 30,000 deer. Even if there weren't any tigers, this boat trip would be fun.

## Best for Scenery

**Sangu River** This beautiful Hill Tracts river passes steep, tree-covered banks, rugged river cliffs and villages so remote you can only get to them by boat.

## Best City Trip

**Dhaka** Bobbing across the Buriganga River – the lifeblood of Dhaka, if not the nation – on board a wooden rowboat, while triple-tiered ferries and oceangoing cargo ships charge past you is among the most surreal (and scary) experiences you'll have.

## Best Boat

**The Rocket** Steeped in almost 100 years of history, Bangladesh's famous paddle-wheel steamer may not be the fastest thing on the waterways these days, but it gets more and more romantic each passing year.

This water-laden country has more than 700 rivers, creating around 8000km of navigable waterways. Travelling by boat has been a way of life in Bangladesh for centuries, and there are said to be more types of boats here than in any other country in the world. It almost goes without saying, then, that taking a boat trip along a river is a quintessential Bangladesh experience, and we recommend you do it as often as you can while you're here.

The most famous boat trip is aboard the old paddle-wheel ferries known as Rockets, but there is an almost unlimited number of boat trips you can take.

# Types of Boats
## The Rocket

The Rocket is a generic name given to the four remaining paddle-wheel steamers that were built in the early 20th century and are run by the BIWTC (Bangladesh Inland Waterway Transport Corporation). Called Rockets because they were once the fastest thing on the waterways, they now plod along, diesel-powered, at a slower rate than more modern ferries, which now also ply the same route, as well as other boats.

### The Route

All four Rockets follow the same set route. They used to go from Dhaka all the way to Khulna in a 30-hour epic trip to the edge of the Sundarbans, but at the time of research the last 10-hour stretch of the trip had been suspended indefinitely, so they were only travelling as far as Morrelganj.

**FROM DHAKA (EVERY DAY EXCEPT FRIDAY)**

| | |
|---|---|
| Dhaka | 6pm |
| Chandpur | midnight |
| Barisal | 6am |
| Hularhat | 10am |
| Morrelganj | 2pm |

**TO DHAKA (EVERY DAY EXCEPT SUNDAY)**

| | |
|---|---|
| Morrelganj | 9am |
| Hularhat | 12.30pm |
| Barisal | 6pm |
| Chandpur | 1.30am |
| Dhaka | 7.30am |

## The Classes

There are three main classes: 1st-class cabins are lovely, and well worth paying extra for. There are twins and singles. Both are carpeted and wood-panelled and come with fans, a TV, a small sink and crisp white bed linen. Shared bathrooms have showers. You also get access to the 1st-class dining room (although meals cost extra) and the wonderful 1st-class deck right at the front of the boat.

Second-class cabins are essentially a more basic version of 1st class. They are twin-bed cabins with bed sheets provided (although it's not quite so crisp and clean as in 1st), and are fan-cooled but have no TV or private sink and the shared bathrooms don't have showers. There are small side decks for you to sit out on, but you can often sneak onto the 1st-class front deck without being told off. Meals cost extra, but are generally pretty good.

Deck class is essentially a ticket onto the boat. It's then up to you to find a spot to sit or sleep on, on the lower, open-sided wooden deck. There are snack stalls down here, which all passengers can use. Deck class is fine for a daytime trip, but extremely uncomfortable if you're travelling overnight.

See p53 for more ticketing information.

## Launches

Private, more modern ferries – known as launches – ply the same route as the Rocket. The overnight ones tend to leave slightly later (from Dhaka between 7pm and 9pm) but are slightly quicker. There are also launches that leave Dhaka throughout the day for closer destinations, such as Chandpur (boxed text p112), in Chittagong division.

**THE HOLIDAY RUSH**

During major national holidays such as Eid ul Adha, passenger ferries can become worryingly overcrowded as locals rush to get home to their families. Safety concerns can be a real issue at these times. Use common sense; if a ferry seems ridiculously packed (even by Bangladesh standards) you should perhaps think twice about boarding it.

Classes are similar to the Rocket, although you may also have the option of 'VIP cabins', with extra room and comfort, and private balconies.

Because there are more of them, you don't usually need to book your launch tickets too far in advance. Head down to Sadarghat – the main river ghat in Dhaka – and inquire about launches to wherever you want to go. If you turn up mid- to late afternoon, you should be able to bag a cabin on a boat that evening.

## Country Boats

Smaller wooden boats, known as *nouka* (country boats), come in all sorts of shapes and sizes and ply the lesser rivers of the more remote regions of Bangladesh. Riding aboard one of these can be a magical experience. They are sometimes rowed and sometimes driven by a small engine. You'll find you often use them just to cross rivers, but you can take short trips on them all over the country. Even if you're not going anywhere in particular, you can just rock up at most river ghats and negotiate a fare with a boathand for a one-hour tour of the river. You'll have to have your best miming skills at the ready because it's very unlikely your boathand will speak any English...but it all adds to the adventure.

# Top River Trips
## Sundarbans National Park

The world's largest mangrove swamp is home to the largest single population of tigers found anywhere in the world, and boarding a boat to go in search of one of them is Bangladesh's undisputed No 1 tourist attraction. It's possible to dip into the mangrove forest on a self-organised day trip from Mongla (p74), but for a true adventure, book yourself onto a three- or four-day boat tour from Khulna (p68).

# Dhaka to Hularhat by Rocket

The first part of this 20-hour trip on the famous Rocket is overnight, so make sure you've booked a cabin! Try not to sleep in, though, because arriving at the large port at Barisal in the early morning mist is a sight worth seeing. Once the boat starts up again, sit back on the deck and lap up the scenery before hopping off at Hularhat and catching a bus to either Bagerhat (p76) or Khulna (p68).

# Buriganga River

For a fun, albeit slightly scary city-river trip, head to the rowboat ghat beside Dhaka's main ferry port at Sadarghat and pay Tk 2 to cross the massive Buriganga in one of the many small wooden rowboats that shuttle passengers across the river. While the cityscape of Dhaka rises in the background, watch in amazement as your tiny boat dodges triple-tiered ferries and enormous cargo ships to get to the opposite bank. Then grab a cup of cha at a tea stall on the other side, take a deep breath and do it all again in reverse.

# Sangu River

The scenery along most rivers is beautiful, but it's particularly special here, on the four-to five-hour stretch of the Sangu River running from Ruma Bazar to Bandarban (p113). This is the Chittagong Hill Tracts, where instead of flat-as-a-pancake paddy fields you'll find dramatic rock faces rising from the water's edge, backed by forested hills teeming with wildlife. It's tough to sort out; you'll need a permit, and if you haven't brought a guide, you'll need your best miming skills because boatmen don't speak English here, but it's a small price to pay for breathtaking scenery and hours of peace and tranquillity.

# Kaptai Lake

Formed when the Kaptai Dam was built in the 1960s, this enormous lake, accessed from the super-relaxed town of Rangamati, offers numerous boating opportunities. The three-hour round trip to Shuvalong Falls is the most popular. See p117 for more ideas.

# Maheshkhali Island

With its village atmosphere and small collection of Hindu and Buddhist temples, the island of Maheskhali makes a wonderfully peaceful escape from the brash beach resort of Cox's Bazaar, but it's the boat trip over to the island that's the real gem. You'll pass pirate-ship lookalike fishing boats, a huge and highly pungent fish market, a small boat-building yard and a string of ice-making houses where huge blocks of ice slide down rollercoaster runners and into waiting boats, before you finally open out into the estuary that leads to Maheskhali. See the boxed text p127 for more details.

# China Clay Hills

Enlist the help of the friendly staff at the YMCA in Birisiri (p64) to help arrange a relaxing three-hour boat trip along the Someswari River to the China Clay Hills: exposed mounds of rock surrounding a picturesque turquoise lake. You'll have to walk the

## SEA VOYAGES

One side of Bangladesh opens out into the Bay of Bengal, so as well as all the amazing river trips outlined here, there are some short sea voyages you can take too.

» **St Martin's Island** Large modern passenger ferries shuttle holidaymakers south to laidback St Martin's Island (p128). Much of the two-hour trip follows the coastline of Myanmar (Burma).

» **Fatra Char** You can take a day trip along the coast from Kuakata (p85) to Fatra Char, a forested Island on the eastern fringes of the Sundarbans.

» **Swatch of No Ground** Excellent tour operator the Guide Tours can help you join a research boat to visit the Swatch of No Ground (boxed text p77), a deep-water canyon south of the Sundarbans, where you can spot whales and dolphins.

## BOAT TOUR OPERATORS

Most of the trips mentioned here can be done independently, but using a tour operator saves you a lot of hassle, allows you added security and gives you the chance to hook up with other travellers.

**» Contic** (www.contic.com) Has restored two elegant traditional Bangladesh boats and runs top-end but informal multiday trips to various places. Highly recommended.

**» The Guide Tours** (www.guidetours.com) Bangladesh's most respected tour company runs day-cruises around the Dhaka area as well as its signature three- or four-day Sundarbans trips.

**» Bengal Tours** (www.bengaltours.com) Also runs well-received multiday trips to the Sundarbans.

**» Bangladesh Ecotours** (www.bangladeshecotours.com) Specialises in the Chittagong Hill Tracts and can help with river trips in hard-to-reach places in this region.

**» Sundarbans Tours & Resort** (www.bangladeshsundarbantours.com) Runs alternative trips to the Sundarbans, which enter the national park from the east, via Kuakata.

last bit, or take a rickshaw, but you can still do the whole round trip in a day.

# Sunamganj Wetlands

The wetlands, or *haors*, of northern Bangladesh are a birder's paradise. Migratory birds flock here in winter and join the resident birds for one big feathered party. Even if you're not a keen bird-watcher, the marshy expanses are fascinating to explore by boat. Tanguar Haor, accessible from Sylhet, is one of the most popular wetland areas to visit. See p138 for details.

# regions at a glance

Bangladesh is relatively small, but unless you're spending a couple of months here, you'll still have to pick and choose which regions to visit.

The megacity of Dhaka sits conveniently at the centre of the country and acts as a gateway to almost everywhere.

Southwest of Dhaka is Bangladesh's biggest draw: the tiger-filled mangrove forests of the Sundarbans National Park.

To the northwest are the history-rich divisions of Rajshahi and Rangpur, home to forgotten kingdoms and dusty ruins, while the east of the country dispels the myth that Bangladesh is completely flat. Here you'll find the gently rolling hills of Sylhet's tea estates and, further south, the stunning forest-covered mountains of the Chittagong Hill Tracts.

## Dhaka

**Food**
**Culture**
**Chaos**

### Biryani & Kebabs

You'll almost certainly have your best food in Dhaka. Biryani houses rule the roost, but you'll also find some excellent kebab joints as well as some decent Western fare.

### Galleries & Museums

Unsurprisingly, Dhaka also packs in the country's best museums, theatres and art galleries. Try to catch a show or an exhibition while you're in town or, at the very least, check out the National Museum.

### Old Dhaka

For some it's too much to handle, but for others the mind-boggling chaos of Old Dhaka is what makes a visit to this most manic of megacities such an experience.

**p34**

## Dhaka Division

**Rural Vistas**
**Villages**
**History**

### Paddy Fields

Especially in the far north, it's glistening paddy field after glistening paddy field as you bus it through this gloriously green region. Rural bliss.

### Garo Settlements

There are around 25,000 villages in Dhaka division, including some in the far north where the population is predominantly Garo. Birisiri is a great place to start.

### Ruins

This is no Rajshahi, but there is a smattering of crumbling ruins to explore in Dhaka division. The pick of the bunch are those at Sonargaon, although Muktagacha is worth a trip.

**p57**

# Khulna & Barisal

**Wildlife**
**Scenery**
**Boats**

### Tigers

You'll see birds galore, spotted deer, maybe some monkeys, but the creature you almost certainly won't see – the Royal Bengal tiger – is what will make your journey into the depths of the Sundarbans such a thrilling adventure.

### Mangroves

Kuakata is a wonderfully natural beach, and the trip down there is full of lush farmland, but it's the pristine mangrove forests of the Sundarbans that steal the show.

### The Rocket

Chances are you'll ride more boats in this river-drenched region than anywhere else in Bangladesh, but if you fall in love with any of them, it will be the old paddle-wheel steamer known as the Rocket.

**p66**

# Rajshahi & Rangpur

**History**
**Architecture**
**Humanity**

### Lost Kingdoms

History buffs get ready. The lost city of Gaud, the ruined kingdom of Mahastangarh and the remains of what was once the largest monastery south of the Himalaya.

### Temples, Mosques & Monasteries

The ancient buildings of this region are an eclectic bunch. You'll find Bangladesh's most exquisite Hindu temple, its largest Buddhist ruins and some of the oldest and most unusual mosques.

### Chars

The poorest people in this highly flood-prone region have been forced off the land and onto the rivers. Many of them are from this region.

**p87**

# Chittagong Division

**Adventure**
**Scenery**
**Adivasi Culture**

### Hiking

This region is full of off-the-beaten-track adventure. Whether it be searching for wild elephants or hiking to the country's highest peaks, Chittagong is a place for those who love the outdoors.

### Chittagong Hill Tracts

Chittagong has coastal beaches, enormous lakes, forest reserves and even a coral island, but it's the rugged mountains of the Chittagong Hill Tracts that dominate the landscape.

### Bandarban & Rangamati

Your chances of meeting Adivasi groups and learning about their ways of life is greater here than anywhere in Bangladesh.

**p106**

# Sylhet Division

**Scenery**
**Wildlife**
**Outdoor Activities**

### Tea Estates

Almost as diverse as Chittagong, Sylhet is home to thick forest reserves, bird-filled wetlands and the majority of the country's 163 tea estates.

### Hoolock Gibbon

Birders will love the wetlands of Sunamganj, and there are a number of types of monkeys to be found in the forests around Srimangal, but the jewel in the crown of Sylhet's wildlife is the very rare Hoolock gibbon, Asia's only species of ape.

### Cycling

There are some wonderful walks and hikes to do here, and a boat trip out to the wetlands is a proper old adventure, but it's tough to beat the freedom of cycling yourself around the tea estates of Srimangal.

**p133**

> **Every listing is recommended by our authors, and their favourite places are listed first**

> **Look out for these icons:**

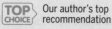 Our author's top recommendation
 A green or sustainable option
 No payment required

See the Index for a full list of destinations covered in this book.

# On the Road

# Dhaka

## Best Places to Stay

» Viator (p45)

» Sabrina's (p45)

» Liebenzell Mission Guesthouse (p45)

» Hotel Pacific (p44)

» White House Hotel (p44)

» Lakeshore (p45)

## Best Places to Eat

» Haji Biryani (p47)

» Star Kebab & Restaurant (p49)

» Spaghetti Jazz (p49)

» Dhaba (p49)

» Santoor (p48)

» Al-Razzaque (p47)

## Why Go?

Dhaka is more than just a city; it's a giant whirlpool that sucks in anything and anyone that comes within its furious grasp. Around and around it sends them, like some wildly spinning fairground ride bursting with energy. Millions of individual pursuits constantly churn together into a frenzy of collective activity – an urban melting pot forever bubbling over.

Dhaka is a city in perpetual motion and the glorious chaos is perhaps best viewed from the back of one of the city's half-a-million fabulously colourful cycle-rickshaws, which fight for space on the city's overcrowded streets with taxis, buses, auto-rickshaws and even horse-drawn carriages.

We can't guarantee you'll fall for Dhaka's many charms, but sooner or later you will start to move to its beat and when that happens Dhaka stops being a terrifying ride and starts to become a unique blend of art and intellect, passion and poverty, love and hate.

## When to Go
### Dhaka

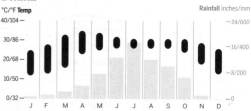

**Jan–Mar** Dry and cool; evenings can become slightly chilly.

**Apr** Getting hot now, but Bengali New Year falls on the 14th so cultural events abound.

**Nov–Dec** Monsoon rains are over, temperatures are cooler and skies are clear.

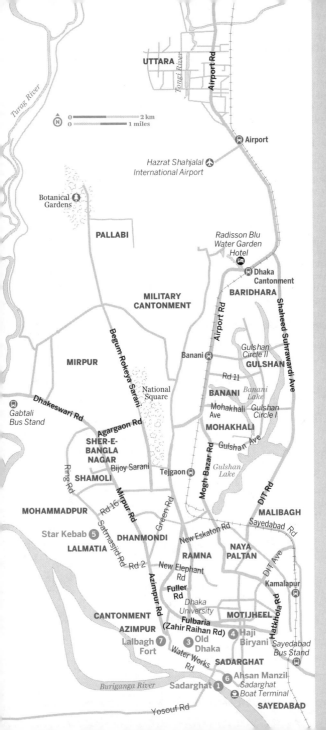

## Dhaka Highlights

**❶** Board a rowboat down at the gritty docks of **Sadarghat** (p37) and cross the manic Buriganga River, the very lifeblood of this enormous city

**❷** Climb aboard one of the city's **cycle-rickshaws** (p56) and watch Dhaka's street life roll by

**❸** Get lost wandering the fascinating, overcrowded alleyways of **Old Dhaka** (Puran Dhaka; p37)

**❹** Tuck into the best biryani in Bangladesh, at **Haji Biryani** (p47)

**❺** Sample some of the country's best kebabs from any streetside kebab stall; or else try the excellent **Star Kebab** (p49)

**❻** Poke around the museum at charming **Ahsan Manzil** (p37), aka the Pink Palace

**❼** Escape Old Dhaka's hustle and bustle and explore the ruins of **Lalbagh Fort** (p38)

DHAKA

## History

Although there were settlements here from as early as the 7th century, ruled first by Buddhist kingdoms and later by Hindu dynasties, Dhaka only really came into its own in 1608 when it was taken over by the Mughals and installed as the capital of Bengal. Under Mughal expansion, the city grew rapidly to over a million people, and some of the city's most famous surviving buildings date from this time. Expansion was brought to an abrupt end when, in 1717, the capital was moved to Murshidabad in today's India. The British East India Company took control of Dhaka later that century (1793), but as Calcutta (Kolkata) rose to prominence, Dhaka continued to decline. At one stage the population was as low as 30,000. There were, nevertheless, some significant developments at this time. A modern water supply system was introduced in 1874. An electricity system followed in 1878. And in 1905, when Lord Curzon, the Governor-General of India, finalised the short-lived partition of Bengal, Dhaka was chosen as the capital of the new state of East Bengal and Assam.

The Partition of India in 1947 saw Dhaka installed as the capital of East Pakistan. A period of major upheaval for the city followed, with a large proportion of Dhaka's Hindus departing for India, while the city received a large influx of Muslims. And as the centre of regional politics, Dhaka saw an increasing number of strikes, demonstrations and incidents of violence.

On 7 March 1971, an estimated one million people attended the nationalist rally at Ramna Racecourse (now Suhrawardi Park), which eventually led to the 26 March declaration of Bangladesh's independence. Nine months of bloody civil war followed before the Pakistani surrender on 16 December, again at Ramna Racecourse, saw the birth of an independent Bangladesh.

As the new nation's capital, Dhaka saw rapid population growth, as migrant work-

## Old Dhaka

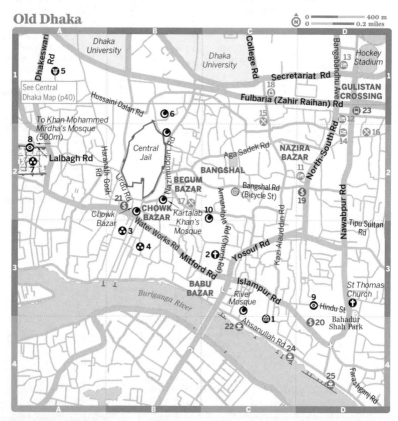

ers from rural areas across Bangladesh flooded into the city, creating new challenges to services and infrastructure that continue to this day.

# ◎ Sights

## OLD DHAKA

No matter where in the world you've just come from, Old Dhaka *(Puran Dhaka)* will side-swipe you with its overwhelming intensity, and leave impressions that will never fade. Time spent getting lost in its streets is time spent falling in love with this city.

### Sadarghat                                    RIVER GHAT

Running calmly through the centre of Old Dhaka, the Buriganga River is the muddy artery of Dhaka and the very lifeblood of both this city and the nation. To explore it from the deck of a small boat is to see Bangladesh at its most raw and gritty. The panorama of river life is fascinating. Triple-towered ferries leer over pint-sized canoes. Country boats bump against the dirty hulks of domineering cargo and fishing boats. On the foreshores, stained with grease and mud, you'll find children fishing with homemade nets in the lee of rusting tankers. Further out, repairmen busy themselves crashing, bashing and scrubbing ship hulls while floating on planks of wood. Barges overloaded with sand and other building materials float down river with barely an inch of clearance above water.

Among all the large ships are the tiny wooden ones that you can hire. These are available almost everywhere along the waterfront, though most people hire them from around **Sadarghat boat terminal** (Map p36; Ahsanullah Rd; admission Tk 4). If you just walk along the jetty here, English-speaking boathands will find you and offer you a one-hour tour of the river. If you can barter the price down to Tk 200 you'll be doing well.

Alternatively, if you don't fancy a price battle with the touts, walk slightly west to the small **rowboat ghat** (admission Tk 1); from here wooden rowboats ferry passengers across the river all day for a set price of Tk 2 per person. The opposite riverbank is of no particular interest – it's packed with clothes shops and stalls, although there are some snack stalls and tea stands, too – but it's the trip over here and back that's the attraction. Note: Sadarghat is pronounced 'shod-or-ghat'.

### Ahsan Manzil                                    PALACE

(Pink Palace; Map p36; Ahsanullah Rd; foreigner/local Tk 75/5; ◎9.30am-4.30pm Sat-Wed & 2.30-7.30pm Fri Oct-Mar, 10.30am-5.30pm Sat-Wed & 3-8pm Fri Apr-Sep) Dating from 1872, the must-see Ahsan Manzil, aka the Pink Palace, was built on the site of an old French factory by Nawab Abdul Ghani, the city's wealthiest zamindar (landowner). Some 16 years after the palace's construction, it was damaged by a tornado. It was altered during restoration,

---

# Old Dhaka

## ORIENTATION

For simplicity, we've divided the city into three areas: Old Dhaka (*Puran Dhaka*), Central Dhaka and North Dhaka.

Old Dhaka is a maze of bustling bazaars and incredibly crowded narrow streets and is by far the most interesting part of the city for tourists. It's packed with historic sights, although hotel facilities are somewhat lacking.

The larger, more modern, central part of the city begins about 2km to the north, with its commercial heart in the district of Motijheel (moh-tee-*jeel*).

North Dhaka includes the more upmarket suburbs of Banani and Gulshan. Here you'll find embassies, expats and Dhaka's nicest guesthouses and restaurants, although there's little in terms of sights.

becoming even grander than before. Lord Curzon stayed here whenever he came to visit. After the death of the nawab and his son, the family fortune was dispersed and the palace eventually fell into disrepair. It was saved from oblivion by massive restoration in the late 1980s, aided by photos of each of the 23 rooms, taken during the high point of the palace's history. The photos are still on display, as are various family portraits and the skull of Nawab Abdul Ghanis's favourite elephant, Feroz Jung.

### Lalbagh Fort                      FORT
(Map p36; foreigner/local Tk 100/10; ☺9am-5pm Oct-Mar, 10am-6pm Apr-Sep, closed Mon morning & Sun) The half-completed Lalbagh Fort and its well-tended gardens are an excuse to escape Old Dhaka's hustle and bustle for an hour or so. Unlike the Sadarghat area, which is full of raw energy, the fort is a slightly melancholic step back into the misty Mughal past of emperors and princesses. It's particularly atmospheric in the early morning light.

Construction began in 1677 under the direction of Prince Mohammed Azam, the third son of Emperor Aurangzeb, although he handed it to Shaista Khan for completion. However, the death of Khan's daughter, Pari Bibi (Fair Lady), was considered such a bad omen that the fort was never completed. Three architectural monuments within the complex were finished, though: the Mausoleum of Pari Bibi (in front of you as you enter), the Diwan, or Hall of Audience (to your left) and the three-domed Quilla Mosque (to your right) all date from 1684.

The only monument you can enter is the Diwan, an elegant two-storey structure containing a small but excellent museum of Mughal miniature paintings, coins, carpets and calligraphy, along with swords and firearms. In the same building, a massive arched

doorway leads to the *hammam* (bath house). Outside is a huge disused bathing tank.

The Mausoleum of Pari Bibi is unusual because of its materials of construction: black basalt, white marble and encaustic tiles of various colours have been used to decorate its interior, while the central chamber, where Pari Bibi is buried, is entirely veneered in white marble.

About 500m past the entrance to the fort, Khan Mohammed Mirdha's Mosque dates from 1706 and is worth a peek, while to the north of the fort is Dhakeswari Temple, the city's main Hindu Temple, and always a lively, colourful affair.

### Shankharia Bazar                   STREET
(Map p36) A crash of drums, a cloud of incense and a bursting paintbox of colours signal a welcome to so-called Hindu Street. Lined on either side with old houses, garlands of lurid orange marigolds, and dark doorways leading to matchbox-sized shops and workshops, this can be an extremely photogenic part of Old Dhaka, as the *shankharis* (Hindu artisans), whose ancestors came here over 300 years ago, busy themselves creating kites, gravestones, wedding hats, and bangles carved out of conch shells. Particularly flamboyant during Hindu festivals, but colourful year round.

### Bara Katra & Chota Katra  HISTORIC BUILDINGS
(Map p36) These dilapidated Mughal-era structures are about the oldest buildings in Dhaka, and searching for them among the high-walled, pinched alleyways of this part of the city is a highlight of a wander around Old Dhaka. Bara Katra, once a palace of monumental dimensions, was built in 1644 and now has a street running through its arched entrance (which houses a cool little tea stand). While only a small portion of the original structure remains standing,

the building is still occupied, used mostly as storerooms (ask to peek inside), and there's a small prayer room on top.

**Chota Katra**, which dates from 1663, was a caravanserai for visiting merchants. It was similar in design to Bara Katra, but there's not much left, save the archways at either end, which now house small shops in their recesses.

To find Bara Katra, walk west along Water Works Rd, then turn left down the alley beside a blue-and-white, mosaic-tiled mosque.

### Hussaini Dalan                                    MOSQUE

(Map p36; www.hussainidalan.com; Hussaini Dalan Rd, Bakshi Bazar) A block north of the central jail is Hussaini Dalan, looking more like a Hindu rajbari (landowner's palace) than an Islamic building. It was built in 1642 as the house of the imam of the Shi'ia community. Though the architecture seems baroque in inspiration, the original building was purely Mughal. It changed somewhat with restorations after the 1897 earthquake, when the roof collapsed. You can see a silver filigree model of the original building in the National Museum (p39).

### Star Mosque                                       MOSQUE

(Sitara Masjid; Map p36; Armanitola Rd) This unusual mosque, with its striking mosaic decoration, dates from the early 18th century, although it has been radically altered. It was originally built in the typical Mughal style, with four corner towers. Around 50 years ago a local businessman financed its redecoration with Japanese and English china tiles, and the addition of a new veranda. If you look hard you can see tiles illustrated with pictures of Mt Fuji!

### Armenian Church of
### the Holy Resurrection                            CHURCH

(আর্মেনিয়ান চার্চ; Map p36; Armanitola Rd) This small area is known as Armanitola, and is named after the Armenian colony that settled here

---

### VISITING MOSQUES

If you are non-Muslim, you are normally still allowed to enter mosques outside prayer times (although you may not be allowed into the main prayer hall itself). You should, however, dress appropriately. Long, baggy clothing is most suitable, and women should bring something along with which to cover their hair.

---

in the late 17th century. The white- and lemon-painted Armenian Church of the Holy Resurrection, dating from 1781, is the soul of this now almost extinct community, and is a tranquil spot. **Mr Martin** (☎731 6953), the caretaker who lives in a house within the grounds, has done much to restore the church, and delights in giving personal tours. In any case, you'll need him to let you in as the gates are always locked.

### Bangshal Road (Bicycle Street)         STREET

For a souvenir of Bangladesh, you can't beat a piece of rickshaw art. The place to find this art is in and around Bangshal Rd, popularly known as Bicycle Street. Even if you don't want to buy anything, it's still interesting to watch workers sawing and hammering away at made-to-order rickshaw accessories.

See p162 for more on rickshaw art.

## CENTRAL DHAKA

### National Museum                                  MUSEUM

(জাতীয় জাদুঘর; Jatio Jadughar; Map p40; Kazi Nazrul Islam Ave; foreigner/local Tk 75/5; ⊙9.30am-4pm Sat-Wed, 3pm-7.30pm Fri) The excellent National Museum, sprawling over several floors, begins with the geological formation of Bangladesh, whisks you through a rundown of the nation's flora and fauna, saunters through a Buddhist and Hindu past, and brings you up to date with the War of Liberation and the creation of the modern state. Opens and closes an hour later from April to September.

### Liberation War Museum                            MUSEUM

(মুক্তিযুদ্ধ জাদুঘর; Mukti-juddha Jadughar; Map p40; 5 Segun Bagicha Rd; admission Tk 5; ⊙10am-5pm Mon-Sat) Housed in a beautiful whitewashed colonial-era building, this small museum chronicles the 1971 War of Independence, one of the 20th century's more deadly wars. The displays start off tame enough but gradually become more graphic before culminating in a room full of personal items (each of which comes with a short story on the owner's life); a large pile of human skulls and bones; and some very disturbing photos of rotting corpses with bound hands being eaten by dogs and vultures. Though the displays might not make for happy holidays, this museum should be a compulsory stop for everyone.

The shaded courtyard out back has a **tea stall** and a small stage where cultural events are held from time to time. There's also a small **bookshop**.

From Topkhana Rd head north up Segun Bagicha Rd and it's on the second street on the right.

DHAKA

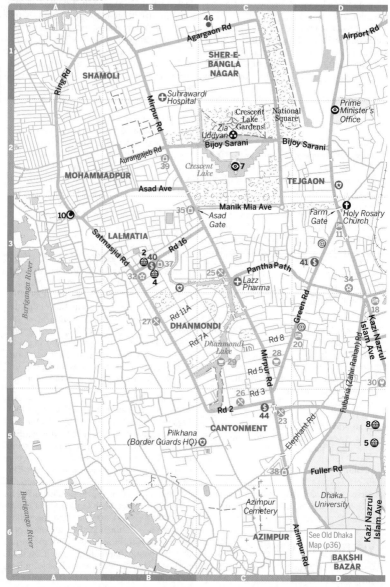

A | B | C | D

SHAMOLI

SHER-E-BANGLA NAGAR

Agargaon Rd

Airport Rd

Ring Rd

Mirpur Rd

Suhrawardi Hospital

Crescent Lake Gardens

National Square

Prime Minister's Office

Aurangajeb Rd

Zia Uddyan

Bijoy Sarani

Bijoy Sarani

**39**

Crescent Lake

**7**

MOHAMMADPUR

Asad Ave

TEJGAON

**10**

Manik Mia Ave

Asad Gate

Farm Gate

Holy Rosary Church

Satmasjid Rd

LALMATIA

Rd 16

**35**

**11**

**2 40**

**37**

Pantha Path

**41 $**

**34**

**32**

**4**

**25**

Lazz Pharma

Green Rd

**27**

Rd 11A

DHANMONDI

@

**20**

Kazi Nazrul Islam Ave

**18**

Rd 7A

Dhanmondi Lake

Rd 8

**29**

Rd 5

**28**

Mirpur Rd

Fulbaria (Zahir Raihan) Rd

**30**

**26** Rd 3

Rd 2

**44 $**

**23**

CANTONMENT

Elephant Rd

**8**

**5**

Pilkhana (Border Guards HQ)

**38**

Fuller Rd

Burganga River

Azimpur Cemetery

Dhaka University

Kazi Nazrul Islam Ave

AZIMPUR

Azimpur Rd

See Old Dhaka Map (p36)

BAKSHI BAZAR

**National Assembly Building**  ARCHITECTURE
(জাতীয় সংসদ ভবন; Jatio Songsod Bhabon; Map p40)
In 1963 the Pakistanis commissioned Louis
Kahn, a world-renowned American archi-
tect, to design a regional capitol for East Pakistan. Due to the liberation movement and

ensuing war, the National Assembly Building wasn't completed until 1982. The building often features in books on modern architecture, and is regarded as among Kahn's
finest works. It's a huge assembly of concrete
cylinders and rectangular boxes, sliced open

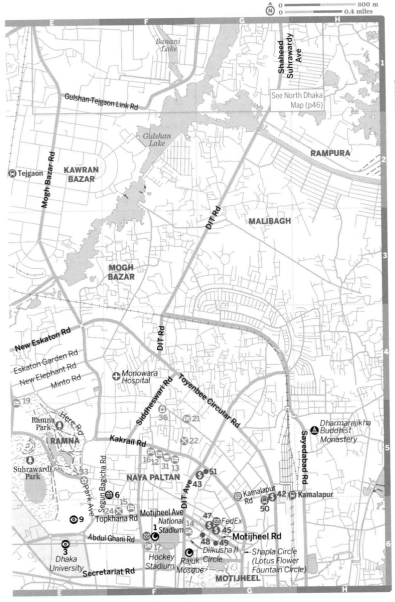

0 — 800 m
0 — 0.4 miles

Banani Lake

Shaheed Suhrawardy Ave

Gulshan-Tejgaon Link Rd

See North Dhaka Map (p46)

RAMPURA

Gulshan Lake

Tejgaon

KAWRAN BAZAR

Mogh Bazar Rd

DIT Rd

MALIBAGH

MOGH BAZAR

New Eskaton Rd

Eskaton Garden Rd

New Elephant Rd

Minto Rd

DIT Rd

Monowara Hospital

Toyenbee Circular Rd

Dharmarajikha Buddhist Monastery

19

Here Rd

Ramna Park

36

21

RAMNA

Siddheswari Rd

Kakrail Rd

Sayedabad Rd

Suhrawardi Park

Segun Bagicha Rd

22

16 12 31 13

NAYA PALTAN

51

DIT Ave

43

6

15

Kamalapur Rd

42 Kamalapur

24

Topkhana Rd

Motijheel Ave

National Stadium

47

FedEx

50

9

14

45

Abdul Ghani Rd

1

48 49

Motijheel Rd

3

17

Hockey Stadium

Rajuk Mosque

Dilkusha II Circle

Shapla Circle (Lotus Flower Fountain Circle)

Dhaka University

Secretariat Rd

MOTIJHEEL

with bold, multi-storey circular and triangular apertures instead of windows.

You can enter the building only on a prearranged four-hour **guided tour** (per person Tk 600), which you must book in advance. You can pick up a booking form at the front gate,

or download it from the parliament website (www.parliament.gov.bd). You also need to bring two copies of your passport and visa. For more information, contact the head of the visitors department **Wares Hossain** (☏01716 479054; waresshaheen@yahoo.com).

# Central Dhaka

**Dhaka University**     HISTORIC BUILDING
(ঢাকা বিশ্ববিদ্যালয়; Dhaka Bisso Biddayaloy; Map p40) Dating from 1921, Dhaka University, or just DU, has some fine old buildings. The architectural masterpiece is the red-brick **Curzon Hall**, a highly impressive example of the European-Mughal style of building erected after the first partition of Bengal in 1905.

**Sat Gumbad Mosque**     MOSQUE
(Map p40) Dating from 1680, Sat Gumbad Mosque is a white-washed onion-dome mosque, and the finest example of the pure Mughal-style mosque in Dhaka.

**Baitul Mukarram Mosque**     MOSQUE
(Map p40) West of Motijheel on Topkhana Rd, this enormous modern mosque is de-signed in the style of the holy Ka'aba of Mecca and is a hard-to-miss landmark. The boisterous market in the surrounding streets stretches around most of the national stadium.

**Old High Court**     HISTORIC BUILDING
(পুরাতন হাই কোর্ট; Map p40) The imposing old High Court, once the governor's residence, is just north of Dhaka University's main campus. It is the finest example in Dhaka of the European Renaissance style.

# 🏃 Activities

See p167 for information about learning Bengali.

### Rickshaw Rides

One of the best ways to see the sights of Dhaka is by cycle-rickshaw, but although taking a rickshaw for a straightforward trip from A to B is easy enough, trying to arrange a city tour with a non-English-speaking rider is well nigh impossible, and finding English-speaking riders is tough. One trick is to hang around outside five-star hotels, where English-speaking riders congregate. Alternatively, wait until you chance upon one who speaks some English and collar him for a future tour. Locals say you can hire rickshaws for around Tk 50 per hour, but you'll do well to get one for less than Tk 100. Expect to pay around Tk 400 for a half-day tour; more if the rider speaks very good English and can therefore also act as a guide. Tour operators can also sometimes arrange sightseeing by rickshaw.

### River Trips

You can take a public rowboat from Sadarghat (p37) across the Buriganga River for just Tk 2, but if you want something a bit more organised, try one of the following.

**Contic**      BOAT TOURS
(☑881 4823; www.contic.com; House 23, Rd 121, Gulshan II) This river-cruise specialist was founded in 1997 by the same people who started Friendship (www.friendship-bd.org) and its floating hospital. Contic has two large but elegant handmade wooden boats, with cooking facilities and accommodation on board, and organises all-inclusive half- and full-day rides as well as overnight trips. Prices start at US$43 and US$50 per person for half- and full-day trips. A three-day, two-night trip costs US$335 per person. Note: they need at least six passengers to run a trip and passengers must book, and pay a 50% deposit, at least one week in advance.

**Guide Tours**      BOAT TOURS
(Map p46; ☑988 6983; www.guidetours.com; 6th fl, Rob Supermarket, Gulshan Circle-II, Gulshan) Offers full-day cruises along the Shitalakkhya River on its yacht, SB *Ruposhi*, with pick-up and drop-off at its office in Gulshan. Prices range from Tk 4200 to Tk 13,000 per person depending on how many are in your group.

## ☞ Tours

**Guide Tours**      TOURS
(p55) The company with the best reputation offers half- and full-day tours in and around Dhaka. Prices for a half-day tour range from Tk 1800 to Tk 4500 per person depending on how many are in your group.

**Bengal Tours**      TOURS
(Map p46; ☑883 4716; www.bengaltours.com; house 45, Rd 27, block A, Banani) Offers half- and full-day city tours. The half-day tours focus on Old Dhaka while the full-day tour spins you around both the commercial city and Old Dhaka. Prices are virtually identical to those of the Guide Tours.

## 🛏 Sleeping

### OLD DHAKA

Many of the very cheapest hotels in Old Dhaka still refuse to accept foreign tourists (although some can be persuaded with a friendly smile and a bit of Bengali). The places we've listed all accepted foreign guests at the time of research.

**Hotel Shadman**      HOTEL $
(Map p36; ☑711 3591; 164 Nawabpur Rd; s/d from Tk 330/510) Shiny-tiled corridors lead to basic but spacious rooms with TV, attached bathroom and lots of natural light (a luxury you don't always get in budget digs in Old Dhaka). Rooms are on the upper floors of a tower block so it's much quieter than at rival hotels. No hot water, no air-con, and squat toilets only.

**Hotel Al-Razzaque International**      HOTEL $
(Map p36; ☑956 6408; 29/1 North-South Rd; s/d Tk 350/550, with air-con Tk 550/800;❄) A welcoming hotel, and as close to the Old Dhaka action as you can get if you're a foreigner. Al-Razzaque has small but tidy rooms with very clean bathrooms. This may be one for your sleeping sheet, though. The hotel sheets were far from spotless when

---

### DHAKA'S ART GALLERIES

**Bengal Gallery of Fine Arts** (Map p40; ☑812 3115; www.bengalfoundation. org; House 275F, Rd 16, Dhanmondi) For art exhibitions.

**DRIK** (Map p40; www.drik.net; Rd 8A, Dhanmondi) For photography.

**Faculty of Fine Art** (Map p40; Kazi Nazrul Islam Ave) For art exhibitions. Housed inside Dhaka University's Institute of Arts and Crafts.

**National Museum** (p39) Also hosts art exhibitions.

## AN IRREPRESSIBLE GIANT

Dhaka's city population is around 7 million, with the population of its metropolitan area double that. This places it in the top 20 largest cities on earth, but perhaps the most worrying statistic is that Dhaka's seemingly irrepressible growth rate shows no signs of abating, and despite its already enormous dimensions, the city continues to expand at a greater rate than most of the world's other large cities. The *Far Eastern Economic Review* has predicted that by 2025 Dhaka will have a population of 26 million people!

we stayed. The attached restaurant is excellent.

### Hotel Ramna                     HOTEL $$
(Map p36; ☎956 2279; 45 Bangabandhu Ave; s/d/tr/q from Tk 500/900/1000/1600;✳) Well-run hotel with bright, spacious rooms and communal balconies overlooking the busy streets below. It's very clean for the price, but is still pretty basic. No hot-water showers, although hot-water buckets can be provided. Squat loos only.

### Hotel Baitus Samir International   HOTEL $
(Map p36; ☎716 2791; 155 Shahid Sayed Nazrul Islam Sarani; s/d from Tk 350/550) Brightly lit, clean rooms with pokey bathrooms represent decent value for Dhaka. As with Shadman, rooms are on upper floors so they're reasonably quiet despite the hectic streets below.

### CENTRAL DHAKA
Central Dhaka, particularly the Motijheel area, has more midrange options, and is still just a short rickshaw ride from the sights and sounds of Old Dhaka.

### Hotel Pacific                    HOTEL $$
(Map p40; ☎716 9842, 01723 821775; www.hotel pacificdhaka.net; 120B Motijheel; r without/with air-con from Tk 1200/2100;✳@☎) A great place to meet other foreign travellers, Pacific is about as close to a backpackers haven as you get in this part of Dhaka, even though prices aren't rock bottom. Staff members are welcoming, very helpful and speak decent English, and there's free internet and wi-fi for all guests. The cheapest rooms are windowless and slightly musty, so it's worth paying Tk 100

more for a window. Hot showers and sit-down toilets are standard.

### White House Hotel                HOTEL $$
(Map p40; ☎832 2973/6; www.whitehousehotelbd. com; 155 Shantinagar Rd; s/d from Tk 1700/1900; ✳@☎) This lovely little hotel has the feel of an English seaside B&B. Bright and breezy corridors lead to homely rooms with rattan furniture and wonderfully comfortable mattresses. There's free wi-fi and the business centre's computers are free, too. Also has car rental in an attached travel centre, plus a decent restaurant.

### Hotel Orchard Plaza              HOTEL $$$
(Map p40; ☎933 0829; www.hotelorchardplaza. com; 71 VIP Rd, Naya Paltan; s/d from US$96/108; ✳@☎) Very smart, well-run hotel with exceptionally friendly staff. Rooms are large, comfortable and spotlessly clean. Wi-fi throughout. Discounts of 30% are the norm. Free airport pick-up.

### Hotel Royal Palace               HOTEL $$
(Map p40; ☎716 8978; www.hrpalace.com; 31D Topkhana Rd; s/d Tk 1100/1500, with air-con Tk 1500/2100;✳✳☎) An olde-worlde hotel with friendly staff, clean and spacious rooms and wi-fi in the lobby. And we love the fact that there's a traditional barber in reception.

### Hotel Midway International       HOTEL $$
(Map p40; ☎831 9315; hotelmidway_30@yahoo. com; 30 VIP Rd, Naya Paltan; s/d Tk 730/1200, with air-con from Tk 1450;✳@) This decent-value hotel is old-fashioned without being too run-down. Rooms are a bit tatty round the edges, but bed sheets, floors and bathrooms are all kept clean, while wooden furniture abounds. Internet costs Tk 60 per hour.

### Hotel Farmgate                   HOTEL $$
(Map p40; ☎911 8538; hotelfarmgate@yahoo.com; 82 West Tejturi Bazar, Farmgate; s/d Tk 1000/1500, with air-con Tk 1500/2000;✳) Small but spotlessly clean rooms are great value in this straight-laced locals' hotel (foreigners are welcome, but don't expect much English). There's a rooftop garden with fabulous views, but no seating. The restaurant on the ground floor is very popular. The hotel is a bit isolated from the main sights, but the area is lively, especially come early evening.

### Hotel Victory                    HOTEL $$$
(Map p40; ☎935 3088; 30A VIP Rd, Naya Paltan; s/d from Tk 2318/3478; ✳@☎) Small, informal hotel with a classic feel to it.

**Imperial Hotel International** HOTEL $$
(Map p40; ☏955 4732; 33-34 Bangabandhu Ave;
r from Tk 1200;❄@☎) Large old-school hotel
facing the enormous Baitul Mukkaram
Mosque.

**SEL Nibash** HOTEL $$
(Map p40; ☏966 1017; www.selrms.com; 30 Green
Rd, Dhanmondi; r from Tk 1950;❄@☎) Slick
business hotel on the fringes of trendy
Dhanmondi.

**NORTH DHAKA**
The main areas of interest here are Banani
and Gulshan, two of Dhaka's most upmarket
residential districts, although most of the best-
value hotels and guesthouses are now concen-
trated in Banani. Prices are higher here than
elsewhere, but the streets are quieter and generally more pleasant places to wander around.
It's also an area where you can find Western-
friendly treats such as international cuisine,
wi-fi cafes and modern supermarkets. This
is still very much the real Bangladesh, but it's
not quite as in-yer-face as the mesmerisingly
hectic streets of Old Dhaka.

**TOP CHOICE Viator** GUESTHOUSE $$$
(Map p46; ☏987 1434, 01717 925272; www.viator
bangladesh.org; House 60, Rd 7A, Block H, Banani;
s/d Tk 1800/2500;❄@) A gem of a guest-
house, Viator is friendly and well run, and
has spotless rooms, which come with bags
of space, plenty of natural light and comfort-
able, quality furniture. Delicious meals are
available at an extra cost (breakfast is free),
and there's an internet and DVD room, al-
though surprisingly no wi-fi. The excellent,
fair-trade handicrafts shop on the ground
floor is perfect for souvenirs. If Viator is full,
you could try neighbouring **Liebenzell Mis-
sion Guesthouse** (☏989 0133; www.liebenzell.

org; House 65, Rd 7A, Block H; r Tk 1250), a small
German-run Christian missionary guest-
house, which also has clean, well-furnished
rooms.

**Sabrina's** HOMESTAY $$
(Map p46; ☏885 6968, 01911 758668; sabhhl@
gmail.com; Apt C1, House 137, Rd 4, Block A, Banani; dm/s/d US$28/35/50;❄@☎) Sabrina, or
Li Mei, is a Chinese expat who has been in
Bangladesh for more than 10 years, and who
recently opened her Banani apartment to
backpackers. It's quickly become one of the
friendliest guesthouses in Dhaka. There are
only four rooms (so make sure you book!),
two with en suite, one without and another
converted into a small bunk-bed dormitory.
All rooms are modern, clean and lovingly
cared for. There's free wi-fi and some great
Chinese home cooking available. There's no
sign, but just say 'guesthouse' to the security
guard at the gate and he'll show the way.
Note: rates are more expensive if you pay in
Bangladeshi taka rather than US dollars.

**Lakeshore** HOTEL $$$
(Map p46; ☏885 9991; www.lakeshorehotel.com.
bd; House 46, Rd 41; r from US$270; ❄@☎☀)
Everything about this small but top-quality
hotel, from the modern glass bathroom fit-
tings to the rooftop pool fit for a New York
millionaire, is simply magnificent. If you fit
into this price category then the chances are
you fit into this hotel. Discounts mean you
should be able to nab standard rooms for
less than US$200.

**Hotel Sarina** HOTEL $$$
(Map p46; ☏885 9604; www.sarinahotel.com; Rd
17, Banani; r from US$200;❄@☎☀) Modern
but refined business hotel with plenty of
class. Small enough to feel intimate, but big

**DHAKA'S 5-STAR HOTELS**

The following offer familiar, international-standard, five-star facilities and services. At the
time of research, Hilton and Marriott were also rumoured to be planning hotels in Dhaka.

**Westin** (Map p46; ☏989 1988; www.starwoodhotels.com/westin; cnr Gulshan Ave & Rd 45;
r from US$199;❄@☎☀) The pick in terms of quality and its Gulshan location.

**Radisson Blu Water Garden Hotel** (☏875 4555; www.radissonblu.com/hotel-dhaka;
Airport Rd, Dhaka Cantonment; r from US$190;❄@☎☀) Best for the airport.

**Pan Pacific Sonargaon** (Map p40; ☏814 0401; www.panpacific.com; 107 Kazi Nazrul Islam
Ave; r from US$350;❄@☎☀) Distinguished. Rates drop to around US$150.

**Ruposhi Bangla Hotel** (Map p40; ☏833 0001; www.ruposhibanglahotel.com; 1 Minto Rd;
r from US$260;❄@☎☀) Former Sheraton, with plans to reopen as an Intercontinental.
Rooms discount to US$150.

# North Dhaka

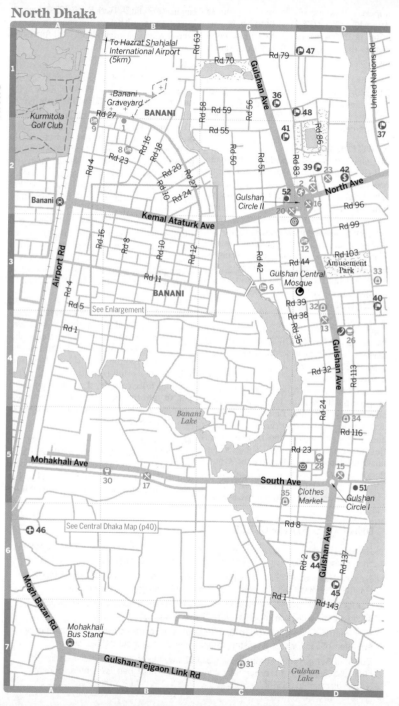

To Hazrat Shahjalal
International Airport
(5km)

Kurmitola
Golf Club

Banani
Graveyard

**BANANI**

Rd 27

Rd 16
Rd 18
Rd 23

Rd 20
Rd 27
Rd 24
Rd 10

Rd 63
Rd 70

Rd 58
Rd 59
Rd 55

Rd 79

Rd 96
Gulshan Ave

36

48

41

Rd 86

37

Rd 50
Rd 51

Rd 83

39
23
42

2
21

North Ave

52

Gulshan
Circle II

20
16

Rd 96

Rd 99

@

Banani

**Kemal Ataturk Ave**

Rd 16
Rd 8
Rd 10
Rd 12

Airport Rd

Rd 4

Rd 11

**BANANI**

See Enlargement

Rd 5

Rd 1

12

Rd 42
Rd 44

Gulshan Central
Mosque

Rd 103
Amusement
Park

33

6

Rd 39
Rd 38
Rd 35

32
13
26

40

Gulshan Ave

Rd 32

Rd 24

Rd III

Banani
Lake

34
Rd 116

Rd 23

28
15

**Mohakhali Ave**

30
17

**South Ave**

35
Clothes
Market

51

Gulshan
Circle I

See Central Dhaka Map (p40)

46

Rd 8

Rd 2
44
Gulshan Ave
Rd 137

Mogh Bazar Rd

Rd 1

45

Rd 143

Mohakhali
Bus Stand

31

**Gulshan-Tejgaon Link Rd**

Gulshan
Lake

47

9

8

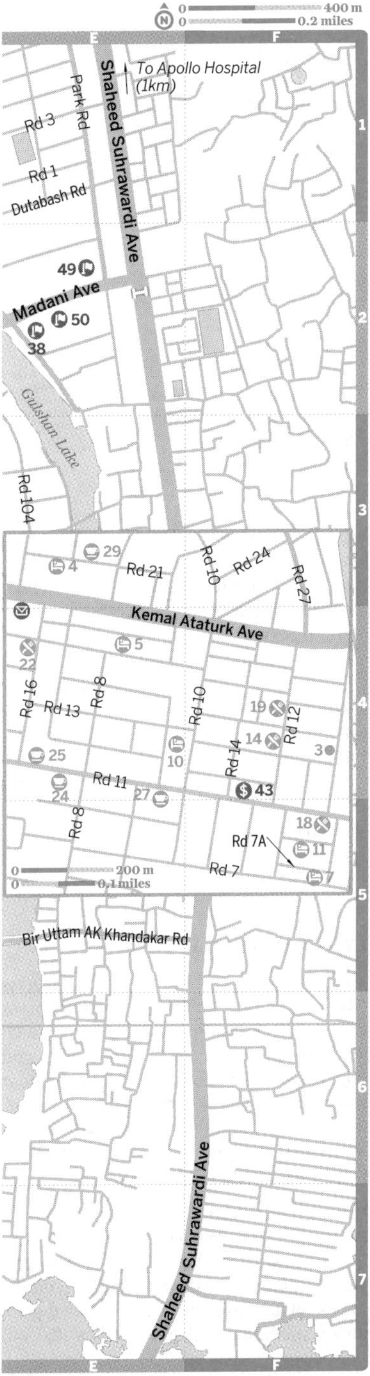


enough to house three quality restaurants, a bar and a small gym and pool as well as large and very comfortable rooms. Service is uniformly excellent. Expect 30% to 40% discounts.

**Royal Park** HOTEL **$$$**
(Map p46; ☎881 5945; www.royalparkbd.com; House 85, Rd 25A, Block A, Banani; r from US$100; ❄@📶🏊) Comfortable rather than luxurious, this small business hotel does still offer good facilities and excellent service. Rates include wi-fi, airport pick-up, as well as use of the gym and pool.

**Hotel De Castle** HOTEL **$$$**
(Map p46; ☎881 2888; www.hoteldecastle.com; House 72, Rd 21, Block B, Banani; r from US$60; ❄@📶) Reliably clean and inviting rooms with a quiet and cool atmosphere. Rates include in-room wi-fi, airport pick-up and breakfast. And you can usually nab rooms for around US$50.

**Sky Park Guesthouse** HOTEL **$$**
(Map p46; ☎989 9894; skyparkbd@yahoo.com; House 65, Rd 15, Block D; Banani; r from Tk 1500; ❄@📶) A mixed bag of rooms.

**Regent Guest House** HOTEL **$$**
(Map p46; ☎881 2858; hotelregentbd@yahoo.com; House 100, Rd 13C, Block E, Banani; s/d from Tk 1700/2200) A bit tatty, but OK if others are full.

## Eating

### OLD DHAKA

TOP CHOICE **Haji Biryani** BANGLADESHI **$$**
(Map p36; Kazi Allaudin Rd, Nazira Bazar; biryani Tk 130; ⌚4.30-9.30pm) An Old Dhaka institution, Haji only does one dish – mutton biryani – but, as you can imagine, it does it exceedingly well. This place is tiny, so you'll almost certainly have to share a table: squeeze in, sit down and just wait for your biryani to arrive. Do as the locals do and drip some lime juice over it before you tuck in, then chomp on a fresh chilly in between mouthfuls. No English sign, but it's next to a mosque, and its green metal shutters are noticeable.

**Al-Razzaque** BANGLADESHI **$**
(Map p36; 29/1 North-South Rd; mains Tk 50-150; ⌚6am-1am) Wildly popular with the locals, and rightly so, Al-Razzaque does delicious curries, biryanis and Bangladeshi breakfasts, but the pièce de résistance here are the plate-sized flaky rotis, which are absolutely magnificent. No English menu, but some English spoken.

# North Dhaka

## 🏃 Activities, Courses & Tours

**Nana Biryani** BANGLADESHI $
(Map p36; Abul Khairat Rd; biryani Tk 90; ⊗7am-1am) Like Haji Biryani, this place has no English sign or menu, and there's little English spoken, but persevere; Nana serves up arguably the best chicken biryani in Dhaka. They also do mutton biryani, plus some tasty mutton-tikka cakes as a side dish.

**Hotel Star** BANGLADESHI $
(Map p36; BCC Rd; meals Tk 100; ⊗6am-2am) Very popular, no-nonsense restaurant with dependable curries and biryanis, though the speciality here is kebabs. Not quite as good as those served up at its sister branch in Dhanmondi (p49), but still more than decent. Has an English menu.

## CENTRAL DHAKA

**TOP CHOICE Santoor** INDIAN $$$
(Map p40; House 2, cnr Rd 11 & Mirpur Rd; mains from Tk 300; ⊗noon-3pm & 6-10.30pm) Named after an Indian stringed instrument and billed as a 'symphony of dining', Santoor serves up mouthwatering Indian dishes, including south Indian favourites such as *dosa, idli, vada* and *uttapam*. The tandoor kebabs also shouldn't be missed.

**Malancha Restaurant** BANGLADESHI $
(Map p40; 50 New Elephant Rd; mains from Tk 100; ⊗7am-midnight) Students from nearby university campuses flock here to fill up on the knockout biryanis and curries. Kebabs are also sometimes available. Food is laid out

buffet style so you can just point and choose, although they do have an English menu.

### Star Hotel & Kebab
BANGLADESHI $

(Map p40; Rd 2, Dhanmondi; mains from Tk 120; ☺5.30am-midnight) One of the most popular of Dhaka's Star Kebab chains, this one does a mutton leg roast to die for, plus the usual tasty biryanis and curries, and very good dhal-and-roti breakfasts. For Star's best kebabs in town, walk round the corner and up Satmasjid Rd for a few hundred metres until you come to the **Star Kebab Stall** (kebabs Tk 60-80; ☺1-11pm), which does stunning beef, chicken and mutton takeaway kebabs and has an English menu stuck up on one wall.

### Dhaka Roti House
BANGLADESHI $

(Map p40; off Inner Circular Rd, Naya Paltan; mains Tk 50-100; ☺7am-midnight) The guys working at the ever-busy tea stalls on Inner Circular Rd recommended this as the best kebab place in the area. You can thank them later. The beef *sheekh* (grilled kebab on a skewer) and the grilled chicken are sumptuous, and the rotis sure aren't bad either. Also does biryani and a few curry dishes, but this place is all about the kebabs. No English sign or menu, but some English spoken. Take the lane down the side of the cinema and it's the first restaurant on your right.

### New Café Jheel
BANGLADESHI $

(Map p40; 18/1 Topkhana Rd; mains Tk 80; ☺6am-midnight) Thick, fiery curries at this bright and clean favourite. Tk 120 will get you a curry, rice and naan bread. Bargain.

## NORTH DHAKA

### ⬒ TOP CHOICE Star Kebab & Restaurant
BANGLADESHI $

(Map p46; House 15, Rd 17, Block C, Banani; mains from Tk 60; ☺6am-midnight) Arguably the best branch of the hugely popular Star Kebab chain, this one is a hit with the local student population, and does ever-dependable and ever-affordable local nosh in a clean, bright and bustling environment. Expect to share a table. Excellent for Bangladeshi breakfasts. English menu, and English spoken.

### Spaghetti Jazz
ITALIAN $$$

(Map p46; 43 North Gulshan II; mains from Tk 600; ☺12.30-3pm & 6.30-10.30pm) A stylish and intimate setting for the best pizza and pasta you'll find anywhere in Bangladesh. Highly recommended.

### Dhaba
INDIAN $$

(Map p46; House 104, Rd 12, Block E, Banani; mains from Tk 100-300; ☺11.30am-10.30pm) Indian street food served in a clean, trendy, air-con restaurant. Everything here is delicious, but the *chaat puchka* (spicy snacks, Tk 50 to Tk 70) are excellent value. Choose a couple of those, and you won't need a main course.

### Gulshan Plaza Restaurant
BANGLADESHI $

(Map p46; Gulshan DIT II; mains Tk 90; ☺7am-midnight) Proving Gulshan isn't just about Western-friendly posh nosh, this no-frills local favourite knocks out tremendous mutton, chicken and beef curries as well as solid biryanis and delicious roast chicken. Also does excellent naan, roti, beef *sheekh* kebabs, dhal and even glasses of *lassi* (yogurt drink). No English menu.

---

## TEA BREAK

There are tea stalls all over Dhaka and beyond, meaning a quick sightseeing pit stop is never far away. Tea here is generally sweet and milky. If you want it without milk ask for *lal cha* (literally, red tea), while *chini na* or *chini sera* means 'without sugar'. A cup of *cha* usually costs around Tk 5. Here are three of our favourite tea stalls:

**Dhanmondi Lake** (Map p40; Dhanmondi Lake, off Satmasjid Rd; ☺6am-10pm) The tea and instant coffee (Tk 20) is nothing special but the location, on a tree-shaded island on Dhanmondi Lake, is certainly cool. Popular young hangout come late afternoon/early evening.

**VIP Rd** (Map p40; VIP Rd, Naya Paltan; ☺9am-10pm) A series of roadside tea stands between Hotel Orchard Plaza and Hotel Victory. Rickshaw riders swear this is the best tea spot in the city.

**Bara Katra** (Map p36; Bara Katra, Chowk Bazar, Old Dhaka) One tiny tea stall (basically an old bloke with a tea pot), set into the ancient arch that once made up part of Bara Katra. Seating for one is available if you don't mind a stone ledge.

### Oh! Calcutta
BANGLADESHI **$$$**

(Map p46; House 49, 6th fl, Rd 11, Block H, Banani; mains Tk 300-600; ⊘noon-3.30pm & 7-11pm) Top-notch Bengali cuisine in a fancy but friendly restaurant. Has an extensive menu.

### Bamboo Shoot
CHINESE **$$$**

(Map p46; RM Centre, 2nd fl, Gulshan Ave; mains Tk 350-600; ⊘noon-3.30pm & 6.30-11pm) The most authentic Chinese restaurant in Dhaka, and well worth a splurge. In the same building as Agora supermarket, which all rickshaw riders know.

### Pan Tau
THAI **$$$**

(Map p46; House 42, Rd 12, Block E, Banani; mains Tk 400-500; ⊘noon-3pm & 6-11pm) Sumptuous Thai curries, a refined atmosphere and excellent service. A relatively new player on the Banani food scene, but already one of the best Thai restaurants around.

### Roti Gosht Aur Chawal
BANGLADESHI **$$**

(Map p46; Gulshan II Circle; mains Tk 100-300; ⊘noon-midnight) Friendly, pocket-sized restaurant with a limited choice of delicious curries to be scooped up with fine *rumali* (extra-thin) roti. The kebabs are excellent, the beef *sheekh* stupendous. English menu. Accessed from the back of Gulshan Circle, not from the main crossroads.

### Nandan Restaurant
BANGLADESHI **$**

(Map p46; Mohakhali Ave, Banani; mains from Tk 80) Does the whole gamut of Bengali dishes, but it's the grilled chicken and the various kebabs that steal the show, as well as the delicious naan bread.

### Sura
KOREAN **$$$**

(Map p46; House 2, Rd 90, Gulshan; mains Tk 500-1000; ⊘noon-3pm & 6-10pm) The best Korean restaurant in town. Expensive, but authentic.

### Fakruddin
BANGLADESHI **$**

(Map p46; 37 Bir Uttam AK Khandakar Rd, Gulshan Circle I; mains Tk 90-150; ⊘12.30-2.30pm & 6.30-8pm) Very popular no-nonsense biryani joint. English menu.

 **Drinking**

Apart from top-end hotels, which have hideously expensive bars, and the embassy clubs, which you need to be invited to by members, Dhaka's only drinking options are a handful of dark, seedy, smoky bars, frequented almost entirely by men. They're an experience to visit, rather than a place for a pleasurable drink, but can be fun if you get a group together. Drinks are mostly cans of beer plus hard spirits such as whisky, tequila and vodka. They all do food, too. In fact, they are, strictly speaking, restaurants. All are closed on Fridays.

### Sakura
BAR

(Map p40; off Kazi Nazrul Islam Ave; ⊘noon-3pm & 5.30-10.30pm) Dark, smoky and woman-less, but very popular. Local beers from Tk 150 and imported beers from Tk 260. Located on 2nd floor of a small handicrafts market opposite Ruposhi Bangla Hotel. After trading hours, you have to enter from around the back of the market.

### La Diplomat
BAR

(Map p46; House 5, Rd 20, Gulshan Circle I; ⊘11.30am-3pm & 6-10.30pm) Typically dark, seedy and smoky, but staff members are welcoming. Local beer from Tk 180.

### Ruchita Restaurant & Bar
BAR

(Map p46; 83-88 Mohakhali Ave; ⊘11am-10.30pm) Another dark, smoky affair, and more of a restaurant set-up than the other two mentioned here. Local beer Tk 170, imported beer Tk 250.

## ☆ Entertainment

### Cinema

### Star Cineplex
CINEMA

(☎913 8260; www.cineplexbd.com; tickets Tk 150-250) On the top floor of the massive shopping centre Bashundhara City (Pantha Path; ⊘9.30am-8pm); often has English-language options for the latest Hollywood blockbusters.

### Sport

Although *kabaddi* is the national sport, it's cricket that the locals go crazy for. If you can catch a Test match, or a one-day international while you're here, count yourself lucky. Check www.banglacricket.com for the latest.

### Theatre, Music & Dance

The best places to search for upcoming arts and music events are the English-language newspapers. The *Daily Star* (www.thedailystar.net) is No 1 for this, and its website has a What's on This Week section, although the *Independent* (www.theindependentbd.com) also has daily listings in the print version of its newspaper.

Venues with regular events include the following:

### Shilpakala Academy
THEATRE

(Map p40; ☎956 2836; www.bdshilpakala.org; 14/3 Segunbagicha, Ramna) City's premier venue for theatre, dance and art.

## WAKE UP & SMELL THE COFFEE

Thought hot drinks in Dhaka would be all about *cha*? Think again. Western-style cafes are all the rage now in upmarket Banani, Gulshan and Dhanmondi. Many serve decent fresh coffee, do comfort food like sandwiches and pasta, and offer free wi-fi. Here are some of our favourites:

**Cafe Mango** (Map p40; Rd 5, off Green Rd, Dhanmondi; ☺10am-10pm; ☏) The coolest cafe in town. Trendy decor, excellent coffee (from Tk 100) and scrummy Western food. Free wi-fi.

**Cofi II** (Map p46; House 6A, Rd 113, Gulshan; ☺noon-midnight; ☏) Sixth-floor cafe with good fresh coffee (from Tk 120), decent food and fabulous views, especially from the garden terrace. Free wi-fi.

**Club Gelato** (Map p46; House 50, Rd 11, Banani; ☺10.30am-11.30pm) No wi-fi, but excellent coffee (from Tk 100) and the best ice cream in Bangladesh (from Tk 120).

**Roll Xpress** (Map p46; House 34, Rd 21; Banani; ☺11am-10.30pm; ☏) Quiet, refined court-yard, good but pricy coffee (from Tk 140), and quality Western food. Free wi-fi.

**Coffee World** (Map p46; House 98, Rd 11, Banani; ☺9am-midnight; ☏) Yeah, so it's a chain, but it's bright, comfortable, does OK coffee (from Tk 95) and opens earlier than most. Free wi-fi.

**King's Confectionary** (Map p46; House 17, Rd 11, Banani; ☺7am-10.30pm) Banani's poor man's cafe, King's doesn't have wi-fi, or particularly good coffee, but it's down to earth, has a small back yard to chill out in, and does loads of good cakes.

**Chhayanaut Auditorium** THEATRE
(Map p40; House 72, Rd 15A, Dhanmondi) The best place in Dhaka to see performances of classical Bengali music and traditional folk music.

## 🛍 Shopping

There are very few things you can buy in Bangladesh that you can't buy in Dhaka, and Dhaka is certainly the place with the largest selection of Bangladesh souvenirs.

### Clothing

**Aarong** CLOTHING & HANDICRAFTS
(www.aarong.com) Gulshan (Map p46; Gulshan-Tejgaon Link Rd, Gulshan 1; ☺10am-8pm, closed Sun); Dhanmondi (Map p40; 1/1, Block A, Mirpur Rd; ☺10am-8pm, closed Thu) If you want to shop for all your Bangladesh souvenirs under one roof, look no further. Aarong is the biggest name in quality Bengali clothing and handicrafts, and is the retail branch of the Bangladesh Rural Advancement Committee (BRAC), which aims to create employment for economically and socially marginalised people through the promotion of traditional Bangladeshi handicrafts. Has half a dozen branches, but the best two are these huge ones south of Gulshan and north of Dhanmondi. Both have a small cafe.

**Kumudini** CLOTHING & HANDICRAFTS
(Map p46; 74 Gulshan Ave; ☺10am-8pm) Three floors of top-quality traditional Bengali clothing and handicrafts, including some lovely children's clothes and toys, as well as a variety of jute products.

**Banga Bazar** MARKET
(Map p36; College Rd) Large, hectic clothing market with seconds, and factory overruns, providing plenty of scope for bargain hunting.

**Prabartana** CLOTHING & HANDICRAFTS
(Map p40; www.prabartana.com; Mirpur Rd, Mohammadpur; ☺10am-8pm, closed Thu) Helping support women in Bangladesh, this quiet shop and cafe sells colourful Bangladeshi clothing and handicrafts.

### Handicrafts

**Viator** HANDICRAFTS
(Map p46; www.viatorbangladesh.org; House 60, Rd 7A, Banani; ☺10am-10pm) The fair-trade handicrafts shop attached to the excellent Viator guesthouse, this place has a selection of trinkets, paintings, textiles and carvings, mostly made by Adivasis from the Chittagong Hill Tracts.

**Folk International** HANDICRAFTS

(Map p46; www.folkinternational.webs.com; House 19, Rd 108, Gulshan; ⊙10am-8pm) A nonprofit with a similar selection to Viator.

**Jatra** HANDICRAFTS

(Map p40; House 39, Rd 16, Dhanmondi; ⊙10am-8pm, closed Tue) Folk handicrafts with a funky modern twist.

## Bookshops

Many of the smaller handicrafts shops, including Viator and Folk International, sell English-language books on Bangladesh history, culture and travel. They also stock Mappa maps, the best maps you can find for Bangladesh.

**First Chain Bookshop** BOOKS

(Map p40; www.pbschain.com; Shantinagar Rd, Naya Paltan; ⊙10am-9pm) Large bookshop with good range of English-language books, especially kids books, and music CDs. It has a small cafe and juice bar, and free wi-fi. Can buy online, too.

**Words 'n' Pages** BOOKS

(Map p46; Rd 7, Gulshan I; ⊙10am-8pm) Decent stock of English-language novels and kids books.

## Other

**Bangshal Rd** RICKSHAWS

(Bicycle St; Map p36) This street in Old Dhaka, and the adjoining Kazi Alauddin Rd, is the place to buy rickshaw parts, rickshaw art or even rickshaws themselves. The art is painted on thin strips of tin (later attached to the back of rickshaws), which can be rolled up to fit nicely inside most suitcases or rucksacks. Expect to pay around Tk 100. Bargaining is required, of course.

**New Market** MARKET

(Map p40; Mirpur Rd; ⊙closed Mon afternoon & Tue all day) Dhaka's largest market. Sells pretty much anything you can imagine.

**Agora** SUPERMARKET

(Map p46; RM Centre, ground fl, Gulshan Ave; ⊙9am-8pm) Dhaka's best Western-style supermarket, with branches all over the city.

## ℹ Information

### Dangers & Annoyances

Considering its massive size, Dhaka is a remarkably safe city and few travellers experience any problems in terms of crime (although you should always take extra care of your belongings in overly crowded places such as markets and train and bus stations).

The biggest danger is road safety. Road accidents are all too common. Take trains rather than buses when you can, and you should be extra vigilant when crossing the city's hectic streets. In fact, in Dhaka you should even have your wits about you when walking along pavements – potholes are not uncommon, nor are low-hanging electricity cables.

One major annoyance, of course, is air pollution, which can be horrendous, particularly if you are prone to allergies.

Hartals (strikes) and accompanying violent demonstrations are common, although as a tourist you won't be targeted. Still, it's sensible not to get involved. Be curious, but from a distance.

Also see p169.

### Emergency

For an ambulance you need to call a private hospital such as Apollo or Monowara. A call-out fee will be charged. See p52.

**Fire** (☑199)

**Police** (☑999)

### Internet Access

Internet cafes are few and far between in Dhaka, and they are always closed on Fridays. However, many of the hotels we've reviewed have internet access and/or wi-fi, and a growing number of Western-style cafes have free wi-fi (see the boxed text p51).

If you're in Bangladesh with your laptop for a month or more, it's also worth considering buying a modem stick from one of the mobile telephone operators (see p53).

**Cyber Cafe** (Map p46; Golden Plaza Market, Gulshan Ave, Gulshan Circle II; per hr Tk 40; ⊙10am-8pm) Inside a small electronics market, just off Gulshan Ave.

**Cyber Cafe** (Map p40; Green Rd, Dhanmondi; per hr Tk 30; ⊙9am-11pm) Next door to SEL Nibash Hotel.

**e-park Cyber Cafe** (Map p40; Toyenbee Circular Rd, Motijheel; per hr Tk 25; ⊙10am-9pm) A short walk from the main train station.

**SM Cyber Cafe** (Bangshal Rd, Old Dhaka; per hr Tk 40; ⊙10am-11pm) Up a narrow staircase to the 2nd floor.

### Medical Services

Dhaka has the best medical facilities in the country but we still advise you go elsewhere for major procedures and surgery.

**Apollo Hospital** (Map p46; ambulance ☑840 1661, 01714 090000, appointments ☑884 5242; www.apollodhaka.com; Plot 81, Block E, Bashundhara Residential Area, off Pragati Ave) Probably the best hospital in Dhaka.

**International Centre for Diarrhoeal Disease Research in Bangladesh Hospital** (ICDDRB; Map p46; ☑989 9620, 01730 019695; www. icddrb.org/clinic; 68 Shahid Tajuddein Ahmed Sharani, Mohakhali; ☉8.30am-5pm Sun-Thu) The travellers' clinic here is excellent for travel health advice and travel-related issues such as vaccinations. A consultation costs Tk 1000 (Tk 4000 if you have medical insurance). You should make an appointment, but if you have an emergency, such as needing a rabies jab, they will see you on the spot.

**Lazz Pharma** (Map p40; ☑911 7839; www. lazzpharma.com; 64/3 Lake Circus, Zubida Super Market, Kalabagan, Dhanmondi; ☉24hr) A 24-hour pharmacy; stocks the anti-malarial drug Doxycycline.

**Monowara Hospital** (Map p40; ☑831 8135; 54 Siddeshwari Rd) Handier for Central and Old Dhaka.

## Money

A growing number of ATMs accept foreign bank cards. At the time of research, the most reliable were AB Bank, Standard Chartered Bank, Trust Bank and HSBC. We've marked foreign-friendly ATMs on our maps. For other money-changing services, try these bank branches. Opening hours are 10am to 4pm and 6pm to 8pm Sunday to Thursday, and 2pm to 4pm on Saturdays.

**HSBC** (☑966 0547; www.hsbc.com.bd) Chowk Bazar (Map p40; Water Works Rd, Chowk Bazar); Gulshan (Map p46; cnr Gulshan Ave & Rd 5, Gulshan Circle I); Motijheel (Map p40; Motijheel Rd, Motijheel)

**Standard Chartered Bank** (Map p40; ☑833 2272; www.standardchartered.com/bd; Motijheel Rd, Motjheel)

## Post

**DHL** (Map p40; ☑955 3511; 93 Motijheel Rd; ☉9am-9pm) More expensive, but far more reliable than the Bangladesh postal service. In a back alley, just off Motijheel Rd. There's a branch of **FedEx** (☑956 5113; ☉9am-10.30pm) next door.

**Main Post Office** (Map p40; cnr Abdul Ghani & North-South Rds; ☉9am-6pm Sat-Thu) Also houses the unusual **Post Museum** (2nd fl; ☉9.30am-4pm Sun-Thu), including old stamps from practically every country in the world.

## Telephone

**Grameenphone** (Map p46; ☑988 5261; www. grameenphone.com; cnr of Gulshan Ave & Rd 113; ☉9am-7pm) For local SIM cards for your mobile phone, and internet modems for your laptop. Staff members speak good English. Also has a SIM card counter as you exit customs at the airport, as well as branches across the country. When you want to top up your phone, the magic phrase is 'flexi-load'.

# ❶ Getting There & Away

## Air

At the time of research there were four main domestic airlines, linking Dhaka with such places such as Chittagong, Cox's Bazar, Sylhet, Rajshahi and Jessore. United is the pick of the bunch. See the relevant regional chapter for domestic flight details.

United services a few international destinations including Kolkata, Kuala Lumpur and Dubai. Biman operates around half a dozen international routes, including direct flights to the UK.

Other more reputable airlines flying in and out of Dhaka include **Emirates** (www.emirates.com), **Malaysia Airlines** (www.malaysiaairlines.com), **Singapore Airlines** (www.singaporeair.com) and **Thai Airways** (www.thaiairways.com). At the time of research, budget airline **Tiger Airways** (www.tigerairways.com) had just started flights between Dhaka and Singapore.

**Biman** (Map p40; ☑956 0151; www.biman airlines.com; Dilkusha II Circle, off Motijheel Rd, Motijheel; ☉9am-5pm)

**GMG Airlines** (☑891 5699; www.gmgairlines. com; airport, domestic terminal) Had temporarily ceased operations at the time of research, but planned to relaunch towards the end of 2012.

**Regent Airlines** (Map p46; ☑895 3003; www.flyregent.com; SA Tower, Bir Uttam AK Khandakar, Gulshan Circle I)

**United Airways** (Map p46; ☑885 4769; www. uabdl.com; Taher Tower Shopping Center, Gulshan Circle II)

## Boat

You're supposed to book 1st-class Rocket (paddle-wheel) tickets at the **Bangladesh Inland Waterway Transport Corporation head office** (BIWTC; Map p40; ☑955 9779, 891 4771; ☉Sun-Thu 9am-4.30pm) in Motijheel. Second-class tickets should be bought at the much-harder-to-find **Badamtoli office** (☑739 0691; ☉8am-4pm), close to the Badamtoli boat terminal, although with a smile and some persistence you may be able to persuade the guys at the head office to sell you 2nd-class tickets, too. Deck-class tickets are bought on board, but are hard to come by for the overnight trips, which start in Dhaka.

The Rocket departs at 6pm from Sadarghat (Map p36) every day except Friday. At the time of research, you could only go as far as Morrel-ganj, not all the way to Khulna, as had traditionally been the case. For more details see the boxed text on p71.

Private ferries, known as launches, also leave Sadarghat daily. Tickets are just bought from the boat in question. Long-distance trips leave in the evening, from around 7pm, and travel overnight. Shorter trips leave throughout the day.

One possible daytime journey is the four-hour trip to Chandpur in Chittagong division. Private launches leave roughly every hour from 6.30am. See the boxed text p112 for more details.

## Bus

The bus system in Bangladesh seems mind-bogglingly chaotic at first, but you soon get used to it. Large bus stations, such as those in Dhaka, are made up of a series of ticket counters, each selling tickets to different destinations. None has English signage. To find the right one, just mention the name of your destination to the first few people you stumble across, and you'll soon be ushered towards the correct ticket counter or, at smaller stations, towards the bus itself. Note: a ticket counter is sometimes just a wooden table.

It's often the case that a number of companies run buses on the route you want, and ticket prices vary slightly from company to company, so treat the prices listed here as guidelines rather than absolute figures.

Also note that bus stations are generally referred to as bus stands.

### GABTALI BUS STAND

Dhaka's largest bus station, **Gabtali** (Map p35) is a madhouse; be on guard for pickpockets (particularly after dark), but in general people are very friendly and helpful. Most buses leave from around 7am until at least 5pm.

**Barisal** Tk 250, six to nine hours

**Bogra** Tk 280, five hours

**Dhamrai** Tk 30, one hour

**Dinajpur** Tk 500, 10 hours

**Jessore** Tk 300, seven hours

**Khulna** Tk 450, eight hours

**Rajshahi** Tk 400, six hours

**Rangpur** Tk 400, seven hours

### SAYEDABAD BUS STAND

**Sayedabad** (Map p35; Hatkhola Rd) is another huge station, which serves many of the same destinations as Gabtali, but is used mostly for accessing places to the east of Dhaka. All of the main coach companies have offices in and around this station, so it's tempting to pay a bit extra for more legroom.

**Cumilla** Tk 100, three hours, 5.30am to 10.30pm

**Chandura** (for border at Akhaura) Tk 120, three hours

**Chittagong** Tk 250, six hours, 5am to midnight

**Sylhet** Tk 300, five hours, 5am to 11.30pm

### MOHAKHALI BUS STAND

The smaller, more manageable **Mohakhali** (Mogh Bazar Rd) serves places in north Dhaka division. If you take a rickshaw from Banani to here (Tk 40), you'll have to walk the last stretch, along Mogh Bazar Rd.

**Birisiri** Tk 200, five to seven hours, 7.30am

**Mymensingh** Tk 160-200, four hours, 6am to 9pm

**Tangail** Tk 120, two hours, 6am to 8pm

### GULISTAN (FULBARIA) BUS STAND

Hectic **Gulistan** (Map p36; Gulistan Crossing, Nawabpur Rd), just north of Old Dhaka, is basically just a series of roadside bus stops. Destinations include Sonargaon (Tk 35, one hour).

### BRTC INTERNATIONAL BUS TERMINAL

This small and orderly **international bus terminal** (Map p40; ☑935 3882; Kamalapur Rd) has two daily buses to Kolkata (Tk 1400, 11 hours, 7.30am), which both leave at the same time. It's best to book a couple of days in advance if you can. Also has thrice-weekly buses to Agartala (Tk 300, four hours, 8am Monday, Wednesday and Thursday). See p22 for more on border crossings.

## Coach

The major coach companies have offices dotted around the city, but two places where there's a concentration of them are on the fringes of Sayedabad bus stand and along Toyenbee Circular Rd, just north of Motijheel. Expect to pay about twice as much as for a normal bus, and three or four times as much if you opt for air-con. The most popular companies are **Green Line** (always air-con), **Soudia**, **Hanif** and **Shohagh Paribahan**, but there are many others.

## Train

Like all train stations in Bangladesh, Dhaka's main train station, **Kamalapur** (Map p40), is relatively well organised and easy to manage (especially if you've just come from India!). Many trains to and from here also stop at the smaller Banani and Airport train stations, both of which are more convenient if you're staying in North Dhaka. Buying tickets is straightforward, although they sell out very quickly. At the time of research tickets were being sold up to 10 days in advance, but this then changed to three days in advance. Check to see if this is still the case because it's worth trying to buy your tickets as soon as they're released. Note that you can buy tickets in advance from Banani train station ticket office even if your train won't be stopping there. You can also book tickets using your mobile phone, through the Grameenphone (www.grameenphone.com) network. Check the 'MobiCash' section of their website for details. Plans to introduce an e-ticketing system had been on the table for a while, but at the time of research had yet to materialise.

See the boxed text p55 for selected trains from Kamalapur Station. All Chittagong trains go via Akhaura (1st seat/*shuvon* Tk 130/75, two to three hours), for the India border, and Comilla (1st seat/*shuvon* Tk 170/75, three to four hours).

## SELECTED TRAINS FROM DHAKA

| DESTINATION | TRAIN NAME | DEPARTS | ARRIVES | FARE (1ST SEAT/ SHUVON) | OFF DAY |
|---|---|---|---|---|---|
| Chittagong | Mahanagar Provati | 7.40am | 2.20pm | Tk 290/125 | none |
| Chittagong | Chittagong Mail | 10.30pm | 7.15am | Tk 450/290/125* | none |
| Dinajpur | Drutajan Ex | 7.40pm | 5am | Tk 535/370/185* | Wed |
| Khulna | Sundarban Ex | 6.20am | 4.50pm | Tk 420/200 | Sat |
| Khulna | Chittra Ex | 7pm | 5.15am | Tk 625/420/200* | Mon |
| Mymensingh | Balaka Commuter | 10.30am | 2.10pm | Tk 110/60 | none |
| Rajshahi | Silkcity Ex | 2.40pm | 8.55pm | Tk 285/140 | Sun |
| Sylhet | Parabat Ex | 6.40am | 1.10pm | Tk 270/150 | Tue |
| Sylhet | Upaban Ex | 9.50pm | 5.10am | Tk 425/270/150* | Wed |

*1st berth/1st seat/shuvon

All Sylhet trains go via Srimangal (1st berth/1st seat/shuvon Tk 300/200/110, five hours). All Khulna trains go via Jessore (1st berth/1st seat/shuvon Tk 535/385/180, eight hours).

Twice a week (Wednesday and Friday), there is a direct train to Kolkata (without/with air-con Tk 910/1353, 11 hours, 8.10am), in India. The train leaves from Dhaka Cantonment train station (Map p35), but you have to buy your tickets at a designated ticket counter (open 9am to 5pm) at Kamalapur Train Station (or at the train station in Chittagong). You will, of course, need a valid Indian visa for this train journey.

## ❶ Getting Around

### To/From Hazrat Shahjalal International Airport

Top-end hotels often include airport pick-up in their room rates. And most midrange hotels will have a pick-up service for a charge (expect at least Tk 1000 to a hotel in Banani).

It's cheaper, of course, to take a taxi. There's a **fixed-rate taxi booth** just outside the airport exit. Expect to pay between Tk 500 and Tk 800, depending on where you are heading. If you walk out to the car park or beyond, you'll be able to negotiate cheaper fares yourself, depending on your levels of patience.

It's cheaper still to catch a CNG (auto-rickshaw). Expect to pay Tk 150 to Tk 200 to Banani (North Dhaka), and about twice that to Motijheel (Central Dhaka). Your bargaining position will increase if you walk further out of the airport towards the main road, where there will be more CNGs to choose from.

Local buses do run from the main road into the city, and are very cheap (Tk 10 to Tk 20), but

they are extremely difficult to negotiate for non-Bengali speakers, and are always packed.

Cycle-rickshaws aren't allowed at the airport or on the main highway leading to it.

### Bus

Cheaper than cheap, local buses have no English signs, and their numbering is in Bengali. They are always overcrowded, so boarding between major bus stops is no mean feat. Fares vary, but around Dhaka you rarely need to pay more than Tk 10.

### CNG

Most auto-rickshaws are run on compressed natural gas in Dhaka, and hence are known as CNGs. Some people also refer to them as baby taxis. They all have meters, but it's very rare to find a driver willing to use one, so get ready for some hard bargaining. Also prepare yourself for some hair-raising rides through the city streets. It seems no gap is too small for a CNG to squeeze through! Here's a rough guide to the sort of fares you can expect:

**Airport to Banani** Tk 150
**Airport to Motijheel** Tk 300
**Banani to Gulistan Crossing** Tk 100
**Banani to Gabtali bus stand** Tk 150
**Banani to Sadarghat** Tk 150

### Car

You'll need an International Driver's Licence to drive here, although we don't recommend you do. Quite a few tourists opt to hire a car with a driver, though.

The **Guide Tours** (p55) and **Bengal Tours** (p43) both offer this service, as do some midrange guesthouses and top-end hotels. Expect to pay around Tk 3000 for a half day, and Tk

4500 for a full day. Add to that at least another Tk 2500 if you also want a guide.

### Rickshaw

Dhaka's fantastically colourful rickshaws (which in Bangladesh means cycle-rickshaws) are a tourist attraction in their own right (see the boxed text p162) and you should go for a spin in them as often as you can. You will find them everywhere (there are around 400,000 of them on the streets on any one day!), and when traffic is crowded (as it usually is) they're not much slower than anything else that moves. Rickshaws are restricted from moving right across the city by traffic regulations and sheer distances, so you can usually travel only short distances, within a particular neighbourhood. Prices are negotiated. We find that Tk 10 per kilometre is normally about right.

### Taxi

Taxis are harder to find than CNGs. There are two types of taxis on the roads of Dhaka. The yellow Navana taxis are more spacious, have air-con and are usually cleaner than their black counterparts, but you pay for the difference. Meters in yellow taxis clock more quickly and at a higher rate than the black taxis, but this is often irrelevant because, as with CNGs, most drivers are reluctant to use the meters.

### Tempo

Fast and cheap to use, tempos (large shared auto-rickshaws) are a convenient way to travel if you know where you're going, aren't carrying much luggage and don't mind rib-cage compression.

A trip from Gabtali bus stand to Farm Gate costs around Tk 10.

### Tomtom

Unashamedly touristy, horse-drawn carriages, or tomtoms, can still be found on the outskirts of Old Dhaka. You'll see them trotting along from the Gulistan Crossing down to Sadarghat (per person Tk 20), picking up whoever they can as they go.

# Dhaka Division

## Best Places for History

» Sonargaon (p59)
» Muktagacha (p63)
» Mymensingh (p61)

## Best Landscapes

» China Clay Hills (p65)
» Someswari River by Birisiri (p64)
» Sonargaon (p59)

## Why Go?

Enveloping the city of Dhaka, and including some destinations that make great day trips from the capital, Dhaka division stretches for more than 250km from south to north, reaching right up to the border with the Garo Hills in India.

It's a rural wonderland, comprising some 25,000 villages, and much of the region is given over to radiant rice paddies, filling your vision with more hues of green than you ever knew existed. A smattering of wonderfully romantic, slowly decaying ruins also lends a historic air to the region, but it's the land in the far north of Dhaka division that has perhaps the greatest pull. This is where glistening paddy fields give way to dappled forests, great rivers and hilly panoramas, and where the indigenous culture of the Garo people awaits the more adventurous traveller.

## When to Go
### Mymensingh

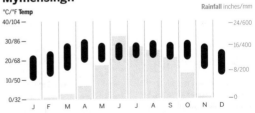

**Oct–Mar**
The dry season means off-the-beaten-track trips in the far north.

**Jun/Jul**
Dhamrai has chariot-pulling during the Rath Jatra festival.

**Jun–Sep**
Monsoon brings boggy roads, but the landscape is a sight in itself.

## Dhaka Division Highlights

**1** Explore charmingly dilapidated ruined mansions, little-visited ancient mosques and a stunning rajbari-turned-museum in Bangladesh's one-time capital of **Sonargaon** (p59)

**2** Plug yourself into the Adivasi way of life at the remote forested village of **Birisiri** (p64)

**3** Hike, boat or ride a rickshaw to the small but stunning turquoise lake at the **China Clay Hills** (p65)

**4** Wander the old-town market streets and enjoy tree-shaded riverside walks in the laidback town of **Mymensingh** (p61)

**5** Meet the craftspeople at the unusual metalcraft workshops in the Hindu village of **Dhamrai** (p60)

**6** Examine the crumbling 300-year-old ruins of the once-magnificent rajbari at **Muktagacha** (p63)

# Sonargaon

Sonargaon, or Golden City, was the eastern capital of Bengal at various times in history. It slipped into decline when Muslim rulers decided to move their capital to Dhaka in the 17th century, and is now little more than a couple of villages with a scattering of ruins. It makes an excellent day drip from Dhaka, though, combining countryside, culture, archaeology and adventure in one easily accessible bundle.

Very little remains of the original city – a couple of mosques and some indistinguishable mounds of earth, most of which are found around the small village of Mograpara to the west of the main highway. What most people now visit for is Painam Nagar, a charmingly decaying street of dilapidated mansions built by wealthy Hindu merchants just over a century ago, and Sadarbari, a beautifully restored rajbari (Raj-era palace) with a gorgeous pondside setting and an interesting folk-art museum.

## ◉ Sights & Activities

**Sadarbari**                                    MUSEUM
(folk-art museum; admission Tk 100; ⊘9am-5pm Fri-Tue) Built in 1901, this stunning rajbari is an appropriate building for a folk-art museum. The building has two facades. The one facing the main road, with steps leading down to the water and life-size English horsemen in stucco on either side, is one of the most picturesque in Bangladesh. The other, at the museum's entrance, is profusely embellished with a mosaic of blue and white tiles, and has an Andalucian look to it.

Inside, the unadorned rooms are stuffed full of folk art and handicrafts from the 17th century onwards. Around the back of the rajbari, and on the opposite side of the lake, is a new building containing another museum of folk-art objects.

The beautiful water-soaked gardens around the back of rajbari are another highlight, and perfect picnic territory.

Your ticket gains you entrance to the grounds as a whole, as well as to both museums.

It takes about 30 minutes to walk here from where the bus drops you off. Rickshaws (Tk 10 to Tk 20) are also widely available.

**Painam Nagar**                                  RUINS
The once-elegant town of Painam Nagar is busy fighting a losing battle with nature, and with every passing year the trees and vines drape themselves a little further over the decaying houses. The result is a delightful ghost-town quality where the buildings appear to hang like exotic fruits from the branches of the trees.

Constructed almost entirely between 1895 and 1905 on a small segment of the ancient capital city, this tiny settlement consists of a single street, lined with around 50 (now dilapidated) mansions built by wealthy Hindu merchants. At the time of Partition, many owners fled to India, leaving their elegant homes in the care of poor tenants, who did nothing to maintain them. Most of the remaining owners pulled out during the anti-Hindu riots of 1964, which led to the 1965 Indo-Pakistan War. Despite the rot, a few people continue to live in some of the houses and their bright shades add a technicolour tint to the village.

**Goaldi Mosque**                                 MOSQUE
Built in 1519, and now virtually hidden behind thick bamboo groves and clusters of mango and jackfruit trees, is the graceful, single-domed Goaldi Mosque. This is the most impressive of the few extant monuments of the original capital city, and a fine example of pre-Mughal architecture. It is one of the oldest surviving mosques in the country.

Opposite, and standing beside a pond, is the still-active Abdul Hamid's Mosque, originally built in 1705, but now with a more modern look to it due to recent renovations.

Few people know about these mosques (including some rickshaw riders) so it's often best to walk here. In any case, it's a lovely walk across farmland from Painam Nagar and only takes around 15 minutes. Just keep asking for 'Goaldi Masjid'.

## ✖ Eating

If you don't bring your own picnic, you can grab lunch from any one of a cluster of roadside restaurants opposite Sadarbari. Expect to pay between Tk 100 and Tk 200 for a simple rice-and-curry meal.

## ℹ Getting There & Away

Buses (Tk 35, one hour) leave frequently from Dhaka's Sayedabad bus stand and drop you at a crossroads on the main Dhaka–Chittagong Hwy, from where rickshaw-wallahs will be keen to show you to the sights. The area also makes for pleasant walking.

# Sonargaon

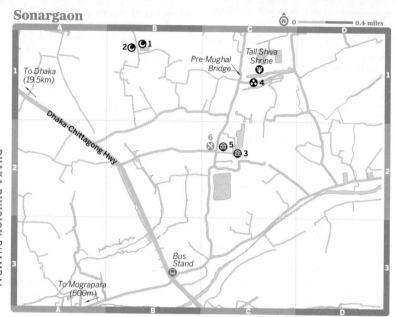

**To Dhaka (19.5km)**

Pre-Mughal Bridge

Tall Shiva Shrine

Dhaka-Chittagong Hwy

Bus Stand

**To Mograpara (500m)**

## Sonargaon

### ⊙ Sights
1 Abdul Hamid's Mosque ....................... B1
2 Goaldi Mosque ..................................... B1
3 New Museum ......................................... C2
4 Painam Nagar ........................................ C1
5 Sadarbari .............................................. C2

### ⊗ Eating
6 Roadside Restaurants ....................... C2

## Dhamrai

This predominantly Hindu village with a few surviving metalcraft workshops makes an unusual day trip from Dhaka and is particularly rewarding during major Hindu festivals. The main strip is a busy market street, but it also contains a dozen or so extravagant century-old houses built by the wealthy Hindu families who once lived here. One such house contains the **Dhamrai Metal Crafts Workshop** (☑01713 003136), the most accessible of three workshops in the village that have revived the ancient lost-wax technique of making brass and bronze statues. The owner, Sukanta Banik, speaks excellent English and is more than happy to give visitors a guided tour of his family's beautiful old house and its fascinating workshop. There is no pressure to buy anything, but there are a number of objects on sale that make excellent souvenirs.

The workshop is at the far end of the town, on the left just after the **Jagannath Chariot**, a multistorey chariot adorned with painted images from Hindu mythology, which sits in the middle of the road and is paraded down the street during the Hindu festival of Rath Jatra (see p17). Just beyond the workshop is an alleyway on your left, which leads to the village's principal Hindu temple, built close to an ancient Shiva temple, which is now being swallowed by the undergrowth.

Buses to Dhamrai pass the **National Martyrs' Memorial** (Jatiyo Smriti Saudha; pronounced 'jat-ee-yo shmree-tee shod-oh'), a tapering 50m-high memorial to the millions who died in the struggle for independence and which is housed in well-kept gardens. The memorial is on the outskirts of the industrial town of Savar.

### ❶ Getting There & Away

Buses (Tk 30, one hour) leave frequently from Dhaka's Gabtali bus stand and drop you at a junction on the main road. Turn right here and keep walking for a few hundred metres until you reach Dhamrai village. Keep walking straight to get to the workshop. Buses between Dhamrai and the National Martyrs' Memorial cost Tk 5.

# Mymensingh

☏091 / 230,000

A leafy town built on the banks of the mighty Brahmaputra River, Mymensingh enjoys a lovely riverside setting, a sprinkling of Raj-era buildings and one of the most interesting old quarters in the country. It also acts as an ideal launchpad for off-the-beaten-track excursions further north – a rarely visited region dotted with Garo villages and swathed in lush, green landscape.

## ⦿ Sights & Activities

**Old Town Area**                            MARKET
The original alleyway-riddled core of the town, located between the train station and the waterfront, is a fascinating place in which to get lost. It's filled with market stalls selling all manner of food and goods. Keep an eye open for the gold workshops, huddled away in the mess of streets, where people hammer down minuscule gold pieces found in the riverbed in order to make jewellery. The town has a large Hindu minority and there are several noticeable Hindu shrines in the old town area. The most obvious is the rotting stone **Shiva temple** just by the water.

**Riverbank Parks**                          PARKS
The thin stretch of park area on the waterfront at the western edge of town makes up one of the most enjoyable public spaces in this part of Bangladesh, and come late afternoon locals take full advantage by decamping down here to lull about in the shade of trees and watch multicoloured boats criss-cross the river. There are several small tea stalls and a few benches dotted around, or else rest up at **Sarinda Park Cafe**. In the playing fields just behind the parkland, numerous cricket matches add their thunk and whack to proceedings. Should you want a closer look at the other side of the river, one of the small wooden **boats** will happily take you over (Tk 2). From the far bank, set off across this rural oil painting towards one of the many little villages whose inhabitants are likely to be overjoyed to have you around. It's a perfect setting in which to create your own adventure!

**Mymensingh Rajbari**              HISTORIC BUILDING
Built between 1905 and 1911, this well-kept former mansion in the middle of the city is now occupied by an organisation that trains female teachers, but much of the original structure remains. An ornamental marble fountain with a classical statue of a semi-nude nymph lies just beyond the arched gateway entrance. Behind the main building is the Jal-Tungi, a small two-storey bathhouse once used as the women's bathing pavilion. You can politely ask the security guard for admittance to the grounds, but

## BANGLADESH'S GOLDEN CITY

The ancient capital of Sonargaon (or 'Golden City' in Hindi) flourished as the region's major inland port and centre of commerce during the pre-Muslim period. By the 13th century it was the Hindu seat of power. With the Muslim invasion and the arrival of the sultan of Elhi in 1280, its importance magnified as the region's de facto Islamic capital. Some 42 years later, the first independent sultan of East Bengal, Fakhruddin Mubarak Shah, officially established his capital in Sonargaon.

For the next 270 years, Sonargaon, known as the 'Seat of the Mighty Majesty', prospered as the capital of East Bengal, and the Muslim rulers minted their money here. An envoy from the Chinese emperor visited Sultan Ghiyasuddin Azam Shah's splendid court here in 1406. He observed that Sonargaon was a walled city with broad streets, great mausoleums and bazaars where business of all kinds was transacted. In 1585, famous traveller Ralph Fitch noted that it was an important centre for the manufacture and export of *kantha* (traditional indigo-dyed muslin), the finest in all of India. Ancient Egyptian mummies were reportedly wrapped in this *kantha* exported from Bengal.

When the invading Mughals ousted the sultans, they regarded Sonargaon's location along the region's major river as too exposed to Portuguese and Mogh pirates. In 1608 they moved the capital to Dhaka, thus initiating Sonargaon's long decline into oblivion. Yet its legendary fame for incredibly fine muslin fabric continued undiminished until foreign competition from the British (and their import quotas) ruined the trade.

# Mymensingh

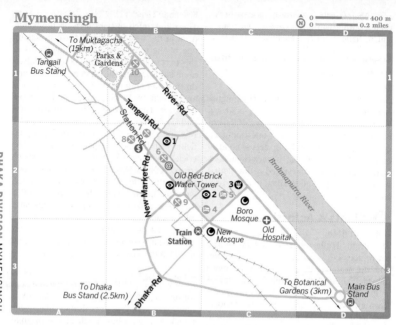

## Mymensingh

**⊙ Sights**

**🛏 Sleeping**

**🍴 Eating**

it is doubtful whether he will grant you a glimpse of the interior of the building.

**Botanical Gardens**                                GARDENS
(বোটানিকাল গার্ডেন; entrance Tk 5; ◷9am-5pm) Three or four kilometres east of town, next to the Agriculture and Fisheries College, are the large and peaceful botanical gardens. Well laid out, although not particularly well maintained, they make a decent place to relax on a bench with a book. You can also get

boats across the river from here. A rickshaw from the town centre costs around Tk 30.

## 🛏 Sleeping

**Hotel Amir International**                       HOTEL $$
(☏51500, 01711 167948; Palika Shopping Centre, 46 Station Rd; s/d Tk 750/1000, d with air-con Tk 1500;❄) Lots of shiny tiled floors make this a neat and clean place to stay. Rooms come with a wooden desk and chair, satellite TV and hot water. The manager speaks some English. You may be told the non-air-con rooms are all taken, but they almost certainly won't be.

**Nirala Rest House**                              HOTEL $
(☏67384; 67 Chotto Bazar; s/d from Tk 200/475) A perfectly acceptable budget option, Nirala – in business now for more than half a century – has rooms that are small and basic but clean enough and that come with their own small attached bathrooms (squat loo only). Coming from the train station, take the first of the two roads on your left opposite the mosque. The hotel is then on your left. Limited English.

## 🍴 Eating

As well as the places listed here you can also pick up a cheap meal or kebab in the train station approach road, while tea stalls set up in the afternoon along the northeastern stretch of the riverbank.

### Sarinda
BANGLADESHI $$

(CK Ghosh Rd; mains from Tk 100; ☺9am-11pm) Kebabs, roast chicken, fish and biryani in one of the town's smartest restaurants. Popular with families.

### Rom III Restaurant
BANGLADESHI $

(1st fl, 25 Shaymachoron Roy Rd; mains from Tk 75; ☺7am-midnight) Tasty curries and delicious kebabs, but not as clean or comfortable as Sarinda. Serves small-sized portions, though, so it's handy for single travellers, but note that rice is sold in double portions unless you ask otherwise. On the opposite side of the road, ROM III Sweets & Bakery curbs all your sugar cravings.

### Sarinda Park Cafe
CAFE $

(River Rd; ☺6am-11pm) The menu is nothing special – instant coffee only, plus a few local snacks such as *shobji* (mixed vegetable curry, pronounced 'sabzee') and, if you're lucky, kebabs, but the very well-maintained garden is a lovely place to rest up if you can't find a suitable bench along the riverbank. Menu in Bengali only, and not much English spoken.

### China Green Restaurant
CHINESE $$

(Station Rd; mains Tk 150; ☺11am-11pm) Pretty standard Chinese fare, but OK if you fancy a break from the local cuisine.

### ⓘ Information

Two or three ATMs around town accept foreign cards. Check email at Toyal Cyber Cafe (Station Rd; per hr Tk 25; ☺9.30am-9.30pm).

### ⓘ Getting There & Away
**Bus**

The Dhaka bus stand, 2km south of town, only serves Dhaka (Tk 200, four hours, 5.40am to 7.30pm). Buses to most other destinations leave from, or at least pass through, the extremely hectic Bridge bus stand; destinations include Birisiri (Tk 65, 3½ hours, 6.30am to 8.30pm) and Bogra (Tk 120, six hours, 6.30am to 8.30pm). Buses to Muktagacha (Tk 20, 30 minutes, 6am to 8pm) leave from the Tangail bus stand.

## Around Mymensingh
### MUKTAGACHA

A wonderful decaying 300-year-old rajbari, and a traditional sweet so lip-smackingly delicious that it's famed across the country, make the quiet village of Muktagacha a worthy half-day trip from Mymensingh.

Spread over 10 acres, the rajbari here is a special estate, even in disrepair. The main structure is bedecked with Corinthian columns, high parapets and floral scrolls in plaster. Inside you'll find, among other things, a former treasury with the last of 50 safes and a room that the caretaker quaintly describes as the 'finishing room', but is actually a less quaint execution chamber. The main audience chamber here has the remnants of a rotating dance floor, while the Rajeswari temple and the stone temple, believed to be dedicated to Shiva, are just two of the finer shrines you'll find within the complex. Just outside are the former stables for the rajbari's 99 elephants; the area is now occupied by the local police. The caretaker here speaks broken English and will probably find you and offer you a guided tour. He's quite a character and well worth the baksheesh he'll ask for. Offering him

### SELECTED DAILY TRAINS FROM MYMENSINGH

| DESTINATION | TRAIN NAME | DEPARTS | ARRIVES | FARE (1ST/SHUVON) |
|---|---|---|---|---|
| Chittagong | Mymensingh Ex | 6.40am | 10.10pm | Tk 76* |
| Dhaka | Jamuna Ex | 5.03am | 8.10am | Tk 110/60 |
| Dhaka | Jamalpur Commuter | 7.10am | 10.30am | Tk 110/60 |
| Dhaka | Balaka Ex | 2.50pm | 6.40pm | Tk 110/60 |
| Dhaka | Dewangonj Ex | 3.55pm | 7.25pm | Tk 110/60 |
| Dhaka | Aghnibina | 6.38pm | 10.05pm | Tk 110/60 |
| Dhaka | Brahmaputra Ex | 8.33pm | 11.45pm | Tk 110/60 |

* *shuvon* class only

## ADIVASI FOCUS: THE GAROS

**Name** They call themselves the A-chik Mandi (literally 'hill people'), although most outsiders refer to them as Garos.

**Population** Around two million in total, of which around 100,000 to 200,000 are thought to live in Bangladesh.

**Current region** Largely in and around the Garo Hills of India.

**Original homeland** The Garo are thought to have migrated from the Tibetan plateau more than 2000 years ago.

**Religion** Thanks to the efforts of 19th-century missionaries, most Garos are now Christians, though they often maintain aspects of a traditional belief system known as Sangshareq.

**Language** A-chick in India, A-beng in Bangladesh. A surprisingly large number of Garo people also speak English.

**Favourite tipple** Rice-beer.

**Unusual fact** The Garo are one of the world's few matrilineal societies – titles and land ownership are passed down through the women of the family, and when a man marries he moves into his wife's house. They are not matriarchal; men still tend to govern Garo communities and manage the properties that the women own.

around Tk 50 for his tour of the complex seems to be fair, but it's entirely your choice.

Few locals visit the rajbari, but they're less likely to miss a chance to stop off at the well-known **Gopal Pali Prosida Monda Sweet Shop** (☎01711 707909), which makes the best *monda* (grainy, sweetened yogurt cake) in the country. Almost 200 years ago the Pal family cooked these delicious sweets for the zamindar (landowner), who liked them so much that he employed the family. When the landowner's family left during Partition, the Pal family opened shop and have been in business ever since. It's a tiny but refined place where you can sample *monda* (per piece Tk 15) on a silver-plated dish, or take away a boxload for ensuing bus journeys.

The rajbari is signposted from the main road where the bus will drop you off. For the sweet shop, walk straight ahead as you exit the rajbari, then turn right at the end of the lane and the shop will be on your left. Look for the lion motif over the door.

## Birisiri

☎09525

Birisiri is a quiet, welcoming Garo village, set in a small forest close to the Someswari River. It offers little in terms of tourist sights, but the journey here, across lush farmland, is extremely picturesque and the village is within striking distance of the highly photogenic China Clay Hills. Most interestingly perhaps, Birisiri offers travellers the chance to meet and learn more about the Garo people.

### ⊙ Sights & Activities

**Tribal Cultural Academy**                    MUSEUM

The only 'sight' in Birisiri, this small research museum is worth poking your head into. You may have to ask around to get someone to unlock the doors, but once you're in you'll find exhibits displaying the culture and traditions of local ethnic minorities such as the Garo. The museum is a short walk north along the main road from the centre of Birisiri.

### 🛏 Sleeping & Eating

Your only food options are the no-frills roadside restaurants on the main street where the bus drops you off. The one next door to, and to the left of, Swarna Guesthouse does the most consistently good dishes. The chicken and rice here is decent. It's open all day and you won't pay more than Tk 100 for a meal. Swarna Guesthouse is easy to spot on the main street and has cheap rooms if the YWCA and YMCA both happen to be full.

**YWCA**                              YOUTH HOSTEL $

(☎0171 2042916; Birisiri; dm/s/d from Tk 200/600/800) Set in the woods surrounding Birisiri village, this well-looked-after hostel has clean, tidy rooms that overlook an attractive garden with a cute bamboo pergola. Very friendly, but sometimes fully booked because of training days held here. Follow the signs down a track from the main road where the bus drops you off and keep walking for a few hundred metres.

### YMCA

(☑56266, 01743 306230; Birisiri; dm from Tk 120, private rooms from Tk 350) Slightly more rundown than the YWCA but just as welcoming and enjoys the same peaceful forest setting. Rooms are pretty basic, with pokey squat-toilet bathrooms, but they overlook a huge garden, which houses the even more basic dorms. It's down the same lane as the YWCA but about 200m closer to the main road, where the lane splits off to the left.

## ❶ Getting There & Away

Buses to Mymensingh (Tk 65, 3½ hours) leave throughout the day from the main road. One bus continues all the way to Dhaka (Tk 200, 3pm, seven to eight hours). It usually leaves at around 3pm, but it's worth checking this when you're here. Coming here from Dhaka, there is one direct bus, which leaves from Mohakhali bus stand at 7am.

## Around Birisiri

### CHINA CLAY HILLS

The cool turquoise-blue waters beside the China Clay Hills are reminiscent of a high-altitude mountain lake, but in fact the hills are no more than small mounds, raised just a few metres above the level of the surrounding farmland and river systems. Despite the small-scale mining that goes on here from time to time, it's still an extremely photogenic spot, and makes a lovely place for tree-shaded picnic, but the main reason to venture this far north is for the journey itself.

Either take a tranquil three-hour rowboat trip up the Someswari River, or else a bone-rattling, but ever such fun two-hour rickshaw ride, crossing the river on a small wooden ferry before passing through a number of remote villages en route. You could even hike all the way from Birisiri and back if you left early enough in the morning. Just keep asking villagers for *cheena mati pahar* (China Clay Hills).

English-speaking staff at Birisiri's YMCA or YWCA can help arrange either a boat or a rickshaw to the China Clay Hills. Expect to pay around Tk 600 for a rowboat (three hours one way) or Tk 1200 for a motorboat (one hour one way). Note that boats can't take you all the way to the China Clay Hills because the site isn't beside the river. They will likely drop you at Ranikhong, from where you'll have to pick up a rickshaw or walk. Hiring a rickshaw for the day from Birisiri costs around Tk 400.

# Khulna & Barisal

## Includes »

## Best Places for Scenery

» Sundarbans National Park (p71)

» Kuakata (p85)

» Villages around Bagerhat (p76)

## Best Places for Boat Trips

» Sundarbans National Park (p71)

» Barisal (p83)

» Kuakata (p85)

## Why Go?

Unexplored jungle swamps teeming with wildlife as danger-ous as it is beautiful make this region stand out as the one many people want most to visit. Comprising in large parts of nothing but marshlands, waterlogged jungles and rivers, this archetypal explorer country is not easy to navigate, but it promises to leave you with some of your most abiding memories of Bangladesh.

The star attraction, of course, is the Sundarbans, the world's largest mangrove forest and home to the largest sin-gle tiger population on earth. If you organise only one trip in Bangladesh, make sure it's a trip to the Sundarbans.

Your tiger-tracking tendencies satisfied, don't shoot straight back to Dhaka. There are historic mosques, seclud-ed beaches and a mesmerising network of rivers to explore, as well as the chance to take some of the best boat trips this water-laden country has to offer.

## When to Go

### Jessore

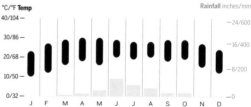

| Oct–Feb | Mar | Apr |
|---------|-----|-----|
| Mildest and most pleasant time to visit the Sundar-bans. | Thousands of pilgrims descend on Kushtia to pay their respects. | Trek through the Sundarbans in honey-harvesting season. |

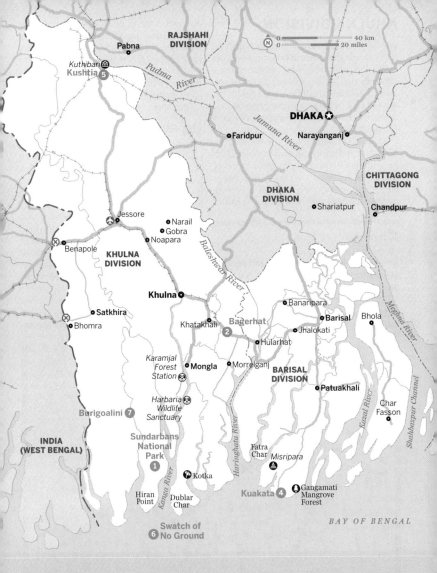

## Khulna & Barisal Highlights

**①** Float through the forests of the **Sundarbans National Park** (p71) in search of the elusive Royal Bengal tiger

**②** Visit the magnificent Islamic architecture at **Bagerhat** (p76) before exploring the forested villages

**③** Ride the **Rocket** (boxed text p71), a paddlewheel steamer and Bangladesh's most famous boat

**④** Travel to the remote beach of **Kuakata** (p85), on the eastern fringes of the Sundarbans

**⑤** Contemplate the poetry of Rabindranath Tagore or the folk songs of the Baul musician Lalon Shah in **Kushtia** (p81)

**⑥** Come in winter and hook up with a research boat to go whale-watching at the **Swatch of No Ground** (boxed text p77)

**⑦** Time your visit for the start of April and join the **honey harvest trail** (boxed text p77) in the depths of the Sundarbans forests

# KHULNA DIVISION

The tigers and mangrove forests of the Sundarbans are the main reason for venturing out to this southwest corner of the country, although the Islamic ruins of Bagerhat are another big draw. Sadly you can't get all the way out here by Rocket steamer any more, but the part-ferry, part-bus journey from Dhaka to Khulna, via Barisal, can be a lot of fun.

Travellers heading to or coming from Kolkata in India will also pass through Khulna – the land border at Benapole is one of Bangladesh's busiest – while Kushtia makes an interesting stop if you're on your way north to the history-rich division of Rajshahi.

## Khulna

☎ 041 / POP 855,000

Khulna, capital of the province, and launchpad for trips into the Sundarbans, is a town on the frontier. Beyond its scraggly streets

awaits a range of extraordinary adventures that, for many travellers, are the sole reason for coming to Bangladesh. Though the town itself offers few tangible sights, this frontier sensation hangs heavy in the air and only the most jaded of travellers won't feel a flutter of excitement as they step off the bus that carried them here.

## 🛏 Sleeping

**New Safe Hotel** HOTEL **$**
(☎813 355; JK Tower, 83 Khan A Sabar Rd; s/d Tk 460/690 with air-con Tk 750/980;❄) This friendly hotel, above a motorbike showroom, was pretty much brand new at the time of research so it should still be in decent condition by the time you read this. Compact but tidy rooms come with white-tiled flooring and sparkling bathrooms with sit-down loos. Even if it's lost some of its newly opened shine by the time you get here, it should still represent good value. Breakfast included.

## Khulna

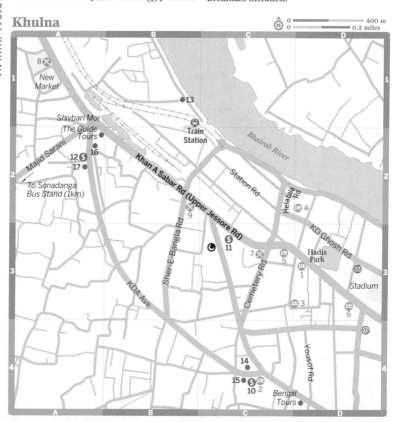

**Western Inn International** HOTEL $$
(☎810 899; western-inn.com; 51 Khan A Sabar Rd; r incl breakfast from Tk 1300; ❄@✆) All in all, this is probably the best hotel in Khulna. Rooms are pricey, admittedly, but they are huge and come with free wi-fi, spotless bathrooms and balconies overlooking a ragged, tree-shaded garden. The restaurant is decent and staff members are generally pretty helpful.

**Hotel Jalico** HOTEL $
(☎811 883; jalickhotel@yahoo.com; 77 Lower Jessore Rd; incl breakfast s/d from Tk 440/690, with air-con Tk 750/1000; ❄) Run by a charming manager (though not all staff share his friendliness), Jalico is one of the best-value hotels in Khulna, with large, spotless rooms and good city views. Air-con and fan rooms are the same; it's just that you can choose not to use the air-con and pay a cheaper rate.

**Hotel Castle Salam** HOTEL $$
(☎732 799; www.hotel-castlesalam.com; cnr Khan Jahan Ali Rd & KDA Ave; r Tk 600-1600; ❄@✆) Rooms are cheaper, but much smaller than those at Western Inn – Castle's main rival – and they don't have the balconies or wi-fi. But this is still a smart, well-run hotel, which is kept very clean, and there is at least wi-fi in the lobby. Also has a good restaurant,

and a trendy coffee shop attached. Breakfast with air-con rooms only.

**Hotel Arcadia** HOTEL $
(☎01751 219130; 76 Khan A Sabar Rd; s/d from Tk 300/600) Concrete floors are swept regularly and sheets are kept clean, and although the singles are cramped, double rooms are reasonably spacious. Only some rooms have sit-down toilets. Staff members are welcoming to foreign guests despite limited English. Decent budget choice.

**Hotel Society** HOTEL $
(☎01731 936466; Helatala Rd; s/d from Tk 150/250) Simple, spartan rooms come with desk, chair, TV and whitewashed walls. Bathrooms are wincey and squat-loo only, but this is the cheapest acceptable place in town. Not much English spoken.

## ✖ Eating

Two of the best restaurants in town are attached to two of Khulna's best hotels, the Western Inn and Castle Salam. Nonguests are welcomed at either. Both serve a good selection of Bengali, Indian and Chinese dishes, from around Tk 100 upwards per dish. And both are open from around 7am to 11pm, although they close during mid-afternoon for a couple of hours.

**Aloka Restaurant** BENGALI $
(1st fl, 1 Khan A Sabar Rd; mains from Tk 80; ☺7.30am-10.30pm) Delicious, no-nonsense main courses – biryanis, kebabs, curries – plus hearty breakfasts – dhal, fried egg, paratha – presided over by a friendly manager who speaks decent English. No English menu, but staff will help you choose.

**Grillhouse** BENGALI $$
(New Market; mains Tk 90-180; ☺10am-11pm) The kebabs here are mouthwatering. Sadly, they are served only from 4.30pm onwards and the last few times we've been here only the chicken tikka ones have been available. Still, they are delicious. Kebabs aside, the menu has a fairly ordinary selection of Bengali and Chinese dishes, but the friendly English-speaking manager ensures a cordial atmosphere.

**Goon Goon Coffee Shop** CAFE $
(Hotel Castle Salam, 1st fl; ☺9am-11pm) Stocks pastries, sandwiches and cakes as well as doing fresh coffee. Floor-to-ceiling windows at one end afford good street views. Located on the 1st floor of Hotel Castle Salam, but open to nonguests.

## Khulna

## FISHING WITH OTTERS

Fishing with otters has been taking place for at least 1000 years and was once fairly wide-spread across the world; in the UK it didn't die out until 1880. There are two techniques employed by the fishermen; one involves the otters individually catching fish and returning them to the fishermen while the other (and the technique employed in Bangladesh) involves a net being lowered into the water and 'shuffled' along the river bed or against clumps of water plants to disturb the fish, which the otters then chase into the net.

The Guide Tours (www.guidetours.com) and Bengal Tours (www.bengaltours.com) organise day trips and overnight trips to villages such as Hariar, where this ancient fishing practice can still be found. For any semblance of authenticity, you need to book yourself on an overnight trip because fishing with otters is a nocturnal practice. Daytime demonstrations are laid on for tourists, but we've received reports that they feel overly contrived.

It is possible to reach these villages yourself (see below), but unless you speak Bengali it's extremely difficult to arrange to spend a night on a boat with a fisherman.

Expect to pay Tk 10,000 for a day trip from Khulna organised through a tour operator, or as much as Tk 30,000 for an all-inclusive overnight trip. If you turn up on your own, fishermen will ask for as much as Tk 8000 for a daytime fishing demonstration. You may be able to get them down to around Tk 1000 to Tk 2000.

### Getting to the Villages

First take a local bus from Khulna to Noapara (Tk 30, 45 minutes), from where you need to hop on a ferry (Tk 2) to cross the river (the ferry ghat is down a lane on the other side of the street from where you get off the bus). From the other side of the river, turn right to catch a bus to Gobra (Tk 30, 40 minutes). You can walk from Gobra to the village of Goyalbari, where there are some otter fishermen. Or you can catch a motorcycle taxi from Gobra to Singasolhur Village (TK 50), from where you hop on another local river ferry (Tk 2) to Hariar.

Note that, if you're heading for Goyalbari, you can easily do a round trip in a day. If you're heading for Hariar, you'll need to leave early (before 9am) to make it back to Khulna the same day.

---

**Meena Bazar**  SUPERMARKET $

(Khan A Sabar Rd) Stock up on extra snacks for your Sundarbans boat trip from this small Western-style supermarket chain.

## ℹ Information

**Bengal Tours** (☎724 355; www.bengaltours.com; 236 Khan Jahan Ali Rd; ☺9.30am-5pm) Housed in a crumbling, blue-washed colonial building.

**Cafe.net** (2/2 Babu Khan Rd; per hr Tk 20; ☺10am-10.30pm)

**Guide Tours** (☎731 384; www.guidetours.com; KDA Bldg, KDA Ave; ☺9am-5pm)

**Standard Chartered Bank** (KDA Ave) Changes money and has an ATM. Two AB Bank ATMs can also be found.

## ℹ Getting There & Away

### Air

The nearest airport is at Jessore.

**United Airways** (☎730 699; 75 KDA Ave, 3rd fl; ☺9am-7pm) Provides a shuttle bus between the airport and its Khulna office (Tk 200 one way). Leaves the office three hours before outbound flights, and meets incoming flights from Dhaka at the airport.

### Boat

The **Bangladesh Inland Waterway Transport Corporation** (BIWTC; ☎721 532) is responsible for all river trips on the Rocket. Its office in Khulna looks like a small house. It's just behind the train station and opens every day at around 9am.

There used to be six Rockets between Khulna and Dhaka (1st/2nd/deck class Tk 1010/610/150) per week in each direction. They all stopped at Mongla (1st/2nd/deck Tk 140/80/15), Barisal (1st/2nd/deck Tk 530/310/70) and several smaller ports. It was always wise to reserve several days in advance to ensure a private cabin.

Departures from Khulna were scheduled at 3am, although you could board the evening before and sleep on board before departure.

However, in the past couple of years the Rocket service hasn't reached as far as Khulna. In fact, it hasn't even reached Mongla. For most of 2011, the Rocket started, as usual, in Dhaka, but travelled only as far as Morrelganj, via Barisal, before turning round and heading back to

# Mongla

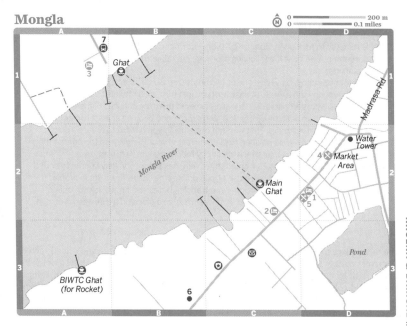

Mnasty incidents involving lost boats. Nowadays, no matter what boatmen in Mongla may tell you, the only way to travel independently into the Sundarbans from Mongla is on a day trip to the **Karamjal Forest Station** or, if you leave early enough, to the **Harbaria Wildlife Sanctuary**. With raised walkways, viewing platforms and a small 'zoo', the Karamjal Forest Station is hardly the back of beyond, but surprisingly in recent years it's been one of the best places to see a tiger. Think of it as a fun boat trip rather than an off-the-beaten-track safari adventure and you won't leave disappointed.

Private tour operators will find you soon after you arrive in Mongla. One guy operates out of Hotel Bangkok, but they'll find you whatever hotel you stay in. Shop around for quotes, and be clear on what is included in the price, where the boat will go and how long it will go for. And don't pay everything up front!

For trustworthy advice on boat trips, seek out **Monowar Ferdous** (✆01816 879874; monowarferdous@yahoo.com), the manager at the Parjatan Hotel. He doesn't run his own trips, but can help you arrange one. When we were last here he quoted us Tk 1000 for a half-day trip (three hours) to Karamjal and back, and Tk 4500 for a full-day trip (8am to 5pm) to Harbaria and back, via Karamjal.

## Mongla

### 😴 Sleeping
| | |
|---|---|
| 1 Hotel Bangkok | D2 |
| 2 Hotel Singapore | C2 |
| 3 Parjatan Hotel (Hotel Pashur) | A1 |

### 🍴 Eating
| | |
|---|---|
| 4 Paradise Hotel | D2 |
| Royal Bengal Restaurant | (see 3) |
| 5 Sureswar Hotel & Restaurant | D2 |

### ℹ️ Transport
| | |
|---|---|
| 6 BIWTC Office | B3 |
| 7 Bus Stand | A1 |

Prices don't include food. Most people just take their own.

Note that you need permits to enter the area beyond Karamjal, hence the full-day trip being much more expensive. Also note that prices will fall if you book as a group because some costs (boat hire, for example) can be shared.

## 🛏️ Sleeping

**Parjatan Hotel**                    HOTEL **$$**
(✆75100, 0181 6879874; monowarferdous@yahoo .com; Khulna Rd; r without/with air-con Tk 1000/ 1700;❄️) Also known as Hotel Pashur, this is

## BOOKING YOUR SUNDARBANS TOUR

While it's easy to rock up in Mongla (p74) one afternoon and be climbing aboard a Sundarbans-bound boat the following morning, multiday trips from Khulna take a lot more planning.

Most tour operators only have one or two boats (the Guide Tours has three), with each boat doing just one trip a week, at best, so if you just turn up in Khulna it may be the best part of a week before a boat is due to leave. And even then, the chances of there being a spare place on that boat are pretty slim. We recommend booking at least two or three weeks in advance, if not more. That way, not only should you be able to ensure a place on a boat, but you'll also be in a position to plan the rest of your Bangladesh trip around the dates of your Sundarbans tour, which are set by tour operators well in advance.

Try to contact tour operators through their websites before you leave home to sound out possible tour dates. Even if you can't book online (the Guide Tours, for example, allows you to book from home through wire transfer, but doesn't have its own online booking system), you should be able to at least reserve a place on a trip, which you can then confirm once you arrive in Dhaka.

the nicest place to stay in Khulna. It's across the river (an easy Tk 2 ferry ride) from town, and is right by the bus stand. It looks a little like an old colonial palace (though it is in fact a modern creation) and is set in peaceful gardens. Rooms are bright and clean, with a small balcony overlooking Mongla River and the busy port beyond. Rooms are sometimes full, so try to book ahead. The manager here speaks good English.

**Hotel Bangkok**                    HOTEL $
(☎0171 3975311; Main Rd; r Tk 300, with shared bathroom Tk 200) The deep-green rooms are small, but well kept. Some rooms have river views – some have road noise. It is the friendliest hotel in Mongla. Some English spoken.

**Hotel Singapore**                  HOTEL $
(☎01911 853724; s/d Tk 250/400, with shared bathroom Tk 200/350) There isn't much to pick between this and the Hotel Bangkok. Singapore might get a little more light but to counter this the rooms are a little tattier. Very little English.

### ✕ Eating

Mongla isn't overflowing with eating options. The local favourite is the Sureswar Hotel and Restaurant (Main Rd; mains Tk 60; ◷24hr), located on the main drag, next to Hotel Bangkok. It stocks the standard Bangladeshi fare and has a handy 'food catalogue' painted onto the wall in English.

Also on the main drag, and identical in almost everyway, is the Paradise Hotel (Main Rd); turn right out of Hotel Bangkok and it's on your left.

If you need an escape, head across the river to the Parjatan Hotel (Hotel Pashur), where you'll find the Royal Bengal Restaurant (mains Tk 100-300; ◷7am-10pm), with a decent selection of Bangladeshi and Western options in a quiet environment.

### ⓘ Getting There & Away

#### Boat
The crumbling **BIWTC office** (☎73193) is on the main drag, south of town. Turn left out of Hotel Bangkok and it'll be on your right. At the time of research, though, all Rocket services to and from Mongla had been suspended indefinitely. The best alternative was to get on or off the Rocket in Hularhat, a couple of hours away from Mongla by bus, via Bagerhat.

Before the suspension of services, the Rocket left Mongla at about 6am, for Barisal (1st/2nd/ deck class Tk 460/285/80, 12 hours) and Dhaka (Tk 1050/625/160, 25 hours), and at around 4pm for Khulna (Tk 170/100/30, three hours).

#### Bus
Buses for Khulna (Tk 55, 90 minutes, 6.30am to 5.30pm) leave every 15 minutes and go via the T-junction known as Khatakhali (Tk 35, one hour) where you can change for Bagerhat.

## Bagerhat
☎401 / POP 45,000

Unesco-protected Bagerhat, with its treasure trove of historical monuments, will send a shiver of excitement down the spines of archaeology buffs. Hidden among the green folds of the surrounding countryside are more ancient mosques and mausoleums than anywhere else in Bangladesh (except Dhaka), but the crowning jewel of this fabulously little-known collection is the Shait Gumbad Mosque – a multi-domed medieval masterpiece.

The creators of such buildings understood the value of good scenery, and the tranquil countryside, full of tropical trees, ponds and birds, is a joy to walk through.

Bagerhat was built in the 15th century by one of the most revered men in Bangladeshi history, Khan Jahan Ali (see the boxed text p79), and is a significant cradle of Islam in Bangladesh.

The town, about 4km from the main sights, lacks decent hotels and restaurants, so it's sensible to visit Bagerhat as a day trip from Khulna or Mongla, both of which are a short bus ride away.

## ◉ Sights

**Shait Gumbad Mosque**          MOSQUE

(admission Tk 100; ◷9am-5pm Tue-Sat & 2.30-5pm Mon Oct-Mar, 9am-6pm Tue-Sat & 2.30-6pm Mon Mar-Sep) Built in 1459, the same year Khan Jahan Ali died, the famous Shait Gumbad

Mosque is the largest and most magnificent traditional mosque in the country. Shait Gumbad means 'the Temple with 60 Domes' – a misnomer given that there are actually 77. This fortresslike structure has unusually thick walls, built in the tapering brick fashion known as Tughlaq, and is a hugely impressive sight. Admission includes entrance to the museum, which is within the grounds of the mosque. Note that women travellers have been known to be refused entry, although this isn't always the case.

**Bagerhat Museum**          MUSEUM

This small, neatly arranged museum, located within the grounds of the Shait Gumbad Mosque (admission is covered by the mosque entrance fee, and it's open the same hours), contains relics from the surrounding area and is a good place to get your bearings before setting out to explore Bagerhat.

**Village Mosques**          MOSQUES

Around Shait Gumbad are two other smaller mosques, both single-domed, in reasonably good condition and a lot of fun to get to. **Bibi Begni's Mosque**, which has some

---

## SPECIALIST TOURS

Tour operators such as the **Guide Tours** (www.guidetours.com) and **Bengal Tours** (www.bengaltours.com) organise a number of specialist trips into the Sundarbans, which can add a touch of the unusual to your trip if you happen to be here at the right time of year.

### The Honey Harvest Trail

Hugely popular and full of adventure, honey-harvest trips are organised in early April and allow tourists to trek on foot through the forest, following local workers, known as *maualis*, as they go in search of the honey produced by the formidable honey bees of this region.

These giant bees, which form colonies sometimes tens of thousands strong, are renowned for their ferocious nature and for chasing attackers long distances in large swarms. In order to get close to their nests, the *maualis* use smoke to subdue the bees, but it takes years of painful practice to get it right.

The honey-gathering season kicks off at Burigoalini on 1 April with a volley of gunshots and much fanfare. The boats of the *maualis* then race off downstream and into the forest in search of the best honey-hunting areas. The season lasts for two months, although tour operators tend to organise only a couple of trips in total, and normally only in April. Expect to pay around Tk 10,000 to Tk 12,000 per person.

### Whale-watching

The Swatch of No Ground, a deep-water canyon a short way offshore from the Sundarbans, acts as something of a magnet to Brydes whales plus three species of dolphin (Pacific bottlenose, spinner and pantropical spotted). Between December and February, the Guide Tours can sometimes arrange for tourists to join scientists on the research boat, which visits the area as part of the **Bangladesh Cetacean Diversity Project** (www.shushuk.org). There's room for only one or two extra passengers, and facilities are cramped and extremely basic, but the experience is one of those once-in-a-lifetime things. Expect to pay around Tk 20,000 per person for a two-day trip.

# Bagerhat

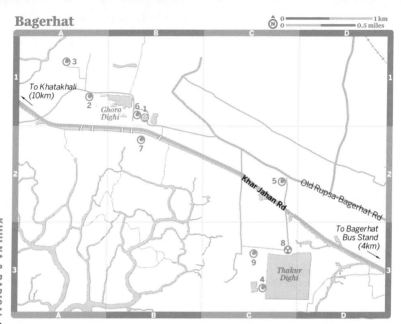

## Bagerhat

interesting floral motifs, and the bulbous **Chunakhola Mosque**, are both located behind Shait Gumbad and make a lovely walk. To get to Bibi Begni, walk anti-clockwise around Ghora Dighi pond. A few hundred metres after leaving behind the lake and entering a small forested area, you'll see the mosque on your left. If you turn right here, and then stay to your left, you'll wind your way through a peaceful forested village until you eventually reach Chunakhola Mosque, situated in a lush paddy field. If you have trouble finding them, remember the Bengali for mosque is *masjid*. Chances are you'll end up being led to them by an energetic gang of friendly village kids.

**Singar Mosque**, across the main road from Shait Gumbad, is much easier to find, but less of an adventure to get to.

### Tomb of Khan Jahan Ali    MAUSOLEUM
Khan Jahan's Tomb (Mazhar Khan Jahan Ali) is the only monument in Bagerhat that retains its original cupolas (domed ceilings). The cenotaph at the entrance is covered with tiles of various colours and inscribed with Quranic verses, but it is usually covered with a red cloth embroidered with gold threads. The single-domed **Dargah Mosque** is enclosed within the same complex by a massive wall with short towers at each corner and archways on the front and back. This is a popular pilgrimage site and therefore has a little more colour and flair than some of the other monuments around here. The pond, known as Thakur Dighi, which the complex overlooks, contains a large crocodile said to be over 100 years old, which has become a bit of a tourist attraction. There used to be two, but one died in 2011.

### Thakur Dighi Mosques    MOSQUES
On the western bank of the pond called Thakur Dighi, and a short walk from Mazhar Khan Jahan Ali, the recently repaired **Nine-Domed Mosque** (Noy Gombuj Masjid; নয় গম্বুজ মসজিদ) is an impressive structure, with

eight small domes on its roof surrounding one larger central dome. The mihrabs (niches) are embellished with terracotta floral scrolls and foliage motifs, with a prominent chain-and-bell terracotta motif in the centre.

You might also want to check out the tumbledown Zinda Pir Mosque, which is about 500m off to the west of Mazhar Khan Jahan Ali, and contains a number of small tombs within its overgrown grounds.

Ronvijoypur Mosque                    MOSQUE

About 1.5km east of Shait Gumbad, and directly north of the road that leads to Mazhar Khan Jahan Ali, this splendidly chunky 15th-century mosque is singularly impressive. It contains the largest single dome in Bangladesh, spanning 11m and supported by 3m-thick brick walls. The mosque's interior is plain, but the main mihrabs are decorated in floral patterns.

## ✖ Eating

Bagerhat's sights and their surrounding villages and ponds make great spots for a picnic, but you'll probably have to bring supplies from, say, Khulna, as there isn't much in the way of shops anywhere close to the main sights here.

There are a number of cheap, no-nonsense Bengali restaurants by the bus stand where you can grab a fish curry and rice meal for around Tk 60.

## ❶ Getting There & Away

The bus from Khulna takes you through some enchanting countryside. It passes the Shait Gumbad Mosque on the left, about 4km before Bagerhat bus stand. Your driver will probably assume you want get off here. If you're going to Khulna, you may be able to wave down a pass-

ing bus from here, but to be sure of a seat you'll need to catch one from the Bagerhat bus stand.

There are no direct buses to Mongla. You have to catch a Khulna-bound bus to the T-junction a few kilometres north of Bagerhat. This junction is known as Khatakhali. Annoyingly, you'll be expected to pay the full Khulna fare (Tk 50). From the Khatakhali T-junction, you can wave down a Khulna-to-Mongla bus for the remaining one hour to Mongla (Tk 35). Don't expect a seat, though.

If you're planning to take the Rocket back to Barisal or Dhaka, take a bus to Hularhat from the bus stand and then take a shared auto-rickshaw (per person Tk 25, 20 minutes) to the ferry ghat. The Rocket leaves Hularhat at 12.30pm.

From Bagerhat bus stand, destinations include Khulna (Tk 50, one hour, until 9pm) and Hularhat (Tk 30, one hour, until 6pm).

## ❶ Getting Around

The bus stand is at least 4km southeast of the Shait Gumbad Mosque, along the main Khan Jahan Rd. Expect to pay about Tk 40 for a rickshaw, or else hop in a shared electric rickshaw (per person Tk 10). Once you're in the vicinity of the main sights you can walk to any of them, although you may want to get the help of a rickshaw to take you between the Shait Gumbad area and the sights by Thakur Dighi Pond (Tk 10).

## Jessore

☎ 0421 / POP 180,000

Apart from some attractive colonial architecture, most notably the huge Court House building, there is little to see in Jessore (pronounced Joshor) in terms of sights. What the town does offer, though, is a bustling yet manageable street-market atmosphere of winding streets, roadside stalls and tea stands. It's a fun place to wander, and makes

---

### THE MAN WHO BUILT BAGERHAT

Khan Jahan Ali was a Sufi (a Muslim mystic, the counterpart of the Hindu sadhus or Indian yogis) from Turkey who settled in Bagerhat in the middle of the 15th century after decades of wandering and learning.

Upon arriving in Bagerhat with thousands of horsemen, clearing the jungle (this area was likely part of the Sundarbans back then) and founding Khalifatabad (as the town was originally named), this warrior-saint quickly initiated a huge construction program. He adorned his capital city with an incredible number of mosques, bridges, brick-paved highways, palaces and other public buildings. Large ponds of water with staircase landings were built in various parts of the township to provide salt-free drinking water in this predominantly saline belt.

When he died, a mausoleum was built in his memory by the banks of the huge Thakur Dighi Pond. Today Khan Jahan Ali is the patron saint of the area and his name equates with a major pre-Mughal architectural style in Bangladesh.

an authentic, non-touristy introduction to Bangladesh if you've just come from the Indian border at Benapole (p23).

## 🛏 Sleeping

**TOP CHOICE Banchte Shekha** GUESTHOUSE $
(☎68885, 01718 940644, 01931 291090; www.banchteshekha.org; off Airport Rd; r without/with air-con Tk 440/880; ❄) Helping fund a local NGO-run women's training centre, which shares the site, this welcoming guesthouse on the peaceful outskirts of town is easily the nicest and best-value place to stay in Jessore. There are two air-con rooms with attached bathroom but the rest of the rooms are simple, fan-cooled dorm-style rooms with shared bathrooms. Some have two beds, some four, but all cost the same, are kept spotlessly clean and overlook a flower-filled courtyard with fishpond. The centre's dining hall whips up simple but tasty **set meals** (breakfast/lunch/dinner Tk 45/130/140), but do tell them in advance if you want to eat here. To get here, hop in a rickshaw, say 'Arabpur' (the name of this part of town) or 'Airport Rd'. Once you're close, start asking for 'Banchte Shekha' (pronounced *bach*-tah *shay*-kah). It's close to the United Airways office (which is on the main road), down a small signposted lane. A rickshaw from the centre costs around Tk 20.

**Hotel Magpie** HOTEL $
(☎68722; MK Rd; s/d Tk 400/600, with air-con Tk 800/1200; ❄) If it weren't for the crazy road noise this would be a real find. It's bright, well lit, clean and friendly. For budget-hotel prices you get midrange standards.

**Hotel RS** HOTEL $$
(☎61881; RS Tower, MK Rd; s/d from Tk 650/1000; ❄) A bit on the shabby side, but a decent budget-to-midrange option with clean, air-conditioned rooms, a very central location and an OK restaurant. Has a few, slightly cheaper non-air-con rooms available too.

## 🍴 Eating

**New Nuru Hotel** BENGALI $
(MK Rd; mains Tk 100; ⊙6am-10pm) The unchallenged curry king of Jessore, but the fiery kebabs are also worthy of mention. The dhal and naan bread breakfasts also hit the spot. No English menu. Not much English spoken.

**Rose Garden** CHINESE $$
(Jess Tower, MK Rd; mains Tk 150-350; ⊙11.30am-10pm) Clean, friendly restaurant with an extensive Chinese menu, including a number of Sichuan specialities. Tucked away on the upper floors of a small shopping centre.

## ℹ Information

There are a couple of foreigner-friendly ATMs in town. Get online at **Oishi Online** (off Shahid Sarak Rd; per hr Tk 20; ⊙9.30am-11pm).

## ℹ Getting There & Away

### Air

A rickshaw from the centre to the airport (30 to 45 minutes) is around Tk 50. From Banchte Shekha guesthouse it's around Tk 30.

**Regent Airlines** (☎51036, 01730 358871; www.flyregent.com; airport; ⊙8am-8pm) Has twice-daily flights to Dhaka from around Tk 2500.

**United Airways** (☎01713 398783; www.uabdl.com; airport; ⊙8.30am-8.30pm) Twice-daily flights to Dhaka for similar prices to Regent. Also has an office close to Banchte Shekha guesthouse.

### Bus

A rickshaw from the centre to Moniher Bus Stand should be only Tk 10. Expect to pay around Tk 20 to the other two bus stands. As well as the public bus services outlined here, you can also get Green Line's air-con coaches to Dhaka from its ticket office in the town centre.

Destinations from Shankapur bus stand include Khulna (Tk 70, 90 minutes, 6am to 6pm) and Kushtia (Tk 120, three hours, 6am to 6.45pm).

Moniher bus stand serves Dhaka (from Tk 300, seven hours, 6am to 10pm), and from Benapole bus stand buses go to Benapole (Tk 45, one hour, 5am to 10pm).

### Train

There are 10 daily trains to Khulna (1st/*shulov* class Tk 85/35; two hours), although it's very easy to take the bus.

Two trains go to Dhaka (1st berth/1st seat/*shuvon* class Tk 535/385/180). The *Sundarban*

---

### TIGERS IN CHITTAGONG?

Tigers were once widespread in Bangladesh. Even up to the 1930s they were present in 11 out of the region's 17 districts. These days, of course, the Sundarbans National Park is their stronghold. Interestingly, though, as part of the Bangladesh Tiger Action Plan, the forest department is assessing the viability of reports that vagrant tigers are still living within parts of the Chittagong Hill Tracts (boxed text p120).

# Jessore

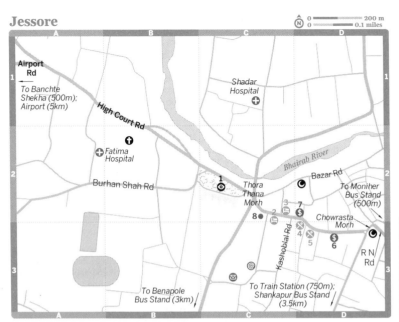

*Express* leaves at 9.29pm and arrives in Dhaka at 5.35am. It doesn't run on Fridays. The *Chitra Express* leaves at 10.05am and arrives at 6.20pm. Its day off is Monday. There are also air-con seats and berths available for around double the price of 1st class.

# Kushtia

📞 071 / POP 85,000

It wouldn't be too far-fetched to dub Kushtia the cultural heart of Bengal. This was once the home of Nobel-laureate poet Rabindranath Tagore and was where he penned some of his most influential works. It is also the final resting place of the great Baul (mystic musician) Lalon Shah, and a hugely popular folk-music festival is held here in his honour twice a year.

## ◉ Sights

**Kuthibari**  MUSEUM

Kuthibari is the former residence of Bengal's most famous poet, Rabindranath Tagore. It was built in the mid-19th century and Tagore lived here for over 10 years from 1880, composing some of his immortal poems, songs and short stories. He returned in 1912 for several years, translating his works into English and earning the Nobel Prize for Literature (1913) in the process.

The house has been turned into a museum (Tk 100; ☺9am-5pm) dedicated to Tagore's life and works, and is set among landscaped gardens – perfect for picnics – where musicians sometimes gather to perform in his honour.

It's an interesting place to visit, but arguably it's the journey over here that's the main attraction. First, make your way down to the river ghat, then cross the river on a small wooden ferry (Tk 2). You'll be greeted at the other side by a strange-looking vehicle called a *nazaman*, a motorised rickshaw-cum-tractor, which is powered by an old boat engine and which shuttles people the remaining 10km to Kuthibari (per person Tk 20; 45 minutes), through picturesque farmland and numerous small villages. It's a fun half-day trip.

There are a few snack stalls outside the entrance to the house, where you can grab lunch, but bringing a picnic to eat in the grounds isn't a bad idea.

A rickshaw from Hotel River View to the river ghat costs Tk 10 to Tk 20. To walk, turn left out of the hotel and walk along NS Rd (Kushtia's main drag) for about 1.5km, passing the easy-to-notice Lovely Shopping Centre on your left. About 200m later turn left down a lane that leads straight to the river.

### Shrine of Lalon Shah SHRINE

The white shrine of Lalon Shah is, for most Bangladeshis, the main reason for visiting Kushtia and come they do, in their hundreds. Lalon Shah is one of the most famous holy men in Bangladesh (see the boxed text p83) and his shrine is a fascinating peek into a mystical side of Bangladeshi life. The shrine centres on the holy man's tomb and that of his adopted parents, while around the perimeter of the shrine are the tombs of various local dignitaries. Behind the tomb complex is a covered area where musicians sometimes play and sing Lalon Shah's songs, while pilgrims burst into dance.

In mid-March and mid-October, the Lalon Utsab festival (p16) is held on the grassy maidan, overlooking the river nearby. It's a multiday folk-music extravaganza and attracts thousands of pilgrims, itinerant vendors and marijuana-smoking holy men who travel from all across the subcontinent to commemorate Lalon Shah's birth (March) and death (October).

The shrine is a Tk 30 rickshaw ride from Hotel River View. Ask for 'Lalon Shah Mazar'.

## 🛏 Sleeping

### Hotel River View HOTEL $

(☎71660; Shapla Chattar, off NS Rd; s/d Tk 400/500, with air-con Tk 800/1000; ❉) Clearly marked, and overlooking the hard-to-miss lotus-flower roundabout at one end of NS Rd (Kushtia's main drag), this friendly hotel is easy to spot and has clean rooms that are

good value despite being a little cramped. The attached restaurant (mains Tk 130-300; ⊙11am-11pm) has a good selection of Bengali and Chinese dishes. It's a Tk 20 rickshaw ride from Terminal bus stand to here. From the Dhaka bus stand, cross over the railway level-crossing and turn right. You'll soon see the lotus flower and the hotel on your left.

### Desha GUESTHOUSE $$

(☎01720 510212; desha_bd@yahoo.com; 317 Jenaidah Rd; r Tk 1035) Disappointingly unwelcoming for an NGO-run guesthouse, Desha does, nevertheless, have the largest and most comfortable rooms in town and can arrange meals if forewarned. It's about 250m before the Dhaka bus stand as you're heading into town, and is diagonally opposite the well-marked Circuit House.

### Hotel Gold Star HOTEL $

(☎61675; 6/1 Khan Bahadur Samsuzuha Rd, Mazampur Gate; s/d from Tk 250/440) Neat and tidy fan-cooled rooms are fine for a night. Bathrooms are very small and squat-loo only. Very close to Dhaka bus stand, this place is down a lane on your right as you walk from the bus stand towards the railway line. Also Tk 20 from Terminal bus stand.

## 🍴 Eating

As well as those listed below, there are a number of cheap and cheerful Bengali restaurants by the Dhaka Bus Stand, most of which open early for breakfast. Expect dhal, roti and fried egg.

### Mouban BENGALI $

(81 NS Rd; mains from Tk 80; ⊙6am-10pm) Very popular roadside restaurant with kebabs, biryani and extremely tasty fried chicken. There's also a lip-smackingly good selection of sweets in an attached shop. English sign, but no English menu. From the lotus-flower roundabout by Hotel River View, walk about 500m along NS Rd and it's on your left.

### Karamai CHINESE $$

(NS Rd; mains Tk 150-300; ⊙noon-3pm & 6-11pm) Decent 1st-floor Chinese restaurant in clean surrounds. Just before Mouban if you're coming from the lotus-flower roundabout and also on your left.

## ℹ Information

There's an **AB Bank ATM** diagonally opposite Karamai restaurant.

## LALON THE SINGING SAINT

Bauls are mystic minstrels who constitute both a quasi-religious sect and a strong musical tradition. Their music celebrates celestial love, but does so in very earthy terms, rather than spiritual ones, and as such Baul ideology is said to transcend religion.

Lalon Shah is regarded as the most important poet-practitioner of the Baul tradition, and is treated as a saint, mystic poet, song composer, social reformer and secular thinker all rolled into one. No one is quite certain when or where he was born. He claimed to have merely 'arrived' and certainly his discovery (aged 16, and suffering from smallpox, he was found by a local farmer floating in the river near Kushtia) lends credence to his claim that he 'came from water'. As the boy recovered, it became clear that he was possessed of great wisdom and he quickly attracted many followers.

Lalon was a humanist and vehemently opposed to all distinctions of religion and caste (throughout his long life he said nothing of the time before his discovery and nobody has ever been able to prove whether he came from an Islamic or Hindu background), though he often spoke positively on aspects of all religions. Instead he encouraged people to look 'into themselves' for answers and, being a talented poet and musician, he used music to get his messages across.

He has become an iconic figure for preaching religious tolerance and secularism. His philosophy, articulated in songs, has inspired and influenced many poets and social and religious thinkers, including Rabindranath Tagore, who references the Baul tradition in much of his writings.

Lalon died in 1890 and is believed to have reached the ripe old age of 116!

### ❶ Getting There & Away

The Dhaka bus stand (not really a bus stand, just a place where buses stop) is close to the main drag, NS Rd. To get to NS Rd from the bus stand walk across the railway line, bear right then turn right at the lotus-flower roundabout. A number of companies with ticket offices at this bus stand have regular services to Dhaka (non-air-con/air-con Tk 250/500, five to six hours).

The Terminal bus stand is about 2km south of town (rickshaw Tk 20) and has services to Jessore (Tk 120, three hours, 6am to 6.45pm) and Rajshahi (Tk 150, two hours, 7am to 5pm).

## BARISAL DIVISION

The river-laden division of Barisal is very much off the radar for the average tourist, but an off-the-beaten-track journey here makes for a wonderfully authentic Bangladesh experience. Barisal has little in the way of must-see sights – although the beach at Kuakata is becoming increasingly popular – but its maze of waterways, luxuriously green farmland and quiet village life make it a beautiful place to travel around.

The small, charming city of Barisal has a busy port, and is a convenient place to base yourself for forays into other parts of the division. You can also catch ferries, including the Rocket, from here to both Dhaka and Chittagong division. If you head further south, to Kuakata, you can even catch boats to the eastern fringes of the Sundarbans National Park; an unusual alternative to the more popular tours that run from Khulna.

## Barisal

☑ 0431 / POP 210,000

Barisal (*bore*-ee-shal) is a major port city and one of the gateways to the world for Bangladesh, yet it's strangely isolated from the rest of the country. Appropriately, perhaps, it's much easier to reach by boat than road, although buses to and from Dhaka are straightforward enough. Barisal is one of the more pleasant cities in the country, with several ponds in the city centre and handsome buildings from the Raj era, crumbling away in quiet backstreets. But it's the busy river port, constantly humming with life, that is the real hub, and to arrive here by boat in the early-morning mist (as you do if you catch the Rocket here from Dhaka) is an unforgettable experience.

### 🛏 Sleeping

**Hotel Athena International**          HOTEL **$$**
(☑65233; Katpotty Rd; s without/with air-con Tk 400/900, d without/with air-con Tk 700/1100;❄)
One of the most popular hotels in town,

Athena has a clean design with equally clean and slick rooms for very reasonable prices.

**Hotel Ali International**  HOTEL **$$**
(☎64732; Sadar Rd; s without/with air-con Tk 700/400, d without/with air-con Tk 700/1000;❄) The cheaper rooms are slightly shabbier than the equivalent at Athena, but the pricier ones are large, clean and well furnished. The English-speaking manager is charming.

**Hotel Ababil**  HOTEL **$**
(East Bogura Rd; ☎0119 8038781; s/d Tk 250/300) Very welcoming for a cheapie, Ababil has rooms that are basic, but kept neat and tidy. Singles without an attached bathroom are also available (Tk 100).

 **Eating**

**Rose Garden Restaurant**  BENGALI **$**
(Sadar Rd; mains Tk 80-120; ☺7am-11pm) A locals' favourite, Rose Garden is clean and comfortable, and does decent Bengali food (biryanis, fried chicken, kebabs) plus a smattering of Chinese dishes. Has a badly translated English menu.

**Sokal Sondha**  BENGALI **$**
(Sadar Rd; mains from Tk 50; ☺5.30am-10pm) No English sign or menu, and no English spoken, but a great place to come for an early morning breakfast of dhal and paratha.

Also does delicious Bengali sweets. Look for white lettering on a green sign, under the NCC Bank.

**Yan Thai Restaurant**  THAI **$$**
(East Bogura Rd; mains Tk 100-200;❄) Bringing the spicy flavours of Thailand to southern Bangladesh, this cosy little restaurant serves OK Thai dishes as well Chinese and Bengali.

## ❶ Information

There are a couple of **AB Bank ATMs**, which accept foreign cards: one near the ferry port, the other just before the main bus stand, on Hospital Rd.

**Cyber Café** (Faisal Huq Ave, 2nd fl; per hr Tk 30; ☺10am-9pm)

**Dutch-Bangla Bank** (Sadar Rd) Changes money.

## ❶ Getting There & Away

### Boat

The Rocket (see p26) runs from Barisal's Rocket Ghat to either Dhaka, in one direction, or Morrelganj in the other. It used to run all the way to Khulna, but at the time of research boats were going only as far as Morrelganj. It would be worth checking when you're here, to see if the Khulna service has resumed. If it hasn't, then you can catch the Rocket as far as Hularhat, then take a bus to Khulna from there (for details, see the boxed text p71).

Note, the Rocket to Dhaka stops off for half an hour in the small fishing town of Chandpur (seven hours), from where you can get to Chittagong by bus (four hours, regular) or train

## Barisal

N 0 — 200 m
0 — 0.1 miles

Hospital Rd
To Main
Bus Stand
(2km)

Kirtonkhol River

Line Rd

Sadar Rd

Chowk Bazar Rd

Fish
Market

Faisal Huq Ave

@

BIWTC Ghat Rd

## FLOATING RICE MARKET

Like the more famous floating markets in Southeast Asia, the small one at Banaripara – just an hour's bus ride from Barisal – is where locals who live in this river-laden part of Bangladesh come to buy and sell groceries without ever having to step off their boats. This particular market deals almost entirely in rice. Not much use for the average tourist, true. But it does make a fascinating and undoubtedly unusual side trip from your forays into southern Bangladesh.

Trading takes place every day, but Saturday is the busiest market day here, when not only is the river full of bobbing 'shops' but also the market stalls in the narrow lanes leading down to the river are at their most colourful.

Buses leave all day from Barisal's main bus stand. To break the journey, you could stop at the large, modern and eye-catching Guthia Mosque (Tk 18, 40 minutes).

(1st seat/*shuvon* Tk 160/80, five hours, 5am and 2.50pm). More convenient for Chittagong, though, is the launch to Moju Chowdhury Hat (boxed text p112).

For daytime Rocket trips, just buy your ticket onboard, half an hour before departure. For overnight trips (especially to Dhaka) you must reserve your ticket at the BITWC office, on the 2nd floor of an unmarked building across the main road from the ferry ghat.

Numerous other passenger ferries, generally known as 'launches', drift slowly upriver from Barisal to Dhaka. Most leave a few hours after the Rocket, at around 8pm or 9pm, and they leave from the main Launch Ghat, not the Rocket Ghat, which is a short walk away. Prices are comparable, although there may be luxury cabins available (Tk 1500 to Tk 2000). There's generally no need to book in advance. Just head to the Launch Ghat in the early evening, ask for a 'Dhaka launch' and you'll be pointed in the right direction. From the Launch Ghat there are also boats to Moju Chowdhury Hat (2nd/deck class Tk 800/200, five hours, hourly from 6am).

From the Rocket Ghat, destinations include the following:

**Chandpur** 1st/2nd/deck class Tk 410/260/80, seven hours, 6.30pm, no service Sunday

**Dhaka** 1st/2nd/deck class Tk 565/355/95, 12 hours, 6.30pm, no service Sunday

**Hularhat** 1st/2nd/deck class Tk 170/105/55, four hours, 6am, no service Saturday

### Bus

A rickshaw from the main bus stand into town is Tk 20 to Tk 30. From the main bus stand buses go to Dhaka (Tk 350, six to nine hours, 8.30am to 10pm) and Banaripara (Tk 35, one hour). Buses for Kuakata (Tk 200, five hours, 6am to 5pm) leave from the Kuakata bus stand.

# Kuakata
☎0441

This largely isolated beach at the southern tip of the delta was named by the original Mogh (Rakhine) Buddhist settlers whose ancestors remain here today. *Kua* means 'well', and *kata* means 'dug'.

The river mouths east and west of the beach ensure the sea is rather murky. In any case, sharks drying on racks along the beach don't augur well for swimming. But although Kuakata isn't the archetypal turquoise-coloured tropical ocean, the vibe is right (it's a lot more shanty than Cox's Bazaar) and the long, palm-tree-lined beach is largely deserted.

The Gangamati Mangrove Forest is a 7km walk east along the beach. You can rent motorbikes (Tk 250 to Tk 300) to get here, but the walk is a lovely one.

You will probably need those motorbikes, though, to get to Misripara Village (about 9km northwest of Kuakata) where you'll find a rustic temple housing a 21ft Buddha statue.

Back in Kuakata itself, the Rakhine Market, by the playing fields just off to the east of the main road, is worth a visit for its locally woven clothes and handicrafts.

A word of warning: some lone women travellers have complained about receiving excessive hassle from groups of men in Kuakata.

## 🛏 Sleeping & Eating

The nicer hotels have restaurants but many people eat at the roadside shacks on the approach road to the beach. Most are open from around 7am to 10pm. As you'd expect, fish is the order of the day, with most places serving a selection of curried fish dishes and fried fish pieces, usually dished up with rice

## SEA CRUISE TO FATRA CHAR

For a great half-day trip, consider hopping aboard a boat to Fatra Char, a forested island about one hour's boat ride west of Kuakata, on the eastern edge of the Sundarbans.

A small clearing beside an oh-so-tempting freshwater lake makes the perfect picnic spot. The **Kuakata Tourist Centre** (☎01734 773580) – little more than a ticket counter on the beach at Kuakata – sells tickets to Fatra Char (Tk 200 return). The trip lasts for around three to four hours, including about an hour on the island.

and a vegetable curry. None has an English sign or an English menu, but you can see the dishes in the large pots they're cooked in, so you can just point and choose. Expect to pay around Tk 100 for a meal. Breakfast tends to be freshly baked paratha, dhal and vegetable curry.

There are no beachside cafes or restaurants, but snack vendors roll their carts down to the beach and serve *chaat* (spicy snacks) and freshly roasted nuts.

**Banani Palace**　　　　　　HOTEL **$$**
(☎56042; r without/with air-con from Tk 800/2000;❄) Set beside a small pond, Banani has clean, white-tiled rooms with TV, sofa and coffee table, and a small attached bathroom. The cheapest rooms, on the ground floor, represent good value for Kuakata. It's on the right as you walk away from the beach along the main approach road.

**Hotel Neelanjana**　　　　　HOTEL **$$**
(☎01712 927904; s/d Tk 1260/1575, with air-con Tk 1950/2150;❄) Kuakata's smartest hotel is far from luxurious, but it has clean, comfortable rooms with private balconies and sit-down toilets in sparkling bathrooms. From the beach, walk over the crossroads then take the next right. Neelanjana will be on your left, after the playing field.

**Hotel Sunrais**　　　　　GUESTHOUSE **$**
(☎01718 120255; s/d Tk 200/400) Simple two-storey wooden shack with very basic rooms. Bathrooms are shared and have squat toilets and tap-and-bucket 'showers'. Some rooms have a sea view, though, and the manager is friendly. On your right as you walk down to the beach from the crossroads.

## ❶ Getting There & Away

Buses to Barisal (Tk 200, five hours, 5.30am to 4.30pm) leave about once an hour from the crossroads just before the beach.

# Rajshahi & Rangpur

## Best Places to Stay

» RDRS Guesthouse (p95)

» Chez Rassak (p101)

» Archaeological Rest House (p93)

## Best Ruins

» Paharpur (p92)

» Puthia (p103)

» Mahasthangarh (p91)

» Natore (p104)

## Why Go?

The rich soils of northwest Bangladesh once held court for powerful Buddhist kingdoms and neutered Hindu empires before falling easily to the embrace of Islam. And all three religions have left their mark in the tumbledown walls of the many ruins that litter this region.

Small villages, colourful markets and remote communities living on fast-eroding sand islands all add to the allure of a trip to this part of the country, but it's the historical narrative that excites the most. Rajshahi and Rangpur contain some of Bangladesh's finest rajbaris (Raj-era palaces), its most exquisitely decorated temples and its largest and most impressive Buddhist ruins. The idyllic rural backdrop to the rest of the country is found here too, but chances are it will be the decaying, moss-hewn ancient architecture that steals the attentions of your camera.

## When to Go

### Bogra

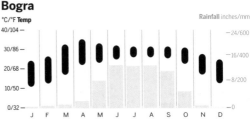

**Oct–May**
Dry season, the best time to visit the flood-prone eastern regions.

**May–Jun**
Mango season in the western areas between Rajshahi and Sona Masjid.

**Nov**
Maha Raas Leela attracts pilgrims to Kantanagar Temple.

## Rajshahi & Rangpur Highlights

**①** Explore the ruined monastery at **Paharpur** (p92), Bangladesh's standout archaeological site

**②** Wander the ruined remains of **Mahasthangarh** (p91), the country's oldest known city

**③** Stroll the ruins of Hindu temples, palaces and former mansions **Puthia** (p103)

**④** Walk through farming villages to the stunning **Kantanagar Temple** (boxed text p98), Bangladesh's finest example of Hindu architecture

**⑤** Track down the scattered Islamic ruins of the lost city of **Gaud (Sona Masjid)** (p102)

**⑥** Discover how one million Bangladeshis are forced to survive on temporary sand islands in the middle of the country's largest rivers by visiting the chars of the **Jamuna** (boxed text p91) or the **Brahmaputra** (boxed text p95)

**⑦** Picnic in the pleasant grounds of the lakeside rajbari of **Natore** (p104)

# Bogra

☎051 / POP 150,000

A sprawling town centred on the hectic Shat Mata (seven-road junction), Bogra acts primarily as a transport hub for most travellers. This is the most convenient place to base yourself for trips to Bangladesh's most famous and impressive archaeological sites – Mahasthangarh (p91) and Paharpur (p92). It's also the closest major town to the Indian border at Hili (p24).

For those with an interest in the lives of people who live on Bangladesh's chars (river islands made of silt), you can visit some of the chars on the Jamuna River in a half-day trip from here, via Sariankandi Ghat.

## ◎ Sights

**Mohammed Ali Palace**
**Museum & Park**                                    MUSEUM
(grounds Tk 20, museum Tk 5; ⊙11am-7pm) This museum is housed inside one of only a handful of furnished rajbaris in Bangladesh – this one is the former home of a line of influential nawabs, which included former foreign minister Mohammed Ali Bogra. The mosaic ceiling of the audience hall is impressive, and the rooms have mannequins dressed to impress in both Bengali and British fashions. The last room you'll see is dedicated to modern art – it's a compelling display, but the lack of English explanation makes it somewhat obscure.

The grounds of the museum have been turned into a mildly pleasant garden and a rundown amusement park with rickety fairground rides. In the far corner is a small row of cages containing monkeys clearly affected by their captivity.

## ☰ Sleeping

**YMCA**                                        GUESTHOUSE $
(☎63058, 01713 368354; Bhai Pagla Masjid Rd; tw without/with air-con Tk 350/700, tr without/with air-con Tk 450/900;❄) Simple but clean and tidy rooms are managed by very welcoming staff. It's on the 3rd floor of a YMCA-run school so it's lively in the daytime. It's down the lane beside the mosque called Bhai Pagla Masjid, which is on the left-hand side of Sherpur Rd as you come from Shat Mata. A rickshaw from Shat Mata costs about Tk 20.

**Red Chillies Guest House**                    HOTEL $$
(☎69777, 62277; Sherpur Rd; s/d from Tk 1000/1250;❄@) Good standard midrange rooms come with TV, air-con and clean bathrooms. It's above the best restaurant in town so makes a smart choice, although staff could be friendlier. The internet was down when we stayed.

**Akboria Hotel & Restaurant**                   HOTEL $
(☎01716 179982; Kazi Nazrul Islam Rd; r without/with air-con from Tk 300/600;❄) In the heart of the action but set back from the main road so not too noisy. Rooms are small but clean and some have terraces. Accessed from the main road through an archway. The attached restaurant does decent kebabs.

**Parjatan Motel**                                HOTEL $$
(☎67024; r without/with air-con Tk 1400/2000;❄@) This colourfully tiled, but rather characterless business conference hotel has clean spacious rooms with balconies and large bathrooms. Internet wasn't working when we were here. The **restaurant** (mains Tk 100-300; ⊙7am-10pm) is also large and clean and does OK Bangladeshi and Chinese dishes. It's a Tk 30 rickshaw ride to Shat Mata, or Tk 10 in a shared auto-rickshaw.

## ✕ Eating

None of the places listed here open for breakfast. For some early morning dhal and roti, try the restaurant attached to Akboria Hotel.

**Red Chillies**                                   THAI $$
(Sherpur Rd; mains Tk 150-400; ⊙11am-10pm) Bogra's smartest restaurant whips up tasty Thai, Chinese and Indian dishes and is the most comfortable place to come for an evening meal.

**Cozy Café**                                    CHINESE $$
(Sherpur Rd; mains Tk 150-300; ⊙10am-11pm) The fried chicken here is tasty, and there's a range of OK Chinese dishes. Does instant coffee (Tk 40) and juices (Tk 50) so, if you can grab a table by the floor-to-ceiling window overlooking Sherpur Rd, it can be a nice place for a pit stop.

**Leziz**                                        WESTERN $$
(Ray Bahadur St; mains Tk 150-300; ⊙11am-10pm) In a quiet back lane, this bright, music-themed cafe–restaurant is run by young, welcoming staff and has burgers, fried chicken, soups, and rice and noodle dishes. The menu also includes juices and lassis, but

RAJSHAHI & RANGPUR BOGRA

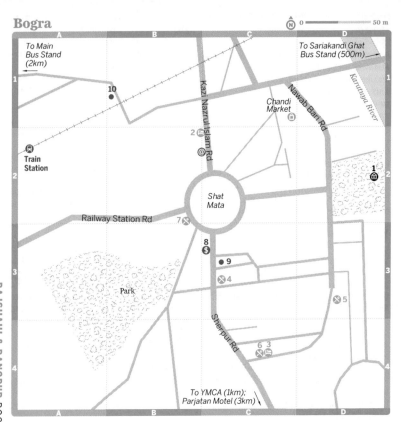

# Bogra

## Bogra

### ◎ Sights
**1** Mohammed Ali Palace
  Museum & Park .................................D2

### 🛏 Sleeping
**2** Akboria Hotel & Restaurant ...............B2
**3** Red Chillies Guest House ..................C4

### 🍴 Eating
**4** Cozy Café.............................................C3
**5** Leziz.....................................................D3
**6** Red Chillies ........................................C4
**7** Rofat Doi Ghar.....................................B2

### ℹ Information
**8** Standard Chartered Bank
  ATM .....................................................C3

### ℹ Transport
**9** Green Line Ticket Office ....................C3
**10** Tempos to Main Bus Stand .............. B1

don't be fooled by the Spanish cappuccino; it's Nescafe with sugar and froth.

**Rofat Doi Ghar**  SWEETS $
(Shat Mata; misti doi per plate Tk 120; ☺24hr) Bogra's best-known *misti doi* (sweet yogurt) stall, this place serves up clay plates of the stuff for you to take away and devour back in your hotel room. There are loads of similar places across town, but locals say this is the best of the lot.

## ℹ Information
**Cyber Zone** (Kazi Nazrul Islam Rd; internet per hr Tk 20; ☺10am-10pm)
**Standard Chartered Bank** (Sherpur Rd) Has an ATM, which accepts foreign cards.

## ℹ Getting There & Away
### Bus
The main bus stand is a Tk 20 rickshaw ride from Shat Mata, or Tk 6 in a shared tempo (note: the tempos take you only as far as the railway cross-

ing, just north of Shat Mata). For Paharpur, go via Jaipurhat.

**Dhaka** Tk 280, five hours, 5am to midnight

**Dinajpur** Tk 170, 3½ hours, 10.30am to 3.30pm

**Jaipurhat** Tk 60, 1½ hours, 6am to 8pm

**Mahastan** Tk 10, 30 minutes, all day

**Natore** Tk 60, 2½ hours, 6.30am to 4pm

**Rangpur** Tk 100, 2½ hours, 7am to 9pm

**Rajshahi** Tk 120, three hours, 6am to 8pm

**Green Line** (☏60477; Sherpur Rd) runs two daily air-con coaches to Dhaka (Tk 500, five hours, 10.30am and 1.15am). The morning coach leaves from the office; the night coach from the Parjatan Motel.

The Sariakandi Ghat bus stand is a Tk 15 rickshaw ride from Shat Mata, or a 20-minute walk, and has regular buses all day to Sariakandi (Tk 20, one hour).

### Train

Rail connections are poor, but two trains run direct to Dhaka. The *Rangpur Express* (10.50pm, eight hours, 1st berth/1st seat/*shuvon* Tk 465/320/160) runs every day except Sunday. The *Lalmoni Express* (1.38pm, 7½ hours, Tk 465/320/160) runs every day except Friday.

## Mahasthangarh

*Garh* means fort or fortified city, and the *garh* of Mahastan is considered the oldest city in Bangladesh. It dates back to at least the 3rd century BC, and is an easy half-day trip from Bogra.

Very few ancient structures remain, so what you'll see is essentially an archaeological site consisting of foundations and hillocks, which merely hint at past riches. Nevertheless, the rural setting is incredibly peaceful so even if you aren't blown away by the historical remains, this still makes a pleasant excursion.

The principal site, the Citadel, contains traces of the ancient city. Many other sites in the vicinity are lumped together under the name Mahasthangarh. The whole area is rich in Hindu, Buddhist and Muslim sites, but most have all but vanished. Buddhists were here until at least the 11th century; their most glorious period was the 8th to the 11th centuries, when the Buddhist Pala emperors of North Bengal ruled. It is from this period that most of the visible remains belong.

**RAJSHAHI & RANGPUR MAHASTHANGARH**

---

**WORTH A TRIP**

### CHARS OF THE JAMUNA

A short bus ride from Bogra brings you to Sariankandi Ghat on the banks of the Jamuna River. From here you can catch boats to any one of a number of **chars**.

Chars (pronounced 'choors') are large sandbank islands, created from silt deposits caused by huge and ongoing river erosion. They are forever being extended and reduced in size by the waters of Bangladesh's largest rivers, and can be found in many parts of the northwest, as well as in Barisal in the south.

An estimated one million people live on chars. These are among the poorest and most vulnerable people in the country. The chars they live on are very fertile strips of land, but are extremely susceptible to flooding and further river erosion. They also have no electricity, no running water and no transport systems.

Chars are not tourist attractions, but visiting them is a fascinating opportunity to learn more about the unusual livelihoods of the people who live on them. To find out more, visit the website of the **Chars Livelihoods Programme** (www.clp-bangladesh.org).

To get to the chars in this area, take a bus from Bogra's Sariankandi Ghat bus stand to Sariankandi (Tk 20, one hour) then take a rickshaw (Tk 10) to the ghat, from where you can rent boats. Local boathands will know what you want to see, so not speaking Bengali won't prevent you from visiting one of the chars. However, if you're able to bring a Bengali-speaking friend or guide with you then you'll obviously increase your chances of being able to have some sort of meaningful interaction with the people who live on these islands.

At the time of research, the going rate for a one-hour boat trip, including a stop at a char, was Tk 150. Alternatively, you could try boarding any of the local ferries that leave from here. They will almost certainly be going to or via one of the chars, and will only cost a couple of taka per person. You may, of course, have some waiting to do for a return ferry but, providing it's not too late in the day, one is bound to materialise.

See also the boxed text p95.

# ◎ Sights

### Citadel
RUIN

Running along the left-hand side of the road as you walk from Mahasthan town towards the museum, the Citadel, or what's left of it, forms a rough rectangle covering more than 2 sq km. It was once surrounded on three sides by the then-mighty Karatuya River. Hindus still make an annual pilgrimage to the river in mid-April.

Probably first constructed under the Mauryan empire in the 3rd century BC, the site shows evidence of various Hindu empires, as well as Buddhist and Muslim occupations. The Citadel fell into disuse around the time of the Mughal invasions.

Most of the visible brickwork dates from the 8th century, apart from that added during restoration. Nowadays there isn't a lot left to see aside from the edge of the exterior walls – some of which rise three or four metres above the ground level – and various unidentifiable grassy mounds.

Not far inside the first entranceway you come to if you walk from Mahasthan town, you'll see *jiyat kunda* (the Well of Life), an 18th-century well, the waters of which were said to have supernatural healing powers. From here you can walk the length of the citadel, roughly following the line of the main road, to the museum, which is located just outside the far entrance to the site. The Citadel's interior is now used mostly as farmland and is good picnic territory.

### Mahasthangarh Museum
MUSEUM

(admission Tk 100; ◎10am-6pm Apr-Sep, 10am-5pm Oct-Mar) This small but well-maintained museum has a lively set of objects discovered in the antique-rich surroundings and is a good place to begin your visit.

The highlights are the statues of Hindu gods, terracotta plaques depicting scenes from daily life, and some well-preserved bronze images found in nearby monastery ruins, which date from the Pala period. Other notable objects are the necklaces that look just like those sold in hippy markets all over the West and the fragments of ancient toilet seats! The gardens too are an attraction in their own right.

The museum is closed all day Sunday, and on Monday mornings. On other days, it usually closes for lunch from 12.30pm to 2.30pm. The main entrance to the Citadel is close by.

### Govinda Bhita Hindu Temple
RUINS

(admission Tk 20) Opposite the museum, the remains of a 6th-century temple overlook a picturesque bend in the river. The temple looks like a broken-down step pyramid and is another peaceful spot. Opening hours are the same as for the museum.

# 🛏 Sleeping & Eating

### Archaeology Department
### Rest House
GUESTHOUSE $

(d Tk 400) There's no need to spend the night here, as Bogra is so close, but this simple rest house has a nice village feel to it if you're sick of busy cities. Located next to the Govinda Bhita Hindu Temple, and overlooking the Karatuya River, it has three clean fan-cooled rooms with mosquito netting and private bathrooms. It's usually empty, and locked, so ask someone at the museum if you want to stay here. There's also a small dining room, although you'll have to give plenty of advance warning if you want to eat here.

There are a couple of roadside restaurants beside the museum where you can grab a simple lunch or breakfast. You'll find more in Mahasthan town, where the bus drops you off.

# ⓘ Getting There & Away

Buses run all day from Bogra to Mahasthan (Tk 10, 30 minutes, 11km). From here you can take a rickshaw (Tk 15 to Tk 20) or walk the 1.7km to the museum, located at the far end of the Citadel. There's a smaller side entrance to the Citadel, which you'll soon see on your left as you walk along the road towards the museum. If you're walking, take the first left after the point where the bus drops you off, and just keep going. You'll soon notice ruins on your left.

# Paharpur

One of only two historic sites in Bangladesh that have been given Unesco World Heritage status (the other is Bagerhat), the Somapuri Vihara at Paharpur was once the biggest Buddhist monastery south of the Himalaya. It dates from the 8th century AD and is the most impressive archaeological site in the country.

# ◎ Sights

### Somapuri Vihara
RUIN

The 20m-high remains of the moss-hewn, red-brick stupa rise from the centre of the huge monastery complex at Somapuri Vihara. The complex is in the shape of a large quadrangle covering 11 hectares, with monks' cells making the outer walls and enclosing an enormous open-air courtyard with the stupa at its centre. The stupa's floor plan is cruciform, and is topped by a three-tier superstructure; the 3rd level has a large tower structure similar to that of Moenjodaro in Pakistan.

Look out for the clay tiles lining the base of the structure, which depict various people and creatures.

Lining the outer perimeter are 177 small monastic cells – once living quarters for monks, and later used as meditation rooms. Ninety-two of these house ornamental pedestals, the purpose of which still eludes archaeologists. It is possible they contained the remains of saintly monks who had once resided here.

On the eastern wing of the south side is an elevated brick base with an eight-pointed star-shaped structure that is thought to have been a shrine. To the west lie the remains of what appears to have been the monks' refectory and kitchen.

Except for the guardhouse to the north, most of the remains outside the courtyard lie to the south. They include an oblong building, linked to the monastery by a causeway, which may have been the wash house and latrines. In the same area is a bathing ghat, probably of Hindu origin. Close to the ghat is the rectangular Temple of Gondeswari, with an octagonal pillar base in the centre and a circular platform to the front.

The monastery is thought to have been successively occupied by Buddhists, Jains and Hindus, which explains the curious mixture of artwork. The Jains would have constructed a *chaturmukhar* (a structure with all four walls decorated with stone bas-reliefs of deities). The Hindus replaced Buddhist terracotta artwork with sculptural stonework of their own deities, and terracotta artwork representing themes from the Mahabharata and the Ramayana. Artefacts discovered at the site range from bronze statues and bas-reliefs of the elephant-headed Hindu god Ganesh, to statues of the Jain god Manzuri, bronze images of the Buddha and statues of the infant Krishna.

**Paharpur Museum**                    MUSEUM
(admission Tk 100;⊙10am-6pm Tue-Sat & 2.30-6pm Mon Apr-Sep, 9am-5pm Tue-Sat & 2.30-5pm Mon Oct-Mar) The small museum gives a good idea of the range of cultures that have used this site. Stucco Buddha heads unearthed here are similar to the Gandhara style of Indo-Hellenic sculpture from what is now northwestern Pakistan. Sculptural work includes sandstone and basalt sculptures, but the stonework of Hevagara in passionate

embrace with Shakti is the collection's finest item. The most important find, a large bronze Buddha, is usually away wooing fans on a seemingly endless world tour.

**Halud Vihara**                    RUIN
Other ruins dot the countryside here, but about 15km southwest of Somapuri Vihara, in the small village of Dwipganj, is the second-most impressive: Halud Vihara. The mound is about 30m wide and 7m high but is badly damaged, with bricks strewn across the village. Nevertheless, it's an interesting place to explore. Expect to pay at least Tk 150 in a rickshaw from Somapuri.

## 🛏 Sleeping & Eating

**Archaeological Rest House**    GUESTHOUSE $
(☑0571 89119, 01711 301274; per person Tk 200) The small white building between the museum and Somapuri Vihar is a rest house. Staff at the museum can point you to the appropriate person if you want to stay. Great-value rooms are large, have attached bathrooms and are kept clean and tidy. But there are only two of them, so call ahead if you can. You can view the stupa from one of the bedroom windows and, as the rest house is inside the grounds of the ruins, you can even go for a night-time stroll around the complex once the rest of the tourists have left.

The caretaker's wife will provide you with tasty home-cooked **meals** (Tk 100) if you ask. Otherwise, there are a couple of shacklike restaurants by the museum.

## ⓘ Getting There & Away

From Bogra, take a bus to Jaipurhat (Tk 60, 1½ hours, 6am to 8pm). From there, buses leave regularly for Paharpur (Tk 10, 30 minutes, 7am to 4pm). To get to the sights from Paharpur village, take a rickshaw (Tk 10).

Don't count on getting a bus from Jaipurhat back to Bogra much after 6pm.

## Rangpur
☑0521 / POP 250,000
Always a major transit point for the northern half of the old Rajshahi division, Rangpur became the capital of the newly created Rangpur division in 2010. The small city houses lovely central streets, but opens up into a quieter, spread-out area, dotted with Raj-era architecture, including the splendid Carmichael College and Tajhat Palace.

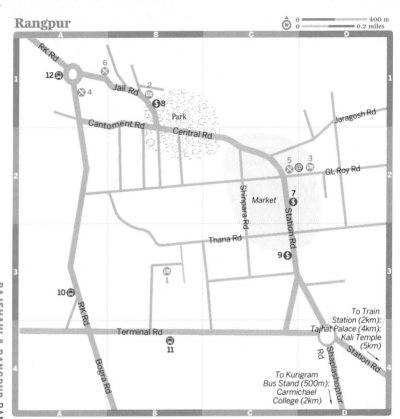

# Rangpur

It's possible to visit some of Bangladesh's fascinating chars (boxed text p95) from here. The beautiful Kantanagar Temple is also within range, and Rangpur is the closest major town to the Indian border at Burimari (p23).

## ◎ Sights

**Tajhat Palace**　　　　　　　　　PALACE
(admission Tk 100; ☺10am-6pm Tue-Sat & 2.30-6pm Mon Apr-Sep, 9am-5pm Tue-Sat & 2.30-5pm Mon Oct-Mar) The domineering Tajhat Palace is one of the finest rajbaris in Bangladesh. During the regime of General Ershad (1982–91) it was used by the High Court division of Bangladesh's Supreme Court, but today it houses a small museum stuffed with old manuscripts and bits and bobs excavated from Paharpur and Mahasthangarh.

The palace, which is structurally intact but deteriorating fast, is similar to Dhaka's Ahsan Manzil (Pink Palace). It has a frontage of about 80m and is crowned by a ribbed conical dome and features an imposing central staircase made of imported white marble. The balustrade originally featured marble sculptures of classical Roman figures, but these have long since disappeared.

The palace was constructed in the 19th century by Manna Lal Ray, a Hindu who was forced to emigrate from the Punjab and found his way to Rangpur. He became a successful jeweller, acquired a lot of land, eventually won the title of raja (landlord or ruler) and built this huge mansion. Local villagers believe there is treasure hidden in its walls.

A rickshaw from the centre costs around Tk 30.

**Carmichael College**　　　　ARCHITECTURE
(কারমাইকেল কলেজ) This famous old college is one of the largest in the country in terms of both area and student enrolment. Situated on the outskirts of town, the college dates from 1916. Similar in inspiration to Curzon Hall in Dhaka and with a grand frontage of over

# Rangpur

### 😴 Sleeping
1 Hotel Tilottama ....................................... B3
2 RDRS Guesthouse ................................. B1
3 The Park Hotel ........................................ D2

### 🍽 Eating
4 Boaishaki Restaurant ........................... A1
5 Mitali Restaurant ................................... C2
6 Trinken ..................................................... A1

### 🛍 Shopping
RDRS Fabrics ............................... (see 2)

### ℹ Information
7 ATM .......................................................... C2
8 ATM .......................................................... B1
9 Sonali Bank ............................................. C3

### 🚌 Transport
10 Bogra Bus Stand .................................... A3
11 Dhaka Bus Stand ................................... B4
12 Medical Morh Bus Stand .................... A1

100m, it is a splendid fusion of classical British and Mughal architecture. Its domes rest on slender columns and a series of arched openings all add to its mosque-like appearance. It is spacious and rural, with cows grazing on the main lawn and students keen to talk of the wider world while resting in the shade.

A rickshaw from the centre is around Tk 20. From Tajhat Palace it's Tk 10.

**Kali Temple**      HINDU TEMPLE

The delightful architectural folly of Kali Temple is modelled on a Florentine dome (or at least a Bengali vision of an English adaptation of a Florentine dome) and is topped with blue-painted Hindu gods. The courtyard also doubles as a village school.

The temple lies about 1km south of Tajhat Palace. A rickshaw from the palace (ask for *kali mondir*) costs Tk 10.

## 🛏 Sleeping

**TOP CHOICE** **RDRS Guesthouse**      GUESTHOUSE $$

(✓66490, 01713 200185; www.rdrsbangla.net; Jail Rd; s/d incl breakfast Tk 1140/1590; ❄@) Run by a highly deserving NGO that works on health, educational and agricultural projects throughout northwest Bangladesh, this fabulous guesthouse, housed in an ivy-clad red-brick building, has polished, spacious rooms, piping-hot showers in modern bathrooms, satellite TV, internet access, a pool table and a team of wonderful chefs. There are plenty of rooms so you shouldn't need to book ahead, but it wouldn't hurt to do so. Sometimes has bicycles available for hire.

**The Park Hotel**      HOTEL $

(✓66718; GL Roy Rd; s/d Tk 260/425, with air-con Tk 600/750;❄) For fancy budget travellers, this central hotel is a delight. The rooms might lack character but this means they are sterile clean. All have wooden bedheads and desks, and the pricier rooms have sit-down toilets.

RAJSHAHI & RANGPUR RANGPUR

---

WORTH A TRIP

## CHARS OF THE BRAHMAPUTRA

Chilmari is a small river ghat not far from Rangpur. From here you can catch boats to a number of chars on the Brahmaputra River. Chars are large islands made of silt, which are heavily prone to river erosion, but which, nevertheless, support communities of people thought to number around one million in total.

One of a number of chars you can reach by boat from Chilmari is known as *char ua para* (pronounced 'chor oowar para'). Around 250 people live here. It's a typically huge sand bank, made up mostly of farmland with small village clusters at its centre. Homes are made of mud, bamboo, jute or a combination of the three. There's a small school, too.

Expect to pay around Tk 100 for a one-hour return trip, including some time to wander around the island. Another option is to ride the wooden passenger boats that ferry between Chulmari and Rowmari (per person Tk 50) on the other side of the river.

As with any trips to places such as this, your visit will be greatly enhanced if you can bring along a Bengali-speaking friend or guide with you. It is possible, though, to get here on your own. Take a bus from Rangpur to Kurigram (Tk 70, 90 minutes) then change for a bus to Chilmari (Tk 35, one hour). Shared autos (Tk 40 to Tk 50) run the same route. The last bus back to Rangpur leaves Kurigram at around 6pm.

**Hotel Tilottama** HOTEL **$**
(☏63482, 01718 938424; Thana Rd; s/d Tk
230/280) This happy budget option is on a
quiet back lane and has welcoming, English-
speaking staff. Simple but tidy rooms come
with a desk and chair, and clean squat-
toilet bathroom. No English sign. Look for
a pastel-blue painted three-storey building.

## ✖ Eating

TOP
CHOICE RDRS Guesthouse BENGALI **$$**
(☏66490, 01713 200185; Jail Rd; meals Tk 250)
Meals here, cooked under the supervision of
guesthouse manager and ace chef Aslam Per-
vez, are supposed to be for guests only, but if
you call ahead and ask nicely, Aslam will let
you eat here even if you're staying elsewhere.
It's worth the hassle of pre-booking because
the food here is delicious. It's a set-priced Tk
250 for lunch or dinner, but you'll be treated
to a range of fabulous Bengali dishes as part
of a set menu. Lunch times are 12.30pm to
2pm. Dinner is 7.30pm to 9pm.

**Mitali Restaurant** BENGALI **$**
(GL Roy Rd; mains from Tk 60; ⊙9am-10pm)
Accessed down a small alley, but with a sign
on the main road, this place – housed in a
run-down, but charming old building – has
been a locals' favourite for years. There's no
menu, but some English is spoken so you
can ask for recommendations. The special-
ity is the *alu chop* (small potato kofta filled
with mutton). The fried chicken is also very
good. There's also biryani and curries as well
as kebabs in the evening.

**Boaishaki Restaurant** BENGALI **$**
(RK Rd; mains Tk 70-100; ⊙7am-1am) Wildly
popular with locals, and well worth the trip
out here, Boaishaki does a great chicken cur-
ry, fine biryani and some mouth-watering
kebabs (evening only). No menu, but at least
one member of staff speaks a little English.

**Trinken** WESTERN **$**
(Jail Rd; mains from Tk 60; ⊙11am-9pm) Clean,
bright, family-friendly cafe–restaurant that
does burgers, chips (fries) and pizza as well
as some Thai-style curries and rice dishes.
Don't expect the cappuccinos to be too au-
thentic. The woman who runs the place
speaks good English.

## 🛍 Shopping

**RDRS Fabrics** CLOTHING
(Jail Rd; ⊙9am-6pm) Run by the same NGO
that runs the guesthouse next door, this

small shop specialises in *satranji* (many
colours) mats and rugs, but also does some
lovely clothing.

## ℹ Information

**Data Link** (GL Roy Rd; internet per hr Tk 20;
⊙10am-10pm)
**Sonali Bank** (Station Rd; ⊙10am-4pm Sun-
Thu) Changes cash and travellers cheques,
but ATM tends not to accept foreign cards.
Foreigner-friendly ATMs are marked on the map.

## ℹ Getting There & Away

### Bus

Buses to Dhaka (non-air-con/air-con Tk
400/600, seven hours, 6.50am to 10pm) go
from the Dhaka bus stand. Bogra (Tk 100, 2½
hours, 7am to 9pm), as well as a number of other
destinations, is served by the Bogra bus stand.

Medical Morh bus stand serves Dinajpur (Tk 60
to Tk 80, two hours, all day); buses to Kurigram
(for the chars near Chilmari; Tk 70, 90 minutes,
until 6pm) leave from the Kurigram bus stand; and
for Patrgram (for the Indian border at Burimari; Tk
140, four hours) go to the Patgram bus stand.

### Train

Rangpur train station is poorly connected, but
there is one direct train to Dhaka (7.40pm,
11 hours, 1st berth/1st seat/*shuvon* Tk
540/375/185) every day except Sunday. The
equivalent train coming to Rangpur leaves
Dhaka at 9am.

# Dinajpur

☏0531 / POP 150,000
Except for a lively Hindu temple inside the
grounds of the town's crumbling rajbari, and
some very colourful market streets packed
with sari shops, there is little of interest for
tourists in this small city. The main reason to
visit Dinajpur is to make the short trip out to
the magnificent Kantanagar Temple.

## ◎ Sights

**Dinajpur Rajbari** RUIN
Mostly in ruins now, the 100-year-old Dinaj-
pur Rajbari still pulls in the crowds, not be-
cause of its crumbling walls and moss-hewn
pillars, but because of the two Hindu temples
standing within its grounds. The one on the
right as you enter – Durga Temple – has a
large peaceful courtyard, but is, like the rest
of the rajbari, largely in ruins. To the left,
though, is the still-active Krishna Temple,
slapped in bright and bold paint, and full of
columns and statues. Thanks to Dinajpur's

# KANTANAGAR TEMPLE

Set in the graceful heart of gorgeous countryside, the rouge sandcastle of Kantanagar Temple, known locally as Kantaji, is a stunning block of religious artwork, and one of the most impressive Hindu monuments in Bangladesh.

Built in 1752 by Pran Nath, a renowned maharaja from Dinajpur, it is the country's finest example of brick and terracotta style. Its most remarkable feature, typical of late Mughal-era temples, is its superb surface decoration, with infinite panels of sculpted terracotta plaques depicting both figural and floral motifs.

The folk artists did not lack imagination or a sense of humour. One demon is depicted swallowing monkeys, which promptly reappear from his ear. Other scenes are more domestic, such as a wife massaging her husband's legs and a lady combing lice from another's hair. Amorous scenes are often placed in obscure corners. These intricate, harmonious scenes are like a richly embroidered carpet.

The 15-sq-m, three-storey edifice was originally crowned with nine ornamental two-storey towers, which collapsed during the great earthquake of 1897 and were never replaced. The building sits in a courtyard surrounded by offices and pilgrims' quarters (now occupied by several Hindu families), all protected by a stout wall. Visitors can no longer go inside the temple, which houses a Krishna shrine, but the intricate detail of its exterior will keep you engaged. The centuries-old Hindu festival of Maha Raas Leela – which celebrates a young Lord Krishna – takes place here around full moon each November, attracting up to 200,000 pilgrims!

Almost as much of an attraction is the utter peace and tranquillity of the site; after you've finished fawning over the temple take a stroll through the fields down to the nearby river. In the dry season the sandbanks exposed by the dropping water levels make a handy cricket pitch for local children.

## Getting There & Away

Buses run regularly all day from Dinajpur's main bus stand to the village of Kantangar (Tk 20, 30 minutes, 7am to 7pm).

From the main road where the bus drops you off it's a lovely 10-minute walk to the temple, over a river, through a couple of mud-hut villages and past stretches of lush farmland. Turn left as you get off the bus and walk towards the river. Cross the rickety bamboo bridge (Tk 10) and just keep following the main path.

with desk, TV, fan and squat-loo bathroom. The manager speaks English.

## ✕ Eating

### Food Garden
CHINESE $$
(Station Rd; mains Tk 150-300; ⊘11am-11pm) A bright and cheerful Chinese restaurant that is popular at both lunch and dinnertime. It's a great respite from the searing intensity of the streets. Does half-portions, too.

### Purnima
BANGLADESHI $
(TNT Rd; meals Tk 100-150; ⊘9am-11pm) This small place, just down from Pabna Sweets, is more of a cafe than a restaurant, but locals say the chef here cooks up the best *kachi biryani* in town, so it's worth coming here for at least one meal. Otherwise, it's a clean, trendy place to stop for a cold drink or an

instant coffee (Tk 20). No English sign, or English menu. Look for the tinted windows.

### New Hotel
BANGLADESHI $
(Station Rd; mains from Tk 40; ⊘7am-11pm) One of the better Bangladeshi restaurants in the town centre, New Hotel's restaurant is very popular and open later than most. There are vegetarian dishes here, too. Not much English.

### Pabna Sweets
SWEETS $
(TNT Rd; ⊘6am-10pm) Dinajpur's best shop for Bengali sweets and *misthi doi* (sweet yogurt).

## ❶ Information

**AB Bank ATM** (Maldapoti Rd) Accepts foreign cards.

**Galaxy Computers** (off Station Rd; per hr Tk 30; ⊘10.30am-9pm)

Dinajpur

Hindu population of around 38% (one of the highest in the country) this place is often heaving with devotees, making it a extremely lively place to visit. Some Hindu families live permanently in the yellow-wash houses built into the walls of the temple enclosure.

You can walk here from town (30 to 45 minutes). A rickshaw costs Tk 20 to Tk 30.

## Sleeping

**Hotel Unique**                                  HOTEL $
(☏52203, 01736 335264; www.hoteluniquebd.com; Nimtola; r without/with air-con from Tk 300/850;❄) Newly opened in 2011, this was comfortably the cleanest and best-value place in town at the time of research. Expect a bit of wear and tear by the time you get here, but it should still be in good nick as the place is well run. Some English spoken.

**Hotel Al-Rashid**                               HOTEL $
(☏65658, 01716 535956; Nimtola; s/d Tk 200/300) Small, basic but tidy singles and doubles

## ❶ Getting There & Away

### Bus

The main bus stand is on Bypass Rd and is a Tk 20 rickshaw ride from town. Destinations include Kantanagar Temple (Kantaji; Tk 20, 30 minutes, 7am to 7pm) and Rangpur (Tk 100, two hours, 6.30am to 6pm).

A short stretch of Station Rd known as Kalitola contains a cluster of offices for coach companies, which have services to Dhaka, and the ticket office for BRTC, which has two daily buses to Rajshahi and regular buses to Bogra.

The BRTC bus stand is close to the main bus stand, on a lane that runs parallel to and west of Bypass Rd. Destinations:

**Dhaka** Tk 500, 10 hours, 7am to midnight
**Rajshahi** Tk 240, six hours, 6.30am and 4pm
**Bogra** Tk 150, 3½ hours, 6.30am to 3pm

### Train

It's quicker to catch buses for other destinations within Rajshahi division, but you might want to consider the train for Dhaka (1st berth/1st seat/*shuvon* Tk 535/370/185, 10 hours, 8.10am and 9.50pm). The 8.10am doesn't run on Wednesday and the 9.50pm doesn't run on Monday.

---

# Rajshahi

☑ 0721 / POP 470,000

Built on the northern bank of the Padma River, Rajshahi is a fun university town with enough colour and attractions to entertain for a short visit. It also makes a sensible base from which to dig through the layers of history in Sona Masjid, Puthia and Natore.

The riverbank by the Padma River affords pleasant views and, in the late afternoon, a carnival-like atmosphere pervades with people strolling and chatting, children playing and vendors selling ice cream and other snacks.

Looking across the vast flood plain, you will see India (the border is about 2km beyond the opposite bank), where the river is called the Ganges. In the dry season it is sometimes possible to walk across the riverbed, which aids the thriving smuggling trade along the border. In any case, you can hop across on a boat (Tk 10). Note: the nearest official border crossing is at Sona Masjid.

## ◉ Sights

**Varendra Research Museum**  MUSEUM
(admission free; ⊙10am-5pm Sat-Wed, 2.30-5pm Fri) Founded in 1910 with the support of the maharaja of Dighapatia, the Varendra Research Museum is managed by Rajshahi University (RU), and is the oldest museum in the country. The predominantly British-style building has some interesting Hindu–Buddhist features, including a trefoil arch over the doorways and windows. A small *rekha* temple forms the roof.

Inside, artefacts from all over the subcontinent are on display, including some rare

---

### THE INFAMOUS INDIGO KUTHIS

In the 18th and early 19th centuries the trade in indigo – the plant that yields the indigo hue for dye – was highly profitable. By the mid-1800s the Rajshahi region alone had more than 150 indigo *kuthis* (factories). The local zamindars (landowners) even loaned money to peasants so they could plant more indigo. Indeed, trade was so lucrative and the *kuthis* so numerous that factory labourers had to be imported.

The farmers, however, didn't profit at all and began changing crops. Using oppression and torture to keep the peasants growing indigo, angry zamindars sometimes went as far as committing murder and burning whole villages. An adage at the time held that 'no indigo box was despatched to England without being smeared in human blood'.

In 1859 the peasants revolted. The Indigo Revolt lasted two years and brought the cultivation of indigo to a halt. Eventually the government had no choice but to decree that the peasants could no longer be forced to plant indigo. As a result, by the end of the century the indigo trade had completely disappeared. Some of the *kuthis* were converted into silk factories but most simply fell into ruin.

High on the riverbank in Rajshahi, although locked away behind gates and walls, Baro Kuthi is one of the last remaining examples of the indigo *kuthis* in this region. Originally built by the Dutch as a silk factory in the early 19th century, Baro Kuthi also served as a fort in times of emergency before being converted into an indigo *kuthi* by the British East India Company. It was in operation for around 25 years before being abandoned and subsequently falling into disrepair.

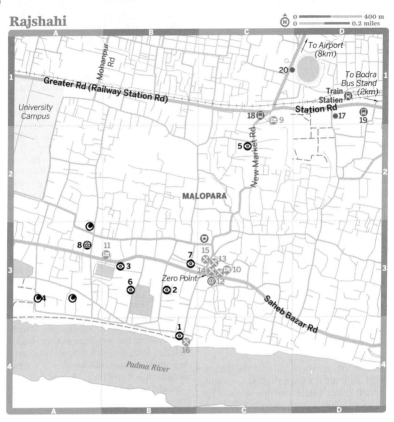

# Rajshahi

## Rajshahi

### ◉ Sights

| | |
|---|---|
| 1 Baro Kuthi | B4 |
| 2 Collegiate School | B3 |
| 3 Fuller House | B3 |
| 4 Mosque | A3 |
| 5 New Market | C2 |
| 6 Rajshahi Government College | B3 |
| 7 Saheb Bazar | B3 |
| 8 Varendra Research Museum | A3 |

### 🛏 Sleeping

| | |
|---|---|
| 9 Hotel Dalas International | C1 |
| 10 Hotel Nice | C3 |
| 11 Red Castle | B3 |

### ✖ Eating

| | |
|---|---|
| 12 Aristocrat Coffee Shop & Restaurant | C3 |
| 13 Bismallah Hotel | C3 |
| 14 Chili's Fast Food | C3 |
| 15 Rajshahi Mistanno Vander | C3 |
| 16 Snack Stalls | B4 |

### ⓘ Information

| | |
|---|---|
| AB Bank ATM | (see 13) |

### ⓘ Transport

| | |
|---|---|
| 17 Bus Booking Offices for Dhaka | D1 |
| 18 Buses to Sona Masjid | C1 |
| 19 Main Bus Stand | D1 |
| 20 Tyaara Travels International | C1 |

examples from the ancient city of Mohenjo-daro in Pakistan, and a superb collection of local Hindu sculpture.

### Buildings of the British Raj
ARCHITECTURE
Near the centre of Rajshahi are some Raj-era buildings. **Rajshahi Government College**, which dates from 1873 when several maharajas donated money for its establishment, is an elegant two-storey edifice with beautiful semicircular arched windows. Others nearby include **Collegiate School** (1836), which consists of two single-storey structures east of the college, with verandas along the facades; and **Fuller House** (1909), a large two-storey red-brick building that is similar in appearance to the college.

### Market
MARKETS
The cube of chaos that is **New Market**, on the way to the train station, is most active in the morning, and is a photographer's paradise. **Saheb Bazar**, immediately northwest of the junction known as Zero Point, is a heady mix of winding alleys and colourful stores, and also great for aimless wandering.

## 🛏 Sleeping

[TOP CHOICE] **Chez Rassak**
GUESTHOUSE $$
(✏762 011, 01711 958708; chezrazzak@gmail.com; House 169, Rd 4, Padma Housing Estate; r incl breakfast Tk 1500-2000;❄@) There are two ways of looking at this well-run guesthouse: either it's a bit out of the way, so rather inconvenient, or it's a quiet escape from the city-centre chaos. Either way, you get spacious, homy rooms with good-quality furniture and modern attached bathrooms. The food here is also very good. The well-to-do residential area is at least a Tk 30 rickshaw ride from the city centre, but is only a short walk from Bodra bus stand (over the rail crossing, right at the end of the road, first left, first left again then first right). Razzak, the owner, speaks good English.

### Hotel Nice
HOTEL $$
(✏776 188; www.hotelnice-raj.com; Saheb Bazar Rd; s/d from Tk 1110/1300;❄@🛜) The most comfortable place to stay in the city centre, newly renovated Nice has reasonably smart, colourful rooms with TV, air-con and clean attached bathrooms with sit-down toilets. There's free internet (including wi-fi) in the lobby, and staff members speak English.

### Hotel Dalas International
HOTEL $
(✏773 839; off Station Rd; s from Tk 300, d without/with air-con Tk 500/800;❄) The best budget option in town by some distance. Rooms are universally spacious and well equipped with TV, chairs and big beds. It's handy for both the town centre and the bus and train stations. The English-speaking management loves a good old chin-wag. Other cheaper, but far less attractive, budget hotels can be found around Saheb Bazar on the road that leads up to New Market Rd.

### Red Castle
GUESTHOUSE $$
(✏810 046, 01714 020124; redcastle@ymail.com; s/d from Tk 1000/2000;❄) Rooms in this attractive, heritage-looking building are absolutely enormous and come with air-con, TV and spotless bathrooms, but the atmosphere is strangely cold and although you're not far from Zero Point, you feel a little bit cut off from the action.

## 🍴 Eating

### Aristocrat Coffee Shop & Restaurant
INDIAN $$
(Saheb Bazar Rd; mains Tk 200-400, cakes & snacks from Tk 50; ⏰cafe 10am-10pm, restaurant noon-3pm & 6-10pm) Modern, relaxed, fan-cooled cafe with coffee (from Tk 30), desserts and ice cream attached to a refined Indian restaurant that does the best food in town. Menu includes Thai and Chinese dishes, too.

### Chili's Fast Food
FAST FOOD $$
(Saheb Bazar Rd; snacks Tk 30-80, mains Tk 200) Burgers, chips and kebabs in a small but clean cafelike restaurant. The main menu has Thai and Chinese dishes, too, but they aren't a scratch on those served at Aristocrat.

### Bismallah Hotel
BANGLADESHI $
(Saheb Bazar; mains from Tk 50) One of the most popular of a host of busy local restaurants just north of Zero Point. Does dhal, roti, curries and rice. No menu. Very little English, but decent food. No English sign, but it's next to Hotel Mukta.

### Rajshahi Mistanno Vander
SWEETS $
(Saheb Bazar; ⏰7am-midnight) The busiest of a number of sweet shops near Zero Point offering *misti doi* (from Tk 60) and a range of other sweets (per piece from Tk 10).

## ℹ️ Information

**AB Bank ATM** (Saheb Bazar) One of a few ATMs that accept foreign cards.

**ehut Chartered Computers** (Saheb Bazar Rd; internet per hr Tk 20; ⊙9am-9pm) Second floor.

## ℹ️ Getting There & Away

### Air

At the time of research, **United Airways** (☎761630; www.uabdl.com; via Tyaara Travels International, Stadium Supermarket 1st fl, Airport Rd) ran three flights a week (Tuesday, Thursday and Saturday) from Rajshahi to Dhaka, but check the website for the latest schedule.

### Bus

Many of the main bus stand services stop at Bodra bus stand on the way out of town. For Sona Masjid (Tk 95, three hours, hourly 7.25am to 4pm), pick up a bus at the crossroads of New Market Rd and Station Rd. For non-air-con (Tk 400) or air-con (Tk 750) coaches to Dhaka (five hours, 6am to midnight), go to the ticket offices just west of the bus stand.

It's Tk 5 per person in a shared auto-rickshaw from main bus stand, also known as 'Terminal', to Bodra bus stand, from where buses go to Kushtia (Tk 140, two hours. 6am to 4.30pm).

From the main bus stand, buses leave for the following destinations:

**Bogra** Tk 120, 2½ hours, 6.30am to 4.30pm
**Rangpur** Tk 220, 4½ hours, 6am to 4pm
**Natore** Tk 50, one hour, 6.30am to 6.30pm
**Puthia** Tk 30, 30 minutes, 6.30am to 6.30pm

### Train

Three trains go to Dhaka (1st berth/1st seat/*shuvon* Tk 405/285/140, six hours, 7.30am, 4pm and 11.20pm). The 7.30pm doesn't run on Sunday, the 4pm breaks on Tuesday and the overnight train on Monday. There should also be air-con seats and berths available on these trains.

One train also runs to Khulna (1st seat/*shuvon* Tk 255/125, 6½ hours, 2pm) every day except Wednesday.

---

# Sona Masjid (Gaud)

A site of great historical importance, Gaud (pronounced Gaur, but known by most people on this side of the border as Sona Masjid, the name of the main mosque here) has more historic mosques than almost any other area in Bangladesh. Some of its sights are in India, some in Bangladesh.

The Hindu Senas established their capital here, after which the Khiljis from Turkistan took control for three centuries, to be followed in the late 15th century by the Afghans. Under the Afghans, Gaud became a prosperous city, surrounded by fortified ramparts and a moat, and spread over 32 sq km. Replete with temples, mosques and palaces, the city was visited by traders and merchants from all over Central Asia, Arabia, Persia and China. A number of mosques are still standing today, and some have been restored, although none of the buildings from the earlier Hindu kingdoms remains.

For information on the Indian border crossing here, see p24.

## ◉ Sights

**Chhota Sona Masjid**                      MOSQUE
Built between 1493 and 1526, the well-preserved 'Small Golden Mosque' is oddly named given that it's actually jet black with just patches of terracotta brickwork. Despite its misleading name, it's a fine specimen of pre-Mughal architecture. The chief attraction here is the superb decoration carved on the black-stone walls. On both the inner and outer walls, ornate stonework in shallow relief covers the surface. It also features an ornate women's gallery, arched gateways and lavishly decorated mihrabs. This living mosque draws in large crowds for Friday prayers, but outside prayer time it's fine for non-Muslims to enter. This mosque is usually just referred to as 'Sona Masjid'. Your bus from Rajshahi will stop beside it.

**Tahkhana Palace Ruins**                      RUIN
About 100m beyond Sona Masjid, turn left down a signposted lane and keep walking for about 250m until you reach this small complex of ruins overlooking a small pond. The principle building is the Tahkhana Palace, built by Shah Shuja in the early 17th century and the area's major Mughal-era building. A large two-storey brick edifice, it once contained more than two dozen rooms as well as a *hammam* (bathhouse) served by terracotta water pipes. Just beyond this is the attractive Shah Niamatullah Mosque, a three-domed mosque built in 1560. Close by is the Mausoleum of Shah Niamatullah Wali, with one dome and four squat towers.

**Darasbari Mosque**                      RUIN
Back on the main road, and about 1km beyond Sona Masjid, turn left down a lane signposted to Darasbari Mosque. About

500m along this lane you'll come to this palace-like mosque built in 1470. It's no longer an active mosque, and is largely in ruins – the domed roof collapsed some time ago – but its red-brick archways are highly attractive, as is the secluded grassy location.

### Khania Dighi Mosque MOSQUE

About 750m beyond the turn-off for Darasbari Mosque, turn right at the bus stand and keep walking for around 250m until you see a sign directing you off to the right to this gorgeous single-domed mosque. Also known as Rajbibi Mosque, it was built in 1490 and is in excellent condition. It has some ornately decorated walls, embellished primarily with terracotta floral designs, but it's the domed roof that is the attraction. Built of thousands of minuscule bricks, it's one of the more arresting mosques in the country. Like the Chhota Sona Masjid, it's a working mosque, in which Friday prayers are especially animated. It's fine for women to enter outside prayer time but they must be respectfully dressed. The mosque's position, crouching under huge stumpy mango trees (May to June is mango season) beside a large lily- and duck-covered pond, only helps to enhance its beauty, and it's a perfect spot for a picnic.

### 🛏 Sleeping & Eating

At the time of research there was nowhere to stay here, barring some extremely basic rooms above one of the small restaurants by the bus stand, but a site for a new Parjatan Motel had been chosen, about halfway between Sona Masjid and the border post. Still, there's no need to stay here as you can get buses back to Rajshahi until 4.40pm.

### ❶ Getting There & Away

Direct buses from Rajshahi to Sona Masjid run from a crossroads near the train station roughly every hour (Tk 95, three hours, 7.25am to 4pm). Note: you may end up having to change at one or more of Godagari, Nawabganj or Kansat en route.

The first place your bus will come to as it enters the area is Sona Masjid. It makes sense to get off here, then walk to the other sights before catching a return bus from the bus stand, which is about 2km down the road, further towards the border post, at a point where the road bears round to the right towards Khania Dighi Mosque.

There are a few rickshaws knocking about if you don't fancy walking. Shared autos ply the main road between Sona Masjid and the border.

Buses from here to Rajshahi run from 7.25am to 4.40pm and leave roughly every hour from the bus stand, which is about 250m from the Indian border post. Buses stop to pick up passengers at Sona Masjid as they leave the area.

## Puthia

The delightful little village of Puthia (*pou-tee-ah*) is positively bursting at the seams with dilapidated palaces and bewitching temples, and is one of the shining highlights of this part of Bangladesh. If Puthia were in almost any other country the ruins here would be seething with camera-snapping tourists, but lost as it is in the remote paddy fields of Bangladesh, you'll have it all to yourself.

The vegetation-chocked village is centred on a cheerful bazaar and a number of lily-covered ponds in which people fish, swim and wash themselves, their clothes and their buffalo.

Mr Bishwana, the caretaker of the temples and a gentleman in the truest sense of the word, works directly for the Archaeology Department and makes a charming guide. If he is not hanging around the Shiva Temple someone will quickly ferret him out for you. Even if you don't want a guide, he is the man with the keys to many of the sights so you will have to find him, or one of his colleagues, anyway.

### ◉ Sights

In addition to the places listed here, there are plenty of other temples and rajbaris, in various states of decay, dotted around the tree-shaded villages and surrounding banana plantations. It's a beautiful place to walk around.

### Puthia Palace RUIN

The stately, multi-columned, two-storey Puthia Palace was built in 1895 by Rani Hemanta Kumari Devi in honour of his illustrious mother-in-law, Maharani Sharat Sundari Devi. She was a major benefactor in the Rajshahi region, having built a boarding house for college students and a Sanskrit college, for which she was given the title 'maharani' in 1877. The building is in just good enough condition to serve as a college today. Though you probably won't be allowed inside, it's enough just to marvel at how grand the exterior is and how perfect the setting, with a large grassy maidan in front and a frog-filled pond behind.

Facing Puthia Palace across the maidan is **Dol Mondir**, a white pyramid-shaped temple with four tiers, built in 1785.

### Govinda Temple
TEMPLE

Arguably the most startling monument in Puthia village is the Govinda Temple, located inside the palace, on the left-hand side of the inner courtyard. Erected between 1823 and 1895 by one of the maharanis of the Puthia estate, it's a large, square structure with intricate terracotta designs embellishing the surface. Most of the terracotta panels depict scenes from the love affair between Radha and Krishna as told in the Hindu epics. The temple now contains a Krishna shrine and is visited by many of the local Hindu population.

There is a second, smaller temple complex on the other side of the pond, which is off to the left as you exit the palace. It contains three beautifully renovated temples – Govinda, Gopala and Anika – with domed, eggshell roofs and carvings that come close to rivalling that of the main Govinda Temple.

### Shiva Temple
TEMPLE

Built in 1823, the towering Shiva Temple sits at the entrance to Puthia village, overlooking a pond. It's an excellent example of the *pancha-ratna* (five-spire) Hindu style common in northern India. Unfortunately, many of the stone carvings and sculptures were disfigured during the 1971 Liberation War. The inside contains a huge black-stone phallic representation of Shiva. Many Hindus come to make *puja* here early in the morning or in the early evening and, with the mist rising off the pond and the light setting everything aflame, this is a beautiful time to come. An even more rewarding time to visit is during one of the two major pilgrimages that take place here – one in March/April and the other during the final week of August.

### ⓘ Getting There & Away

There are numerous buses from Rajshahi to Natore and they all stop at Puthia (Tk 30, 30 minutes, 6.30am to 6.30pm). From the main road follow the sign for 'Puthia Temple' and keep walking for about 500m.

It's easy to pick up buses on the side of the main road here to either Rajshahi or Natore (Tk 20, 30 minutes) from where you can catch buses to Dhaka.

# Natore

☏ 0771 / POP 70,000

The small town of Natore is a place of split personality. On the one hand you've got the town centre itself, a nondescript, dusty small town.

On the other hand you have elegant Natore Rajbari with its fanciful gardens and temple-hemmed ponds, which, when combined with nearby Puthia, makes for an enchanting day trip from Rajshahi or even Bogra.

## ◉ Sights

### Natore Rajbari
PALACES

One of the oldest rajbaris in Bangladesh (dating from around the mid-1700s), the magnificent but dilapidated Natore Rajbari is actually a series of seven rajbaris, four of which remain largely intact. The main block, called Boro Taraf (big palace), is approached via a long avenue lined with impressively tall bottle palms, the white trunks of which resemble temple columns.

To the rear of Boro Taraf is a second block called Chotto Taraf (small palace), consisting of two rajbaris. The principal one faces a pond and is one of the most beautifully proportioned buildings in Bangladesh.

The peaceful and idyllic gardens around the rajbari are as much an attraction as the building itself; bring a picnic to eat in the shade of a gnarled old tree. There are several large ponds here that form an interesting centrepiece, around which are a couple of Hindu temples, one dedicated to Kali, one to Shiva. Both are still used by the many Hindus in the area and attract the odd sadhu (itinerant holy man), unusually for Bangladesh.

Natore Rajbari is at the northern edge of town. You can walk to it in about half an hour (just keep asking for directions) or take a rickshaw (Tk 10 to Tk 20).

## 🛏 Sleeping & Eating

As with Puthia, eating options are thin on the ground in Natore. There are snack stalls around the rajbari, and a few very basic restaurants on the main road, but for a proper meal head to VIP Hotel.

### VIP Hotel
HOTEL **$**

(☏ 66097, 01718 673735; Seb Plaza, Baraharispur; s/d Tk 350/600, with air-con Tk 600/1000; ❋) Simple but neat and clean, rooms here have sit-down toilets in small bathrooms and come with a balcony. Staff are welcoming and the restaurant does OK food (meals from Tk 150).

### ⓘ Getting There & Away

Buses between Rajshahi and Dhaka drop off and pick up passengers at the intersection of the main highway at the eastern end of town. From here it's a few hundred metres along the main drag to get to the right-hand turning, which leads to the Bogra bus stand. The rajbari complex is about 15 to 20 minutes walk from here.

If you're heading to Pabna (Tk 35, 90 minutes) or Rajshahi (Tk 50, 90 minutes, until 7pm) catch a bus at the highway intersection. For Dhaka (non-air-con/air-con Tk 400/700, six hours, 5.30am to midnight), there are some ticket offices just beyond the Bogra bus stand turning, at the far west end of the main drag.

Bogra bus stand has regular buses to Bogra (Tk 60, two hours, 6.30am to 10pm).

# Pabna

☏ 01731 / POP 120,000

Of less appeal to travellers than Natore and certainly Puthia, Pabna does, nevertheless, have a couple of fine old buildings, a very unusual Hindu temple and two well-known rajbaris that make a quick stop worthwhile.

## ⊙ Sights

### Jor Bangla Temple                           TEMPLE
Built in the 18th century in the form of two traditional village huts intertwined and standing on a platform, this temple, 2km east of the town centre, is the best remaining example of the *jor bangla* (twin hut) style. However, the once-beautiful terracotta plaques carved with scenes of daily life are badly weathered and only of appeal to serious history buffs. It's a fun rickshaw ride (from the bus stand Tk 40, from the town centre Tk 20 to Tk 30), along bumpy winding backstreets.

### Rajbaris                                  PALACES
The **Taras Rajbari**, viewed from the street through an unusually impressive archway,

is a few hundred metres south of the town centre on the main road. Dating from the late 19th century, this grand red-and-white building with a crazy coat of arms was evidently once an elegant palace, but it's now all too obviously the drab home of government offices.

Very close by is a fairground-style **mosque** that is as bright and gaudy as you'll find in Bangladesh.

East of town, on the banks of the Padma River, **Sitlai Palace**, dating from 1900, is a grand rajbari that's fairly well preserved. Today it's occupied by a drug company, so you can't see the 30-room interior. The exterior is interesting, however, with a broad staircase flagged with white marble, leading to a second-storey arched portico.

### Shahzadpur Mosque                          MOSQUE
Just outside Pabna is this splendid 15-dome pre-Mughal mosque, built in 1528 in traditional *bangla* (pre-Mauryan and Mauryan) style with thick walls and various arched entrances.

## 🛏 Sleeping & Eating

### Dream Palace                           HOTEL $$
(☏ 66352, 01713 228798; s/d Tk 1000/1400; ☀) About 200m from the main 'Terminal' bus stand, towards the town centre, is this bright new hotel with small but clean air-con rooms. Also does food.

## ⊙ Getting There & Away

The main bus stand, known as 'Terminal', is at the east end of town, on the main highway. Buses include Natore (Tk 35), Rajshahi (Tk 80 to Tk 90) and Dhaka (Tk 360, five hours, regular until 6pm).

# Chittagong Division

## Includes »

## Best Places for Walks or Hikes

» Bandarban (p113)

» Teknaf Game Reserve (boxed text p129)

» St Martin's Island (p128)

## Best Places for Boat Trips

» Sangu River (p115)

» Kaptai Lake (p117)

» St Martin's Island (p128)

» Maheskhali Island (boxed text p127)

## Why Go?

The most diverse region of Bangladesh, Chittagong is a land that stretches from forested hills and scenic lakes to sandy beaches and coral islands. It's a land of off-the-beaten-track adventure, with great hiking and remote boat trips, but also one of cultural contrasts – around a dozen Adivasi groups live here.

Home to Bangladesh's largest port, Chittagong is a place where you can see wooden fishing boats being pieced together on one beach, while disused ocean liners are picked apart on the next. You can trek through forests where elephants roam wild, or walk along the world's longest natural beach before retreating to your hotel's rooftop pool.

Some travellers are put off by the hassles of permits (actually very easy to arrange) or the dangers of social unrest (check the latest before you come). But those who persist are rewarded with experiences you simply can't find in any other region of Bangladesh.

## When to Go
### Chittagong

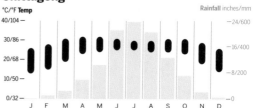

**Oct–Feb**
Best time for hiking the Hill Tracts.

**Oct–March**
Best time for St Martin's Island, before tropical storms start.

**Jun–Sep**
Rainy season. Quietest and cheapest time to visit Cox's Bazar.

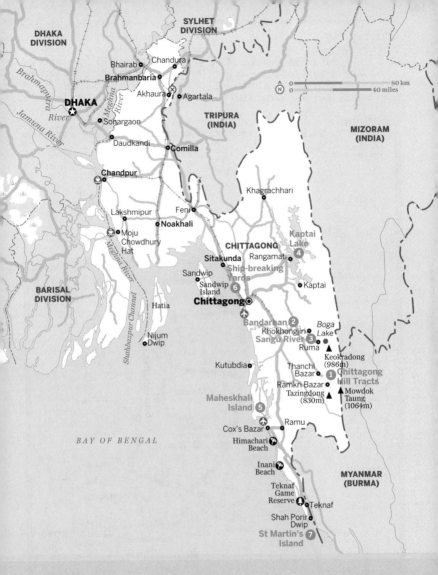

# Chittagong Division Highlights

① Hook up with a trusted guide and hike your way into the depths of the **Chittagong Hill Tracts** (boxed text p120)

② Learn about Adivasi culture by visiting some of the tribal villages around the forested hillside town of **Bandarban** (p113)

③ Enjoy what's arguably the most scenic river trip in Bangladesh by taking a boat ride along the serene **Sangu River** (p115)

④ Spend a day floating across the enormous **Kaptai Lake** (p117)

⑤ Bounce along the waves to rarely visited **Maheskhali Island** (boxed text p127)

⑥ Take a sneak peak at Chittagong's controversial **ship-breaking yards** (p111)

⑦ Enjoy the tropical beach vibe at **St Martin's Island** (p128), Bangladesh's only coral island

# Chittagong

🎵 31 / POP 2.5 MILLION

Often sticky, and terribly polluted, Chittagong, Bangladesh's second-largest city and the country's largest port, is an interesting rather than pleasant place to stay. There's a gritty feel to its city streets, especially those that wind their way down to the river at Sadarghat (*shod-or-ghat*), and the markets in the Old City are great fun to get lost in. But the traffic here is appalling, and with less regulations than Dhaka about which vehicles can and can't spew their fumes into the

## Chittagong

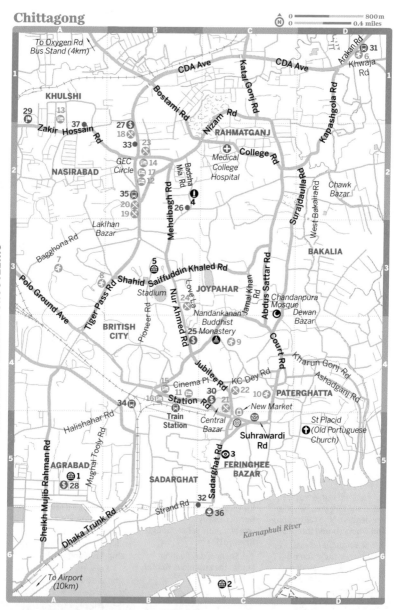

city centre, the pollution here really is eye-streamingly bad.

However, this city is the gateway to one of the most beautiful and fascinating corners of Bangladesh: the Chittagong Hill Tracts. And unless you've paid for a tour operator to do all the paperwork for you, you'll have to stop off here to sort out your permits for the hill tracts region. It also makes sense to rest up in Chittagong for at least one night if you're planning to hit the beaches of Cox's Bazar or St Martin's Island.

### History

Locals say the word 'Chittagong' originated from *chattagram* (small village), though it more likely comes from the Rakhaing (Arakanese) phrase *tsi-tsi-gong* ('war should never be fought') inscribed on a tablet brought by an invading Buddhist army.

Despite its name, Chittagong has been consistently fought over. In 1299 Muslims occupied the city, until the Rakhaing retook it and retained it until 1660. The Mughals took possession next, only to be expelled by the Rakhaing in 1715. Finally, in 1766, the British raised their flag.

The evolution of the city followed a similar pattern to Dhaka, except that the oldest parts (where the city of Sadarghat now stands) were wiped out during the British and post-Independence periods. The Pakistani navy shelled the city during the Liberation War.

## ◉ Sights & Activities

### OLD CITY
**Sadarghat**                                    RIVER GHAT

As in Dhaka, the city's oldest area is the waterfront part called Sadarghat, and as in Dhaka, it's a cacophony of sensual assaults. The early arrival of the Portuguese is evinced by the proximity of the Paterghatta District, just next to Sadarghat, which remains a Christian area. There isn't much to see in Paterghatta, but it's a quiet, clean place to walk around.

If you're walking here from Station Rd, notice the **rickshaw makers**, with their tiny streetside workshops, hammering away on Sadarghat Rd.

For a fun, albeit perhaps slightly scary side trip, hop on a wooden **rowboat** (per person Tk 5) from Sadarghat and cross the ship-laden river to the **fish harbour and market**. The **Marine Fisheries Academy** is housed in a new building here with a small museum.

## Chittagong

### ◉ Sights
| | |
|---|---|
| **1** Ethnological Museum | A5 |
| Fish Harbour & Market | (see 2) |
| **2** Marine Fisheries Academy | C6 |
| **3** Rickshaw Workshops | C5 |
| **4** WWII Memorial Cemetery | B2 |
| **5** Zia Memorial Museum | B3 |

### ◉ Activities, Courses & Tours
| | |
|---|---|
| **6** Bangladesh Ecotours | D1 |
| **7** Battali Hill | A3 |
| **8** Battali Hills Park | A3 |
| **9** DC Hill | C4 |
| **10** Fairy Hill | C4 |

### ◉ Sleeping
| | |
|---|---|
| **11** Asian SR Hotel | B4 |
| **12** Grand Park Hotel | B2 |
| **13** Hilltop Inn | A1 |
| **14** Hotel Abakash | B2 |
| **15** Hotel Golden Inn | B4 |
| **16** Hotel Sylhet Super | B4 |
| **17** Peninsula Chittagong | B2 |

### ◉ Eating
| | |
|---|---|
| **18** Bonanza Food Plus | B2 |
| **19** Dhaba | B2 |
| **20** Handi | B2 |
| **21** Hotel ABP | C4 |
| **22** Hotel Zaman | C4 |
| Niribilee | (see 14) |
| **23** Rio Coffee Corner | B2 |
| **24** Tai Wah Restaurant | B3 |

### ◉ Information
| | |
|---|---|
| **25** AB Bank ATM | B4 |
| **26** Divisional Commissioner's Office | B2 |
| **27** HSBC | B2 |
| **28** HSBC | A5 |
| **29** Indian High Commission | A1 |
| **30** Standard Chartered Bank | C4 |

### ◉ Transport
| | |
|---|---|
| **31** Bahaddarhat Bus Stand | D1 |
| **32** BIWTC Ticket Office | C5 |
| **33** GMG Airlines | B2 |
| **34** Kadamtali Bus Stand | B4 |
| **35** Private Coach Companies | B2 |
| **36** Sadarghat | C6 |
| **37** United Airways (Hotel Agrabad) | A2 |

### Central Bazar
MARKET

The Central Bazar is a warren of alleyways between the lower ends of Jubilee and Station Rds. It's almost impossible not to lose your way among the densely packed rows of clothing shops, but it's a lot of fun trying to find your way out again.

### BRITISH CITY

The British originally occupied the area just northwest of Sadarghat, a slightly hilly section where they built their usual collection of administrative and cultural edifices. Distances here make walking a hard slog, so you'll probably want to take rickshaws between sights.

### Zia Memorial Museum
MUSEUM

(admission local/foreigner Tk 5/75; ☉10.30am-4.30pm Sat-Wed, 3.30-7.30pm Fri) This museum is housed in an interesting mock-Tudor mansion. Among its much-revered collection is the microphone and transmitter with which President Zia proclaimed the country's independence in 1971.

### WWII Memorial Cemetery
CEMETERY

(ওয়ার সিমেট্রি; Badsha Mia Rd; ☉8am-noon & 2-5pm) This tear-inducing cemetery contains the graves of hundreds of soldiers from both Allied and Japanese forces who died on the Burma front. Many are inscribed with simple and powerful epitaphs of loss and love. The cemetery is maintained by the Commonwealth War Graves Commission.

### Hilltop Walks
HILLS

If you're desperate to escape the worst of the traffic fumes, consider climbing one of the small hills that dot this part of the city. **Fairy Hill** (climb the path leading off Jubilee Rd just north of the pedestrian bridge, and ask for the High Court, which sits on top of it, if you get lost), **Battali Hill** (from Tiger Pass Rd) and **DC Hill** all command views of the city and make for pleasant walks.

### AGRABAD

This more modern commercial section of the city has little in the way of interest for tourists.

### Ethnological Museum
MUSEUM

(জাতিতাত্ত্বিক জাদুঘর; Jatitantik Jadhughar; ☉9am-5pm Tue-Sat & 1.30-5pm Mon Oct-Mar, 10am-6pm Tue-Sat & 1.30-6pm Mon Apr-Sep) The interesting Ethnological Museum has displays on Bangladesh's tribal people. Unfortunately, it isn't always open when it should be. Some of the exhibits are looking a bit tattered, but it covers all the major tribal groups of the nearby Chittagong Hill Tracts.

## 🛏 Sleeping

The main areas where tourists stay are Station Rd, which is full of budget hotels and has a grittier old-town feel to it, and the GEC Circle area, which enjoys a wider variety of restaurants.

### STATION ROAD AREA

#### Hotel Golden Inn
HOTEL $$

(☏611 004; 336 Station Rd; s/d/t/q Tk 500/950/1250/1900, with air-con Tk 1000/1400/1700/2800; ❊@) Well run by helpful staff who speak good English, Golden Inn has long been a favourite for budget travellers, though prices are hardly budget these days. It's a vast, echoing place with enough rooms to ensure it's rarely full, and the triples and quads are handy for groups of friends. The restaurant is decent (if poorly lit) and there's a rooftop courtyard with city views. Internet costs Tk 60 per hour.

#### Asian SR Hotel
HOTEL $$

(☏285 0346; www.asiansrhotel.com; 291 Station Rd; s/d from Tk 720/1300, with air-con Tk 1200/2000; ❊@🛜) Very smart and well run, this is probably the best hotel on Station Rd. Rooms are slick and clean and some of them come with either broadband internet access or wi-fi. Add 15% tax to room rates.

#### Hotel Sylhet Super
HOTEL $

(☏632 265; 16 Station Rd; s/d from Tk 350/550, with air-con Tk 800/1200; ❊) The best of a huge number of budget offerings on Station Rd, Sylhet Super has cool-blue tiling and small but clean-enough rooms (although in some rooms you might want to ask for clean bedding). Staff members are welcoming and speak a bit of English.

### GEC CIRCLE AREA

#### Hilltop Inn
GUESTHOUSE $$

(☏655 762, 0181 4885230; hilltopctg@yahoo.com; House 6, Rd 2, Khulshi; r from Tk 2500; ❊@🛜) Housed in a peaceful upmarket residential area called Khulshi, this guesthouse has rooms which are like those you'd expect to find in a decent city-centre apartment: bright, clean, spacious and with TV and wi-fi. Expect 20% discounts and a homey atmosphere.

#### Grand Park Hotel
HOTEL $$$

(☏620 044; www.pavilliongrandpark.com; 787 CDA Ave; s/d from Tk 3162/3795; ❊@🛜) Not as good quality as nearby Peninsula, but much better value as this is still a very smart place to stay.

## SHIP-BREAKING YARDS

Chittagong's controversial industry of ship breaking takes place along the coast northwest of the city. Here, beached along the shore, you can find every kind of ocean-going vessel, from tugboat to super tanker, each one lying stranded as an army of workers dismantles it, section by section, piece by piece. It's controversial because the whole operation is done by hand by workers who, according to both the EU and local watchdog groups, are ill-equipped, under-trained and, in many cases, under age. Accidents, some fatal, are common, and because of the high injury rate the average working life is short, but the work is relatively well paid, so the ship-breaking yards seem to have little difficulty recruiting.

The yards have received bad press in recent years, and are reluctant to let members of the public stroll along the beach, taking photos of kids tearing apart the giant hulls of rusting ships. It is, nevertheless, an incredible sight. Stranded on land as they are, some of the super tankers seem impossibly large.

If you're intent on seeing the ship-breaking yards, prepare to be disappointed because you may well be turned away. Your chances of being allowed to walk around will increase if you haven't got a professional-looking zoom-lens camera slung across your shoulder, and if you visit with a local who has contacts at one of the yards. Ask at your hotel; they may be able to help. Fridays are also easier as management and security staff are likely to be taking the day off.

It's advisable to wear strong, covered shoes. The beach here is, in places, a mushy mess of mud, chemicals and ship debris.

### How To

Expect to pay around Tk 100 to Tk 150 in a CNG to get to the yards. Aim for Bhatiary. Some travellers have reported having more success getting into the yards further north in Sitakunda (CNG one way Tk 250).

The Bengali script for 'ship-breaking yards' is শিপ বেকিং ইয়ার্ড.

For a less confrontational peek, search for Chittagong on Google Maps then zoom in on the coast at Jahanabad. You'll be able to see quite clearly about 20 monstrous ship carcasses, all in various stages of decay.

Rooms are huge and rates include breakfast, wi-fi and laundry. The attached restaurant, the Pavilion, has a good reputation.

**Hotel Abakash**  HOTEL $
(2863 120, 650 OR Nizam Rd; s/d from Tk 500/700;❋) The best budget choice in the GEC area, Abakash has small but clean, well-looked-after rooms with TV and attached bathroom (sit-down toilets). Road noise may be an issue if you're a light sleeper.

**Peninsula Chittagong**  HOTEL $$$
(285 0860/9; www.peninsulactg.com; 486 CDA Ave; r from Tk 14,000;❋@✿❀) This is probably the best hotel in Chittagong, but even after discounts (expect the cheapest rooms to go for around Tk 12,000) it's still hideously expensive. Rooms are very smart, with super-shiny wood flooring and decent wood furniture. There's free wi-fi, coffee and breakfast, and a rooftop pool, plus a choice of restaurants and one of the few spas in the city, Tararom Spa (01758 319773; treatments

from Tk 2000; ⊘10am-10pm). Unless your company is paying, you'll probably want to head down the road to Grand Park instead.

### ✗ Eating & Drinking
#### STATION ROAD AREA

TOP CHOICE **Tai Wah Restaurant**  CHINESE $$$
(1052 Jubilee Rd; mains TK 200-400; ⊘noon-3pm & 6-10pm) With soups, noodles, rice dishes and dumplings, this is probably the most authentic Chinese in Chittagong. The atmosphere is pleasant, with red lanterns creating just the right level of lighting, and walls adorned with giant Chinese knots and decorative fans. The food is spot-on, and they sometimes have beer (ask discreetly).

**Hotel ABP**  BENGALI $
(Jubilee Rd; meals TK 150-200; ⊘6am-midnight) Tuck in to tandoori masala-spiced chicken, grilled by the entrance, and mop up some dhal or curried vegetables with the freshly baked paratha. You'll have to bluff your

way through ordering as there's no English menu, but at least one member of staff speaks a little English.

## GEC CIRCLE AREA

**TOP CHOICE** **Bonanza Food Plus** ASIAN **$$$**
(1692 CDA Ave; mains TK 200-400; ⊘noon-3.30pm & 6-11pm) One of Chittagong's best dining options, this swish, air-conditioned restaurant has an excellent pan-Asian menu, including Chinese, Indian, Thai and Korean. The Indian dishes are particularly good. You can also eat in between the official lunch and dinner times, but from the Chinese menu only.

**Hotel Zamen** BENGALI **$**
(CDA Ave; mains Tk 100-250; ⊘9am-midnight) With branches all over Chittagong division, Zamen is a clean, dependable option for those wishing to sample decent-quality Bengali dishes in a family-friendly environment. It's mostly biryani and curries (chicken, mutton or fish), but there are a few Chinese dishes too. Also has a branch on Jubilee Rd.

**Rio Coffee Corner** CAFE **$$**
(OR Nizam Rd, Well Food Centre, 2nd fl; ⊘10am-11pm; 🛜) Housed in a corner of the 2nd floor of a clean, multi-level fast-food complex, Rio is the only cafe we know of in Chittagong (outside the top-notch hotels) that does proper fresh coffee (from Tk 60). As if that wasn't enticing enough, there's a Baskin Robbins ice-cream counter next to it, as well as free wi-fi.

**Dhaba** INDIAN **$**
(CDA Ave; mains Tk 100-250; ⊘1.30-10.30pm) Not as popular as its Banani branch in Dhaka,

this Dhaba nevertheless still knocks out some tasty curries, kebabs, paratha rolls and *chaat* (spicy snacks). It's basically Indian street food in a clean restaurant environment. Wash it down with a *lassi* (yogurt drink).

**Handi** INDIAN **$$**
(CDA Ave; mains Tk 150-250; ⊘1pm-11pm) Similar menu to next-door Dhaba, although more extensive and slightly pricier. The trendier decor ensures Handi is the more popular of the two. Has decent-value set lunches (1pm to 4pm).

**Niribilee** BENGALI **$**
(650 OR Nizam Rd, 2nd fl; mains from Tk 80; ⊘6am-1am) Cheap, no-nonsense local grub with dhal, omelette and paratha for breakfast before the curries and biryanis are rolled out later in the day. No English menu, but some English spoken.

## ❶ Information

The ATMs at the banks we've marked on our map all accept foreign cards. To change money, you're best trying one of the HSBCs.

**Cyber Cafe** (Suhrawardi Rd; per hr Tk 20; ⊘9am-10pm)

**Cyber World** (650 OR Nizam Rd, 3rd fl; per hr Tk 25; ⊘10am-10pm) Above Niribilee restaurant.

**Divisional Commissioner's Office** (☏634 022, 01734 859390; samiul_masud@yahoo.com; 718 Chatteshwari Rd, 1st fl; ⊘9am-5pm Sun-Thu) Housed in old colonial building on the corner of Badshi Mia Rd and Chatteswari Rd. No English sign.

**Indian High Commission** (☏654 201; www.ahcictg.net; Zakir Hossain Rd; ⊘9am-4pm

---

## CHITTAGONG BY BOAT

Passenger ferries from Dhaka, including the famous Rocket steamer, don't go all the way to the city of Chittagong, but you can still catch ferries to the fishing town of Chandpur, in Chittagong division, and then connect by bus or train.

Boats leave from Sadarghat in Dhaka roughly every hour from 6.30am until midnight, and take around four hours to reach Chandpur (cabin/chair/deck class Tk 350/220/90).

Once you get to Chandpur, you can continue to Chittagong by bus (Tk 200, four hours) or train (1st seat/*shuvon* Tk 160/80, five hours, 5am and 2.50pm).

In the other direction, regular boat services from Chandpur to Dhaka start drying up at around 4.30pm, although there is usually a late-evening boat at around 11.30pm.

Passenger ferries from Barisal to Chandpur arrive in the middle of the night, so you're better off catching a launch (ferry) from Barisal to Moju Chowdhury Hat (deck/single cabin/double cabin Tk 200/400/800, five hours, hourly from 6am), also in Chittagong division. You can buy bus tickets to the city of Chittagong (Tk 200, five hours) on the boat. The bus stand is a 300m walk from the ferry ghat. Buses leave when full.

Note, the Barisal to Moju Chowdhury Hat ferries only run from mid-October to mid-March.

## SELECTED TRAINS FROM CHITTAGONG

| DESTINATION | TRAIN NAME | DEPARTS | ARRIVES | FARE (1ST/SHUVON) | OFF DAY |
|---|---|---|---|---|---|
| Chandpur | Sagharika Ex | 8.30am | 2.10pm | Tk 160/80 | none |
| Chandpur | Meghna Ex | 5pm | 10.05pm | Tk 160/80 | none |
| Dhaka | Subarna Ex | 7am | 12.40pm | Tk 290/125 | Fri |
| Dhaka | Mohanagar Provati | 7.20am | 2.05pm | Tk 290/125 | Sun |
| Dhaka | Mohanagar Godhuli | 3pm | 9.25pm | Tk 290/125 | none |
| Dhaka | Dhaka Mail | 10.30pm | 7.10am | Tk 455/290/125* | none |
| Dhaka | Turna Ex | 11pm | 6.15am | Tk 455/290/125* | none |
| Sylhet | Udayan Ex | 9pm | 6am | Tk 465/320/190* | Sat |
| Sylhet | Paharika | 8am | 5pm | Tk 320/190 | Mon |

*1st berth/1st seat/*shuvon*

Sun-Thu) Can issue Indian visas. See website for application details.

**Main post office** (Suhrawardi Rd; ☺8am-8.30pm Sat-Thu)

## ℹ Getting There & Away

The Dhaka–Chittagong Hwy is the most dangerous stretch of road in Bangladesh and catching a bus between the two cities is a heart-in-mouth experience for much of the way. If you can, take the train or a boat, or fly.

### Air

**GMG Airlines** (✆655 659; www.gmgairlines.com; 1702 CDA Ave, 2nd fl; ☺9am-7pm) Daily flights to Dhaka (from Tk 4000) and Kolkata (from Tk 7700).

**United Airways** (✆251 8177; www.uabdl.com; ground fl, Hotel Agrabad, Zakir Hossain Rd) Also flies daily to Dhaka.

### Boat

The **Bangladesh Inland Waterway Transport Corporation office** (BIWTC; ✆613358; ☺Sun-Thu) is near the end of Sadarghat Rd, about 100m to the west. The administration office is marked in English, but tickets are sold from a nondescript building just before the office.

Ferries from Chittagong only go as far as Hatiya Island (1st/2nd/deck class Tk 988/374/110, seven hours, departs 9am daily except Friday and Sunday), via Sandwip Island (four hours). To get to Barisal or Dhaka by boat, you have to leave from Chandpur.

### Bus

Destinations from Bahaddarhat bus stand include Cox's Bazar (Tk 190, five hours, 6am to 9pm) and Bandarban (Tk 90, three hours, 6am to 6pm).

Oxygen Rd bus stand serves Rangamati (Tk 80 to TK 120, 2½ hours) and Kadamtali bus stand serves Chandpur (Tk 200, four hours).

As well as the public bus services, a number of private coach companies run from Chittagong, with offices just south of GEC Circle. **Green Line** (✆630551) has air-con coaches to Dhaka (Tk 750 to Tk 1050, seven to eight hours, 10 daily 7am to 12.30am), Cox's Bazar (Tk 500, five hours, 9am) and Sylhet (Tk 1000, eight hours, 9pm). Nearby **Soudia** (✆2863399) has a very similar timetable with slightly cheaper prices.

### Train

See the boxed text for major trains from Chittagong. Note that all Dhaka and Sylhet trains go through Comilla (1st/*shuvon* Tk 140/80, three hours) and, for the Indian border, Akhaura (1st/*shuvon* Tk 180/105, four to five hours).

## ℹ Getting Around

**TO/FROM THE AIRPORT** There isn't always a bus to meet incoming flights and the airport is a long way out from town – CNGs cost at least Tk 150. You could try catching a bus to New Market (Tk 10) at the T-junction, 500m from the airport.

**LOCAL TRANSPORT** A rickshaw between Station Rd and GEC Circle is about Tk 40. Further afield you'll have to take a CNG: from Station Rd to Bahaddarhat bus stand and Oxygen Rd bus stand cost Tk 100 and Tk 70 respectively.

## Bandarban

 ✆0361 / POP 30,000

Put simply, there is no better place in which to experience the magic of the Hill Tracts than in the lively small town of Bandarban, which lies on the Sangu River, 92km from

Chittagong. The river is the centre of local life: bamboo rafts up to 500m long, steered by a solitary boatman, drift leisurely downstream, while country boats make slow trips to neighbouring villages. Many of the inhabitants belong to the Buddhist Marma tribe, and there are villages in the hills, which you can easily hike to. The town itself, which has a couple of interesting sights, isn't overly attractive, but the surrounding countryside is some of the finest in Bangladesh and offers one of the few opportunities to really escape the masses.

At the time of writing, all foreigners needed a permit to visit Bandarban. This could be arranged in Chittagong. At the checkpoint before coming into town, officials may request that you call upon the district commissioner in town.

## ◉ Sights

**Dhatu Jadi**  BUDDHIST MONASTERY
(Golden Temple; admission Tk 10) Perched on a hilltop about three kilometres north of town, in a village called Bala Gata, is the large glowing Dhatu Jadi, also known as the Golden Temple *(shorna mondir)* because of its beautiful golden stupa. The monastery complex, Arakanese in style, was only built in 2000, but visiting it is a Burmese blast

## Bandarban

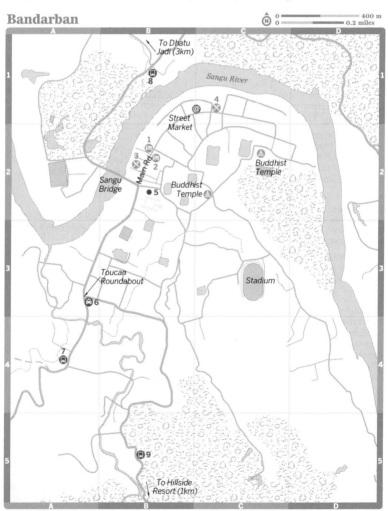

through and through, and the stupa is one of the most impressive in the country. The complex also houses the second-largest Buddha in Bangladesh. It's a one-hour uphill walk from Sangu Bridge, or Tk 150 in a CNG.

## 🏃 Activities

There are a number of short, half-day and full-day walks and hikes you can take in and around Bandarban. The forested scenery is beautiful and is dotted with small Adivasi villages. Hillside Resort, the excellent guesthouse run by the Guide Tours (www.guidetours.com), is the best place to enquire about possible places to visit. They also have guides (per hour/day Tk 100/1000). For more serious, multiday hikes around the Bandarban region, see the boxed text p122. Again, Hillside Resort may be able to help with some of these. Otherwise, try to get in touch with the amateur hikers who run Bangla Trek (www.banglatrek.org).

### Shailapropat Falls                      WALKING
This easy walk follows the quiet road that leads uphill away from Hillside Resort. It takes about an hour to reach Shailapropat Falls, a small waterfall, which trickles from the roadside down into a ravine below. It's popular with local tourists (although they tend to drive here rather than walk) so there are tea and snack stalls set up. Close to the falls is the Bawm village of Faruk Para, where you can buy handwoven baskets, fish traps and rugs.

### Sangu River Walk                        HIKING
An easy-to-follow but pretty steep pathway snakes its way down from the dormitory building at Hillside Resort all the way to the

### Bandarban

#### 🛏 Sleeping
1 Hotel Paharika .......................................B2
2 Hotel Purbani .......................................B2

#### 🍴 Eating
3 Hotel Zamen & Biryani House .............B2
4 Tohzah Restaurant...............................C1

#### ℹ Information
5 District Commissioner's Office ..........B2

#### ℹ Transport
6 Jeep Stand............................................A3
7 Main Bus Stand....................................A4
8 Rangamati Bus Stand ..........................B1
9 Ruma Bus Stand ..................................B5

Sangu River below. It takes about half an hour to climb down to the river. From there, you can either walk (left), or try to catch a wooden rowboat on towards Bandarban town centre. You may catch sight of one of the incredible bamboo rafts, which float their way down river to Bandarban. Some are literally hundreds of metres long!

### Haatibandha & Sangiya Villages    HIKING
These two villages are a short walk through the forest from Hillside Resort. Walk uphill along the road leading away from the guesthouse then take the first track on your right. Follow a narrow brick path down the hill. The first turn on your left winds its way down to Sangiya Village, crossing a small stream a few times. Around a dozen families live here – some Tripuri, some Marma – in bamboo huts on stilts. No one here speaks English. Back up on the brick path, continue straight past the turn to Sangiya and take the first right, again down a part-brick pathway. You'll notice a green-painted church on your right as you enter the pretty village of Haatibandha, home to 28 Marma families. The people here are more Burmese-looking than Bangladeshi, and some of the elder women are decked out in hundreds of bead necklaces, bangles that coil serpent-like around their arms, and strange earrings that look more like bolts and which stretch out the wearer's ear lobes. Look out for the small yellow-and-green-painted hut – the village school, which was built with UNICEF funding. Remember to ask before you take photos. Two villagers here speak some English. You'll need around two or three hours to see both villages from Hillside Resort.

If you go straight rather than turning left to Sangiya Village, or right to Haatibandha, the track from the main road takes you all the way up to Tiger Hill, a popular viewpoint in this area.

### Boga Lake                               HIKING
Hillside Resort organises a trip to the beautiful, tree-lined Boga Lake, which is very popular, although depending on the current permit situation you can usually reach the lake on your own via Ruma Bazar. It takes around four hours to hike to the lake from Ruma. There is basic accommodation by the lake.

### Sangu River                          BOAT TOUR
A boat trip along the Sangu River, upstream from Bandarban, is about as exquisitely picturesque and fabulously peaceful as you can possibly get in Bangladesh. Guides at

## PERMITS FOR CHITTAGONG HILL TRACTS

The permit situation for the hill tracts region is in a constant state of flux. In previous years, foreigners have needed permits, guides and even armed escorts to visit some areas, but at the time of research just a permit was needed and, unless you were going way off the beaten track, you could easily arrange it yourself.

The divisional commissioner's private secretary, Samiul Masud, is the man to find for getting your permit. He is very friendly and helpful, and was able to sort out our documents within 15 minutes of us turning up at the **Divisional Commissioner's Office** (718 Chatteshwari Rd, 1st fl; ☏634 022, 01734 859390; samiul_masud@yahoo.com; ⊗9am-5pm Sun-Thu) in Chittagong. Just bring your passport and have an itinerary in mind, which you will have to outline on the form you are given.

You will then be given copies of your permit, which you should keep handy to dish out to any checkpoint guards who start asking too many questions. Keep Mr Masud's phone number handy too.

Note that if you are visiting the hill tracts on a guided trip, your tour operator should be able to arrange all necessary permits.

Because of the frequent changes in permit regulations, we advise you get on the Bangladesh branch of Lonely Planet's Thorn Tree forum before you leave for Chittagong division, just to double-check the latest.

Hillside Resort can take you on a trip, but it's possible (though difficult) to do it on your own. First take a bus towards **Ruma Bazar** (Tk 80, three hours, once every two hours from 8am) from the Ruma Bus Stand. Depending on the state of the road, it may only go as far as **Khokhongjiri** (two hours). If so, from here, clamber down to the river, past a cluster of tea stalls and small restaurants. At the riverbank, you can either catch a wooden ferry (known as a 'service boat') upstream to Ruma Bazar (per person Tk 30, two hours), or downstream back to Bandarban (per person Tk 120, 3½ hours). The lazy ride back to Bandarban is magical, as you pass villages only accessible by boat and enjoy some mesmerising scenery; sometimes rugged, sometimes rural, but always stunning. There may be no service boats, in which case you'll have to try to pay for your own 'reserved boat'. Expect to pay at least Tk 3000. It's worth every penny. A boat all the way from Ruma Bazar will obviously cost more, although you may only be able to get one when the water is at its highest levels, between May and November. That stretch of the river is equally stunning.

## 🛏 Sleeping

TOP
CHOICE **Hillside Resort**   GUESTHOUSE $$
(Milonchhori; ☏02-988 6983, 01730 045083; Chimbuk Rd; dm Tk 400, s Tk 1150-2300, d Tk 1500-3000, tr Tk 1750-3500;❄) Thrown haphazardly across a steep jungle-smothered hillside,

this wonderful guesthouse, run by the Guide Tours and managed by the lovely Mr Hasan Mahmood Khokon, is easily the best place to stay in Bandarban. Cottages – some with air-con – are fun and comfortable, and the dorm allows for budget travellers to enjoy its choice location, perched up in the forested hills, 4km from the town centre. Showers are cold water only, although the cottages have hot-water taps. The food is excellent (mains Tk 150 to Tk 300), as are the views, and there are guides available, plus great travel advice about the area should you want it. It costs Tk 150 to get here from town in a CNG. The walk is a 45-minute uphill slog, but you pass a number of interesting villages (with excited-to-see-you children) en route. Call ahead, because this place is often full. And note there is a much less environmentally friendly place slightly downhill from Hillside Resort. It's called Sakura Hill Resort, and comes with caged monkeys in the garden, and we don't cover it.

**Hotel Purbani**   HOTEL $
(☏63424; Main Rd; s/d/tr Tk 300/600/850;❄) Very clean tiled rooms with TV and attached bathroom (squat loo) run by friendly staff members who, unlike staff at some other hotels in town, are happy to welcome foreign guests. If it's full, try nearby **Hotel Paharika** (☏62155; Main Rd; s/d/tr Tk 600/800/1200;❄), which after discounts has similarly priced rooms, although less English is spoken.

## ✕ Eating

Even if you don't stay at Hillside Resort, it's worth going there for a meal. The food is excellent – with largely Western-friendly versions of Bengali cuisine on offer – but it's pricier than in town.

**Tohzah Restaurant**                   MARMA $
(Main Rd; mains Tk 40-60; ⊘8am-10pm) This modest restaurant, on the stretch of Main Rd where you'll find Bandarban's street market, is the best place in town to sample Marma cuisine. Expect lots of ginger and chillies! The menu, written in Bengali on a whiteboard at the back, is extremely limited. There were just three main dishes when we ate here; fish, wild pig and lizard. Vegetable side dishes and rice are also available. The manager, who like all the staff is very welcoming, speaks some English so can help translate. He isn't always around, though, so you may have to bluff your way through ordering.

**Hotel Zamen & Biryani House** BANGLADESHI $
(off Main Rd; mains Tk 50-100; ⊘5am-11pm) This rather popular chain, found all over Chittagong, knocks up reliable Bengali dishes including fish, chicken, mutton and beef curries, plus biryanis, of course. Decent spot for dhal-and-paratha breakfasts. No English menu, but some staff members speak a little English.

## ➊ Information

At the time of research, there were no ATMs and nowhere to change money in Bandarban.
**Ching Computer Centre** (Main Rd; internet per hr Tk 30; ⊘3-8pm)

## ➊ Getting There & Away

There's a jeep stand just down from the main bus stand where you can hire jeeps, known here as *chander gari*, to places such as Ruma Bazar (return/overnight Tk 3000/4500, two hours each way).

**Bus**
From Ruma bus stand buses go to Ruma Bazar (Tk 80, three hours, every two hours from 8am). Rangamati (Tk 110, four hours, 8am and 2pm) buses leave from the Rangamati bus stand. From the main bus stand, destinations include the following:
**Chittagong** Tk 90, three hours, 5.45am to 6pm
**Cox's Bazar** Tk 120, three hours, 7.30am to 5pm

**Dhaka** Tk 480, nine hours, 10am, 9.30pm and 10pm

# Rangamati

♫ 0351 / POP 65,000

The main reason for coming to Rangamati is to enjoy the scenic splendour of Kaptai Lake, the country's largest artificial lake, which was created, not without controversy, in 1960. The lake, dotted with islands, is unquestionably beautiful, and a boat trip across it is a fantastic way to spend a day out here, but it's worth knowing that approximately 100,000 Adivasis – mostly Chakma – were displaced when it was created, and around 40% of the land they previously cultivated was submerged forever.

## ◉ Sights & Activities

**Kaptai Lake**                             LAKE
Because of permit restrictions, there are only a few places around the lake to which boatmen are willing to take foreigners. At the time of research, there were six main places to visit, and you could tailor your trip to see any number of them.

The most popular trip was Shuvalong Falls (90 minutes one way). This largely disappointing waterfall is little more than a trickle for most of the year, but the boat trip out to it is fabulous; first crossing the vast expanse of the main lake, then entering an area of islands covered with banana plants, and finally a more dramatic scene as you pass through a steep-sided gorge.

About half way to Shuvalong, you'll pass the restaurant Peda Ting Ting (p120), on a small island, which makes an unusual place for lunch.

The Hanging Bridge, not far from the Parjatan Holiday Complex, is another popular boat-trip destination.

The small Chakma islands at the other end of Rangamati (p119) are another popular boat stop, although, like the Hanging Bridge, they can also be reached by land.

Another popular trip with local tourists is the two-hour ride to Kaptai Town, but the town itself is a bit of a dump.

There are small boat ghats all around the lake, but the main two are Reserve-Bazar Ghat and Tobolchuri Ghat. Passenger ferries shuttle locals from Reserve-Bazar to places such as Kaptai Town. They're sometimes reluctant to take foreigners, but you can get to Shuvalong Falls for Tk 40 if they

CHITTAGONG DIVISION RANGAMATI

# Rangamati

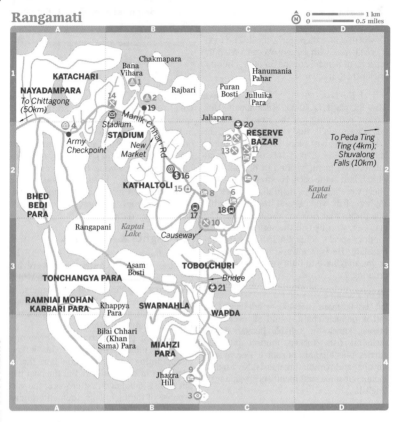

# Ragamati

## ⊙ Sights
1 Bana Vihara .................................. B1
2 Chakma King's Modern Palace ............. B1
3 Hanging Bridge ........................ B4
4 Tribal Cultural Institute Museum.......... A2

## ⊟ Sleeping
5 Hotel Golden Hill ..................... C2
6 Hotel Green Castle ................. C2
7 Hotel Lake View....................... C2
8 Hotel Sufia ............................... C2
9 Parjatan Holiday Complex .................... B4

## ⊗ Eating
10 Girishova Restaurant ............................ C3
11 Hotel Green Restaurant ........................ C2

12 Hotel Shundarban & Biryani
    House .....................................C2
13 Taiping Restaurant................................C2
14 Thai Mart ............................................ B1

## 🔒 Shopping
15 Souvenir Shops .......................................B2

## ℹ Information
16 Trust Bank ATM.....................................B2

## ℹ Transport
17 Bandarban Buses ...................................B2
18 Chittagong Buses....................................C2
19 Rajbari Ghat ........................................ B1
20 Reserve Bazar Ghat ..............................C2
21 Tobolchuri Ghat......................................C3

let you on. Otherwise, you'll have to hire your own boat. Prices depend largely on your bargaining skills. At the time of research, Tk 400 per boat per hour was the going rate.

### Chakma Islands                                     ISLANDS

This whole area is a Chakma stronghold, but two islands in particular are interesting to visit. **Rajbari** (which means palace) is where the Chakma king has his rather unimpressive, recently rebuilt palace. You can't enter the palace, but you can peek inside the nearby Buddhist temple. There are stalls set up here selling brightly coloured handmade Chakma fabrics, and if you follow the road down behind the stalls you eventually reach some small Chakma settlements. A **rowboat** (Tk 2) brings people across to Rajbari from Rajbari Ghat. You can also be rowed across to Bana Vihara, although a bridge also connects that island to the mainland.

**Bana Vihara**, which can be reached, either via Rajbari Ghat, or via a bridge slightly further west, houses a large Buddhist monastery, constructed by Chakma Buddhist monks in 1972. You can wander the grounds, peek inside the temples (ask first) and see monks making wooden boats by the water's edge on the eastern side of the island.

The lane leading from the main road to Rajbari Ghat is signposted UNDP. The United Nations Development Program has an office here.

### Tribal Cultural Institute Museum     MUSEUM

(Manik Charri Rd; admission Tk 20; ◷9.30am-4.30pm, closed Sat) Has well-thought-out displays on the Adivasis of the Hill Tracts, including costumes, bamboo flutes, coins, silver-and-ivory necklaces and animal traps. There is also a map showing where the different people of the region live. Look out for the Marma and Chakma 'books' carved onto palm leaves, which date from the 1860s.

## 🛏 Sleeping

### Hotel Sufia                                  HOTEL $$

(📞62145; Kathaltoli; s/d from Tk 450/900;🕸) All in, this is probably the best-value place in Rangamati, and an extension was being built when we were here, which when finished will add some much-needed lake views. Rooms are clean and well looked after, with sit-down toilets but cold-water

showers, and the location in the busiest part of town (still very quiet, though) is handy for food, internet access and finding CNGs. Also has a good restaurant.

### Parjatan Holiday Complex           HOTEL $$

(📞63126; Deer Park; d without/with air-con Tk 1400/2200, cottages Tk 1700-5200; 🕸) It may be a bit out of the way, and it's the priciest place in town, but this is the best accommodation in Rangamati. The location, overlooking a quiet hyacinth-clogged backwater of the lake, is a lovely spot and friendly management ensure service is good. Rooms are quaint and clean and some come with balconies overlooking the lake. Has hot water, a decent restaurant, a bar (which isn't always stocked) and private boat rental (per hour Tk 600).

### Hotel Lake View                         HOTEL $

(📞62063; Reserve Bazar; s/d/tr Tk 200/400/500) Rooms are extremely basic, and a bit grubby, but if you get one with a window overlooking the lake you probably won't care. The shared balconies on some floors have magnificent lake views. It's also known as Hotel Al-Amin.

### Hotel Golden Hill                        HOTEL $

(📞01820 304714; Reserve Bazar; s/d from Tk 200/400) A mixed bag of rooms – some tiny, some more spacious, while some open out onto shared balconies with views that match those at Hotel Lake View. All rooms have attached bathroom with cold-water shower and squat toilet. As at Hotel Lake View, you'll probably want to bring your own sleeping sheet.

### Hotel Green Castle                     HOTEL $$

(📞61200; Reserve Bazar s/d from Tk 400/800, r with air-con from Tk 1200;🕸) The non-air-con singles are good value – small, but neat and tidy. Twins and doubles are large but not cheap. No lake views from rooms, but OK ones from communal balconies out back.

##  Eating

As well as the places reviewed here, the restaurants at **Hotel Sufia** (mains Tk 150-250; ◷8am-10pm) and the **Parjatan Holiday Complex** (mains Tk 100-250; ◷7am-10pm) are also well regarded.

### Thai Mart                                    ADIVASI $$

(Stadium; mains from Tk 150; ◷8am-11pm) Run by a young and friendly group of Chakma

# CHITTAGONG HILL TRACTS

Decidedly untypical of Bangladesh, both in topography and culture, this Adivasi (tribal) stronghold is a stunning region of hills, ravines and cliffs covered with dense jungles of bamboo, creepers and shrubs, and dotted with tall, slender waterfalls.

The whole region is full of the flavours of neighbouring Myanmar (Burma); it's utterly fascinating and exceedingly beautiful. It also offers a chance to stretch the legs with some of the country's best hiking on offer.

There are three districts: Khagrachari, Rangamati and Bandarban. Most tourists visit only the latter two, which are the more scenic, and are the two we cover here.

## Hill Tribes

A dozen or so different Adivasi groups live in the region, and make up about half the total population. Major groups include the Chakma, the Marma and the Tripuri.

About half of Bangladesh's Adivasi population is Chakma (roughly 240,000 people), while roughly one-third is Marma. Among the many much smaller groups, the Mru (called Murung by Bangladeshis) stand out as the most ancient inhabitants of the area.

The culture and lifestyle of the Adivasis are very different from that of the Bangladeshi farmers of the plains. Some tribes are matriarchal, for example, and most make their homes from bamboo, covered by thatched roofs of dried leaves. Housing aside, Adivasi groups are quite different from each other in many respects, each having their own distinctive rites, rituals, dialect and dress. Chakma women, for example, wear indigo-and-red-striped sarongs.

Adivasi women are particularly skilled in making handicrafts, while some of the men still take pride in hunting with bows and arrows.

Adivasi people you're mostly likely to meet in this region are the Chakma, in Rangamati, and the Marma, Tripuri and Bawm in and around Bandarban. Most of the Bawm people have converted to Christianity and you'll find a handful who speak decent English in Bandarban. The last time we visited, all of the guides at Hillside Resort in Bandarban were Bawm.

## A Troubled History

Under the British, the Hill Tracts gained special status and only Adivasis could own land here, but the Pakistani government abolished the special status of the Hill Tracts as a 'tribal area' in 1964. The construction of Kaptai Lake (in Rangamati) for hydroelectricity in 1960 was an earlier blow, submerging 40% of the land used by the Adivasis for cultivation, and displacing 100,000 people. The land provided for resettlement was not sufficient and many Adivasis became refugees in neighbouring northeastern India.

During the 1971 Liberation War, the then Chakma king sided with the Pakistanis, so when independence came the Adivasis' plea for special status fell on deaf ears. The Chakma king left for Pakistan and later became that country's ambassador to Argentina.

Meanwhile, more and more Bengalis were migrating into the area, taking the land. In 1973 the Adivasis initiated an insurgency. To counter it, the government, in 1979, started issuing permits to landless Bengalis to settle here, with titles to Adivasi land. This practice continued for six years and resulted in a mass migration of approximately 400,000 people into the area – almost as many as all the Adivasi groups combined. Countless human-rights abuses occurred as the army tried to put down the revolt.

staff and cooks, this relaxed restaurant with bamboo roofing does a mix of Chakma and Bengali dishes. English menu. English spoken.

**Peda Ting Ting**　　　　ADIVASI $$
(Kaptai Lake; mains from Tk 180; ⊘9am-5pm)
A popular stop on boat trips to Shuvalong Falls, this shanty-looking restaurant, on a small low-lying island, does good-quality

From 1973 until 1997 the Hill Tracts area was the scene of a guerrilla war between the Bangladeshi army and the Shanti Bahini rebels. The troubles stemmed from the cultural clash between the Adivasi groups and the plains people.

Sheikh Hasina's government cemented an internationally acclaimed peace accord in December 1997 with Adivasi leader Jyotirindriyo Bodhipriya (Shantu) Larma. Rebel fighters were given land, Tk 50,000 and a range of other benefits in return for handing in their weapons. The peace deal handed much of the administration of Khagrachhari, Rangamati and Bandarban districts to a regional council. The struggle to have the accord fully honoured continues today.

## Hiking

There are some fantastic hikes to take in this part of Bangladesh. None is technically challenging, but some are multiday trips, which require hikers to be fit and adventurous. It's not unusual, for example, to find yourself having to wade through rivers en route to your ultimate destination, and hikers to more remote areas will have to be prepared to rough it. Accommodation will either be in tents (if you bring your own) or in small villages with almost no facilities.

Also bear in mind that many of the more remote areas are often off-limits to foreigners. If you apply for permits to climb some of the peaks in these areas, you may be denied them. That doesn't stop some foreigners having a go, though.

Blazing a trail through previously unhiked areas of the Hill Tracts is the community-run hiking group, Bangla Trek (www.banglatrek.org). They're a very welcoming group of amateur hikers, most of whom are based in Dhaka, and many of them speak good English. If you're looking for ideas for places to hike to, or just want to hook up with like-minded walking enthusiasts, try contacting them through their website.

For more on Bangladesh hikes, see the boxed text on p122.

## Guides & Permits

At the time of research you could arrange your own Hill Tracts permit (see boxed text p116) then explore much of the region on your own, but in previous years it's been necessary for foreigners to be accompanied by a guide and sometimes even an armed escort. Check the latest before you leave.

Regardless, some travellers still prefer to use a guide. The following companies operate reliable tours to the region.

» Bangladesh Ecotours (Map p108; ☏031-257 3257, 01819 318 345; www.bangladesheco tours.com; Riad Center, 4th fl, 4508A Arakan Rd, Chittagong) Specialises in the Hill Tracts, and is based in Chittagong. Rates range from US$75 to US$120 per person per day.

» Bengal Tours (Map p46; ☏02-883 4716; www.bengaltours.com; House 45, Rd 27, Block A, Banani, Dhaka) Well established Bangladesh-wide tour company with offices in Dhaka and Khulna.

» The Guide Tours (Map p46; ☏02-988 6983; www.guidetours.com; 6th fl, Rob Supermarket, Gulshan Circle II, Gulshan, Dhaka) The country's most respected tour operator. In addition to tours, it also runs the excellent Hillside Resort (p116) in Bandarban. Guides and tours of the Bandarban area can be arranged at Hillside Resort. For anything more involved, including arranging permits, contact the Dhaka office. A two-day, three-night trip to Bandarban, including transport to and from Dhaka, costs Tk 8000 to Tk 16,000 per person, depending on how many people are in your group.

indigenous food in an unmatched location. Has an English menu. Expect a round trip from Reserve Bazar, including eating time, to take at least two hours.

**Girishova Restaurant** BANGLADESHI $$
(Kathaltoli; mains Tk 100-250; ⊗9am-10pm) This unusual restaurant on a floating platform moored to the shoreline has a pretty much unbeatable location, with fabulous lake

views. It's a perfect spot for a late breakfast, a tea break or a sunset snack, but mosquitoes are a bit of an issue in the evening so you might want to think twice about coming here for dinner.

**Hotel Shundarban & Biryani House**　BANGLADESHI $
(Reserve Bazar; mains Tk 50-150; ⏱5am-11pm) Pocket-sized locals' favourite with no English menu but a manager who can talk you through which curries and biryanis are on of-

fer that day. Great fun, good value, and also a good bet for dhal-and-roti breakfasts. Nearby **Hotel Green Restaurant** (no English sign) and the slightly less popular **Taiping Restaurant** have very similar menus, atmospheres and opening hours.

 **Shopping**

Rangamati is the best place in the Hill Tracts in which to buy souvenirs, particularly hand-woven textiles and clothing.

## BANGLADESH'S BEST HIKES

Fazlay Rabby is one of the co-founders of the amateur hiking group **Bangla Trek** (www.banglatrek.org). These are some of his favourite hikes:

### Easy

#### LOWACHERRA NATIONAL PARK

Beautiful monkey-filled forest in Sylhet division.

**Duration** Half-day trip.

**How To** See p141.

#### HUM HUM FALLS

Remote waterfall deep inside Rajkandi Forest Reserve, also in Sylhet.

**Duration** Day trip.

**How To** See boxed text p144.

### Moderate

#### MT KEOKRADONG

This has traditionally been referred to as the tallest peak in Bangladesh, although at 986m above sea level, it is in fact lower than Mowdok Taung. Keokradong is one of the most-climbed peaks in the country, and the trail is wonderfully scenic. You need to climb various hillocks and cross a number of streams en route. You will also pass Chingri Jhiri waterfall.

**Duration** Three days, two nights from Bandarban (p113).

**How To** On day one, head from Bandarban to Ruma Bazar by local bus or jeep (three to four hours). Trek from Ruma Bazar to Boga Lake (four to six hours), and overnight in an Adivasi guesthouse at Boga Lake. On day two, hike to Keokradong via Chingri Jhiri waterfall, and return to Boga Lake for the second night. On day three, hike back to Ruma Bazar then bus back to Bandarban. Note that in winter some jeeps will take you all the way from Bandarban to Boga Lake.

#### NAFAKHUM FALLS

Located at a picturesque river spot in Thanchi, in Bandarban District, this is one of the most beautiful waterfalls in the country.

**Duration** Three days, two nights from Bandarban (p113).

**How to** Day one takes you from Bandarban to Thanchi Bazar by local bus or jeep (four to five hours) then to Ramakri Bazar by private wooden boat. Overnight at Ramakri guesthouse. On day two, hike to Nafakhum Falls and back to Ramakri Bazar. Stay in the same guesthouse. On day three, return to Thanchi Bazar then Bandarban.

### Hard

#### THANCHI TO RUMA CIRCUIT

This circular trail will allow you to summit two of the Hill Tracts' most popular peaks (Tazing-dong and Keokradong).

There's a cluster of shops close to Hotel Sufia, towards the Trust Bank ATM. You can also buy textiles from stalls on the Chakma island of Rajbari.

 **Information**

A couple of ATMs accept foreign cards – one is next to Hotel Green Castle, the other a short walk from Hotel Sufia – but there's nowhere to change money.

**ehut** (Kathaltoli; internet per hr Tk 25; ⊗10am-9pm)

 **Getting There & Away**

Buses leave regularly for Chittagong (Tk 80 to Tk 120, 2½ hours, 7am to 4pm) from outside Hotel Green Castle. Some buses from Chittagong will drive all the way to Reserve Bazar Ghat. You can also catch some buses from here.

Two buses a day leave for Bandarban (Tk 110, four hours, 7.30am and 2pm) from the

**Duration** Five days, four nights from Bandarban (p113).

**How To** On day one, go from Bandarban to Thanchi Bazar by bus jeep (four to five hours) then trek up to Boarding Headman Para village (four to five hours) to stay the night. On day two, hike to Prata Para village, summiting Tazingdong en route. Day three is a hike to Thaikhong Para village, including a 20-minute detour to Baklai Falls. Overnight in Thaikhong Para. On day four, hike to Boga Lake Para, summiting Keokradong en route. On day five, hike to Ruma Bazar from where you can catch a bus or jeep back to Bandarban.

**MOWDOK TAUNG**

Situated in Mowdok Mual range, and now largely recognised as the highest peak in Bangladesh, having been measured at 1064m, this peak is also known as Shaka Haphong/Tlangmoy. The last leg of the trail is inside dense forest and bamboo bush, while the peak is on the Bangladesh–Myanmar border.

**Duration** Seven days, six nights from Bandarban (p113).

**How To** Day one starts from Bandarban to Thanchi Bazar by bus or jeep (four to five hours), then hike to Boarding Headman Para (four to five hours) where you overnight. Day two, hike to Siplampi Para village (five to six hours) and overnight. You can detour (about one hour) to summit Mount Tazingdong (829m) en route. Day three, hike to Nefew Para village (seven to eight hours), including wading through a stream called Ramakri Khal. On day four, hike to Mowdok Taung peak then back to Nefew Para, and on day five hike to Serkor Para village for an overnight stay (this is a very long day, so start early). Day six: hike back to Thanchi Bazar for an overnight stay, and on day seven take a bus or jeep back to Bandarban.

**Need to Know**

» **Permits** At the time of research, foreigners needed permits to visit anywhere in Bandarban District. Permits were tricky to get for Mount Tazingdong and Mowdok Taung. Your chances will improve if you get an established tour operator to apply for you (see boxed text p120), but you will then have an obligation to use their guides (you may want to, of course).

» **Police** All visitors should report to the local police upon arrival in Bandarban, Ruma and Thanchi.

» **Guides** Unless you've brought your own guide from Bandarban, Chittagong or Dhaka, you will need to hire a local guide (per day Tk 500) in Thanchi Bazar or Ruma Bazar before you continue towards the peaks mentioned above. Don't worry about finding them. They'll find you.

» **Malaria** Malaria is a genuine threat in the Chittagong Hill Tracts. If you haven't brought your own malaria drugs, you can buy Doxycycline at Lazz Pharma (p52), a 24-hour pharmacy in Dhaka.

bus stand between Hotel Sufia and Girishova Restaurant.

# Cox's Bazar

🎵 0341 / POP 50,000

Bangladesh's pride and joy, Cox's Bazar is lauded throughout the land as if it's a contender for one of the natural wonders of the world. It is the longest continual natural beach on the planet (125km), but a world wonder it isn't. In fact, it's not even the nicest beach in Bangladesh (the beaches on nearby St Martin's Island and at Kuakata in Barisal division are far more scenic). However, Cox's Bazar is the most developed of any holiday destination in Bangladesh and as such you'll find tourist facilities that are better than anywhere outside Dhaka. Don't come here expecting to find a piece of southern Thailand, but if your travels are getting the better of you and you just fancy some home comforts and a bit of fresh air, consider swinging by for a couple of days.

## ◉ Sights & Activities

### Beach                                           BEACH
The main reason to come to Cox's Bazar is for the beach. It's a very long, very exposed stretch of sand, rather than a picturesque tropical-island type of affair. Don't expect to be able to shade under a palm tree as the waves lap over your ankles. It is fun for a quick paddle, though, and there are sun loungers and umbrellas you can rent (from Tk 10). The main attraction, though, is being able to take lazy sunset walks along the sand. There is also a handful of decent beach cafes.

If you want more secluded spots for either sunbathing or swimming, try heading about 10km south to Himachari Beach (Tk 200 in a CNG from Kolatoli Circle) or, better still, a further 15km to Inani Beach (Tk 300).

### Aggameda Khyang          BUDDHIST MONASTERY
Founded in 1812, the current structure of this monastery – Burmese in style – was built in 1898. The main sanctuary is built around massive timber columns. The teak flooring adds an air of timelessness to the place. Behind the monastery, and hidden among the trees is Maha Thin Daw Gree, a shrine housing a number of Buddhist effigies, including one (called Cathat Ashun) which is dedicated to Captain Hiram Cox, the British East India Company representative who endeared himself to the indigenous Arakanese and after whom Cox's Bazar is now named.

## 🛏 Sleeping

It may not be pretty, but the rapid (over)development in the Kolatoli area means you can find better hotel and tourist facilities in Cox's Bazar than in any other place in Bangladesh outside Dhaka. Expect spotless rooms and bathrooms (with hot-water showers), free wi-fi in some places, good hotel restaurants, decent English-language skills, and swimming pools in the more expensive hotels. A Radisson is due to open in 2014, further expanding the top end of the market. Budget hotels are tough to find, although there are a few in Laldighi, but if you're looking for a clean, comfortable, midrange hotel, you'll be spoilt for choice. There are literally dozens.

### Hotel Silver Shine                      HOTEL $$
(🎵 64610; www.hotelsilvershine.com; 26 Motel Rd; r from Tk 1750; ❄@🛜🏊) Out of the way, but better value because of it, Silver Shine has very clean, spacious rooms, a good restaurant and a rooftop pool (guests/nonguests Tk 100/150). Good discounts mean you can sometimes nab rooms for as little as Tk 1000.

### Nitol Bay Resort                         HOTEL $$
(🎵 64278; Kolatoli Rd; r from Tk 2000; ❄🏊) One of Cox's Bazar's original hotels, Nitol opened in 1997 and is still a friendly option. Rooms are looking a little tired these days, but it's clean enough and has one of the few pools in town which is free for guests to use. Good food too.

### Kingfisher Cox's Bay Resort      BEACH HUT $$
(🎵 01714 025497; beach; r Tk 1000-1500) The only accommodation in Cox's Bazar that is actu-

---

## BIKINI ALERT!

While on the face of it Cox's Bazar looks like other beach resorts across the world, this is still Bangladesh. Although Bangladeshi men may strip down to their shorts to go for a quick dip in the shallows – and foreign men won't cause offence by doing the same – women here normally paddle in the sea wearing their full *salwar kameez* (long, dress-like tunic worn over baggy trousers). Foreign women who don't want to attract unwanted attention or risk offending the local population should try to wear something similarly modest. And men should probably put their T-shirts back on as soon as they leave the water.

## MAHESKHALI ISLAND

With its small-village atmosphere and collection of serene Hindu and Buddhist temples, the island of Maheskhali (*Mosh-khal-ee*) makes a wonderfully peaceful escape from the brash beach resort of Cox's Bazar. It's also a lot of fun to get to.

First walk along the rickety jetty (Tk 2) to reach Kastura Ghat from where speedboats (Tk 70, 15 minutes) or large traditional wooden ferries (Tk 25, 45 minutes) wait to take passengers to Maheskhali. As you leave the ghat, you'll have to dodge an array of pirate-ship-lookalike wooden fishing boats. Cameras at the ready! Also notice on your left the huge fish market that services all those hotels in Cox's Bazar, and the unusual ice-making houses shooting oversized blocks of ice down runners and into waiting boats.

When you get to Maheskhali, you'll almost certainly be collared by English-speaking touts. Unless you want a guided tour of the island, ignore them, and walk the 500m or so to Goroghata, the island's main town, from where you can pick up an ordinary tout-less rickshaw.

Most people head to Adinath Temple (rickshaw Tk 20), a Buddhist and Hindu temple combined, situated halfway up a holy hill. Round the back of the temple you'll find two tree-shaded holy ponds with great views of mangrove swamps stretching out to sea. There are more great views at the top of the hill as well as a golden stupa and some dusty pathways, which you can follow as far as your legs will carry you.

On your way to Adinath Temple, look out for the boat-builders working largely by hand beside the river. You can also take a rickshaw to Maheskhali Beach (Tk 20), a completely deserted beach on the south of the island.

Goroghata has plenty of cheap roadside restaurants selling the usual Bengali fare, and a couple of very basic accommodation options. Hotel Al-Hossain (☎01826 574370; r Tk 300) has spartan rooms with small attached tap-and-bucket bathrooms, and is on your right as you leave the town. No English.

The last boats back to Cox's Bazar leave at around 6pm.

ally on the beach, this ramshackle wooden building on stilts, next to Beach Cafe, has four large but simple fan-cooled rooms. The two at the back cost Tk 1000. The two at the front cost Tk 1500, but share a verandah with a fabulous sea view. Attached bathrooms are a bit of a squeeze and only have cold showers.

**Ocean Paradise**    HOTEL $$$
(☎52370; www.oceanparadisehotel.com; Kolatoli Rd; r from Tk 6000; ❋@☎⚟) The Radisson might have something to say about it when it opens in 2014, but for now this is the best hotel in town. Service and facilities are both excellent (although of a slightly lower standard than you'd expect from a top-end hotel in a big city). Rooms are immaculate and there's a good choice of restaurants. The pool is free for guests, and a spa was due to open when we were here. Expect 20% discounts.

**Blue Ocean**    HOTEL $$
(☎63207; off Kolatoli Rd; r from Tk 1000; ❋) Set back from the main drag, and a fair walk from the beach, but this is probably the cheapest of the proper hotels in Kolatoli. Rooms are clean. It's often full.

**Hotel Panowa**    HOTEL $
(☎63282; Laldighi Par; s/d from Tk 100/350) Down a lane beside Laldighi Lake, Panowa is a solid budget choice. It's as basic as the prices suggest, and the cheapest rooms have common bathrooms only, but it's well run and often full.

## ✖ Eating & Drinking

Most hotels have their own restaurants, and the nicer ones have open-air barbecue evenings. There's a cluster of cheap roadside restaurants by Kolatoli Circle.

**TOP CHOICE / Mermaid Café**    INTERNATIONAL $$$
(beach; mains Tk 350-750; ⊙noon-midnight) This sprawling, shaded, Goa-style beach shack serves such tasty food in such cool surroundings that you probably won't eat anywhere else once you've tried it. The fish dishes are sumptuous, but everything is top-notch, including the delicious desserts and fresh juices. The only downside: it's just a bit too far back for sea views.

# Cox's Bazar

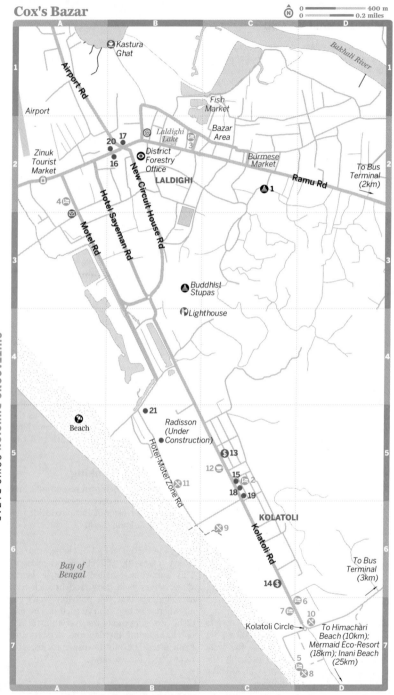

Airport Rd

Kastura Ghat

Airport

Fish Market

Bazar Area

Laldighi Lake

Zinuk Tourist Market

20 17

16

District Forestry Office

LALDIGHI

Burmese Market

Ramu Rd

To Bus Terminal (2km)

1

Motel Rd

Hotel Sayeman Rd

New Circuit House Rd

4

Buddhist Stupas

Lighthouse

21

Radisson (Under Construction)

Hotel-Motel Zone Rd

Beach

11

13

12

15 2

18 19

9

KOLATOLI

Bay of Bengal

Kolatoli Rd

To Bus Terminal (3km)

14

6

7 10

Kolatoli Circle

To Himachari Beach (10km); Mermaid Eco-Resort (18km); Inani Beach (25km)

5

8

0          400 m
0          0.2 miles

# Cox's Bazar

| Sights | |
|---|---|
| **1** Aggameda Khyang | C2 |
| Maha Thin Daw Gree | (see 1) |

| Sleeping | |
|---|---|
| **2** Blue Ocean | C5 |
| **3** Hotel Panowa | B2 |
| **4** Hotel Silver Shine | A2 |
| **5** Kingfisher Cox's Bay Resort | D7 |
| **6** Nitol Bay Resort | D7 |
| **7** Ocean Paradise | C7 |

| Eating | |
|---|---|
| **8** Beach Café | D7 |
| **9** Mermaid Café | C6 |
| **10** Roadside Restaurants | D7 |
| **11** Taranga | B5 |

| Drinking | |
|---|---|
| **12** Cafe 14 | C5 |

| Information | |
|---|---|
| **13** AB Bank ATM | C5 |
| **14** Mercantile Bank ATM | C6 |

| Transport | |
|---|---|
| **15** Green Line Coaches | C5 |
| **16** Green Line Coaches | B2 |
| **17** Hanif Coaches | B2 |
| **18** Hanif Coaches | C5 |
| **19** Soudia Coaches | C5 |
| **20** Soudia Coaches | B2 |
| **21** United Airways (Hotel Kollol) | B5 |

**Beach Café** INTERNATIONAL $$
(beach; mains Tk 150-350; ⊙noon-midnight) A wooden shack on stilts, right on the beach, this cafe has a cheaper version of the menu at Mermaid Café. The food isn't as good, but this is still a top spot for a drink (juices, shakes, instant coffee) or a lunchtime snack.

**Taranga** BARBECUE $$
(Hotel-Motel Zone Rd; mains from Tk 100; ⊙7am-midnight) Has a fairly standard menu of Bengali and Chinese dishes, but the added attraction of garden seating. Evening is the time to come, because from 5pm onwards they stoke up the barbecue and dish out a range of very tasty kebabs.

**Cafe 14** CAFE $$
(Kolatoli Rd; ⊙10am-2am) The only cafe with real fresh coffee (from Tk 150), this Western-style coffee shop, attached to Long Beach Hotel, also does ice cream, cakes and sandwiches.

 **Information**

A few ATMs accept foreign cards; some are marked on the map.
**Sky Lark Cyber Café** (internet per hr Tk 30; ⊙9am-midnight)

 **Getting There & Away**

### Air

**United Airways** (Hotel-Motel Zone Rd; ⊙9am-6pm) By reception at Hotel Kollol, with daily flights to Dhaka (from Tk 4800).

### Bus

The main bus stand, a few kilometres from town, is known as Bus Terminal. From here to either Laldighi or Kolatoli Circle, a rickshaw costs Tk 30 to Tk 40. A shared auto is Tk 10.
**Chittagong** Tk 200, five hours, 8am to 3.30pm
**Dhaka** Tk 600, nine to 10 hours, 10pm
**Teknaf** Tk 120, two hours, 6.30am to 8pm

### Coach

Various coach companies (including Green Line, Hanif and Soudia) have offices clustered on Kolatoli Rd and on Beach Rd in Laldighi. Each has three or four daily air-con services to Dhaka (Tk 1200 to Tk 1600) and Chittagong (Tk 450 to Tk 600), which tend to leave either midmorning or midevening.

# Around Cox's Bazar

Ramu and Lamapara are noted for their Buddhist *khyangs* (temples), and some hills in this area are topped with pagodas.

Ramu, a subsidiary capital of the Rakhaing (Arakan) kingdom for nearly three centuries, is noted for a beautiful monastery containing images of the Buddha in bronze, silver and gold, and inlaid with precious and semiprecious stones. Start at the far end of the street of Buddhist buildings, at the lovely U Chitsan Rakhina Temple, and work your way back towards the town centre.

The beautiful Burmese Bara Khyang at Lamapara has the country's largest bronze Buddha statue. The temple's three wooden

## MERMAID ECO-RESORT

The people behind the wonderful Mermaid Café also run a fabulous eco-resort about 15km south of Cox's Bazar. Unlike most of the accommodation in town, Mermaid Eco-Resort (☎01841 416464; www.mermaidecoresort.com; bungalows US$65-250;@☎) is very low impact, with one-storey wooden huts, raised on stilts above the swampland they're dotted around and connected to each other by wooden walkways. Recycled materials are used when possible – some of the flooring, for example, has been taken from the planks of disused boats.

The resort is peaceful and environmentally friendly, rather than luxurious, but the bungalows all offer a good level of comfort and the setting is magical, in among undisturbed nature and with a private beach just a short boat trip away.

The food is excellent, and there's internet available, including wi-fi, plus film screenings in the evenings.

### Getting There & Away

Catch a CNG (Tk 200, 30 minutes) from Kolatoli Circle. You'll see the sign for the eco-resort on your right, about 7km after Himachari Beach. Don't confuse the eco-resort with the other Mermaid Café, which is on your left near Himachari Beach, or Club Mermaid, the company's latest venture, also in the Himachari Beach area. Coming back from the eco-resort, staff will help you nab a seat in a shared auto (Tk 50).

At the time of research, there were also plans to open a third branch of Mermaid Café in Gulshan, in Dhaka.

buildings house a number of precious Buddhist images in silver and gold, set with gems. Lamapara is a palm-shaded village about 5km from Ramu, and accessible only by zigzagging paved village paths. It's tough to find it on your own, so take a rickshaw or a CNG (Tk 100 to Tk 200 return).

About 2km from Lamapara, at the village of Ramkot, there are Buddhist and Hindu temples perched on adjacent forested hills.

Shared autos to Ramu (per person Tk 25) leave regularly from Bus Terminal in Cox's Bazar.

## St Martin's Island

Idyllic St Martin's Island is everything that brash Cox's Bazar is not. It's the country's only coral island and its beaches do actually match the hype. It also has more bungalow-style accommodation, which adds to the beach vibe. St Martin's is home to a friendly, tomorrow-never-comes population of around 7000, the majority of whom are Muslim, and live primarily off fishing, although the small amount of land on the centre of the island is also farmed.

The island is fairly small – about 6km in length and rarely more than 1km wide – so it's easy to navigate. Rickshaws are available, but you can also just walk around it from beach to beach. The area around the jetty, on

the northeast tip of the island, is called Narikeldia; there there are a few hotels and restaurants. From here, you'll pass through the small village of Uttarpara en route to West Beach, which is the nicest place to stay. The southern part of the island is called Dakshinpara. Even further south is Cherradhip, a thin strip of untouched land which is cut off from the rest of the island at high tide.

The boat trip over here is as interesting as it is scenic. Look out for traditional fishing boats as you sail along the Myanmar coastline. And get your camera ready for some magical sunset shots on the return trip.

## ◉ Sights & Activities

The main attraction is, of course, the beach. Most people head to West Beach (walk straight on from the ferry jetty for 20 minutes, or take a Tk 20 rickshaw), as there's some decent accommodation there, but all the beaches are nice, and you can walk along the beach around the whole island in just a few hours. Boats from the main jetty can take you south to Cherradhip (Tk 150 return), which is the most remote and undeveloped part of St Martin's. It takes around two hours to walk there.

You can dive and snorkel between November and March with the dive group Oceanic (☎01711 867991; www.bddiver.com; single dives Tk 2000-3500, 4-day open-water course Tk 18,000, snorkel Tk 600-800), based on East

Beach, which stretches away to your left as you step off the ferry.

## 🛏 Sleeping & Eating

Beachside restaurants or cafes are sadly lacking on St Martin's. There are snack and drinks stalls, but if you want a meal you'll have to eat at one of the hotels or guest-houses, or in Narikeldia by the jetty.

**TOP CHOICE** Shemana Pereye          BUNGALOW $$
(☎0181 9018027, 0191 1121292; r Tk 2000-2500; ❄) Eight cottages dotted around a well-tend-ed, tree-shaded garden, right beside West Beach. Cottages go for as little as Tk 1200 if it's quiet. Does food. Walk through Abakash to West Beach, turn left and it's just past Panna.

**Panna Resort**          GUESTHOUSE $$
(☎01816 172615; r Tk 2000; ❄) A handful of clean, hotel-standard rooms lining either side of a small garden. Lacks character, but is right on West Beach. Discounts bring rooms down to Tk 1500. Walk through Aba-kash to West Beach and turn left.

**Abakash Parjatan**          HOTEL $$
(☎01713 145584; r Tk 1800-2200, cottages Tk 1200; ❄) Popular with domestic tourists, this three-storey building has ordinary ho-tel rooms as well as a handful of good-value concrete cottages in the garden. The restaur-

ant here is decent (mains from Tk 100), and you can eat your meals in the garden. The road from the jetty ends at the back gate to this place, so to access West Beach – and the other accommodation listed here – you need to walk through its garden.

## ❶ Getting There & Away

Three or four large **passenger ferries** (lower deck/upper deck/lounge Tk 550/700/900) leave for St Martin's (two hours) at 9.30am daily from a

**WORTH A TRIP**

## TEKNAF GAME RESERVE

This rarely visited game reserve (টেকনাফ গেম রিজার্ভ; entrance US$5; ⊙dawn-dusk), which stretches down towards Bangladesh's furthest southern tip, is home to some of the coun-try's few remaining wild elephants. Your chances of seeing one of them are, of course, slim (best chance is in the evening, which unfortunately is also the best time for getting lost!), but hiking into the hilly forest is an adventure in itself. The chances are you'll be the only tourist walking the forest trails, although you may bump into local villagers as they venture into the hills to collect firewood. There are guides available, but they don't speak English and they're often nowhere to be seen. The trails, though, are marked on wooden sign-boards (albeit in Bengali only), so it's reasonably easy to find your way around.

There's an Interpretation Centre by the entrance, but it always seems to be closed, and some basic accommodation (r Tk 600), although it had no running water when we last visited, so you're probably better off at Hotel Ne-Taung.

### Getting There & Away

Take a Teknaf-bound bus from Cox's Bazar (Tk 120, two hours, 6.30am to 8pm). Get off when you see the sign with an elephant on it on the right-hand side of the road, about 8km before Teknaf. If you go too far, you can catch a shared auto-rickshaw (Tk 30) back to the reserve from the bus stand in Teknaf.

The reserve is about 4km before the St Martin's ferry ghat and about 5km before Hotel Ne-Taung.

ferry ghat on the main road between Cox's Bazar and the nondescript town of Teknaf. The ghat is about 5km before Teknaf. Tell your bus driver you want 'St Martin's launch' or just 'St Martin's' and he'll know where you want to be dropped. If you go too far, it's about Tk 20 in a shared auto from Teknaf bus stand back to the ferry ghat.

The ferry ticket counters open at around 7am. The best-value ticket is the upper-deck one. The closed lower deck is a bit stuffy, but there's no need for the air-conditioned lounge because the sea breeze on the open deck keeps everyone cool.

Smaller, more expensive **private ferries** (Tk 1000-1500) leave from a ghat a few hundred metres further towards Teknaf. During monsoon season, these may be the only boats available, and sometimes even these may be cancelled. If you're still really intent on reaching St Martin's at this time of year, some local wooden boat operators offer trips to St Martin's from Shah Porir Dwip, a totally undeveloped beach used by fishermen, 13km south of Teknaf.

Ferries return from St Martin's at 3pm, allowing plenty of time to hop on a bus back to Cox's Bazar. Either go to Teknaf bus stand, or just wave one down on the main road.

# Comilla

☑ 081 / POP 165,000

The only reason for tourists to visit the boisterous and bustling market town of Comilla is to see the Buddhist ruins of Mainimati. Sadly, most of them are located within a military camp on the outskirts of town, so are off-limits to the general public. Salban Vihara, the most impressive of them all, is just outside the military boundary and can be visited.

## ◉ Sights

Hidden away for years in the low Mainimati-Lalmai ridge of hills are the remains of the bygone Buddhist splendour of Mainimati. Between the 6th and 13th centuries, Mainimati was famous as an important centre of Buddhist culture and today the scattered ruins count as some of the most impressive in Bangladesh. The three most important of the 50-odd Buddhist sites are Salban Vihara, Kotila Mura and Charpatra Mura, although only Salban Vihara can be visited.

### Salban Vihara                          RUIN

(admission local/foreigner Tk 10/100; ⊙9am-5pm Oct-Mar, 10am-6pm Apr-Sep) While the ruined monastery of Salban Vihara lacks the imposing stupa of the ruins in Paharpur (p92), the remains give a better idea of the extent of the structure, as they were rebuilt more recently.

This 170-sq-m monastery has 115 cells for monks, facing a temple in the centre of the courtyard. The royal copper plates of Deva kings and a terracotta seal bearing a royal inscription found here indicate that the monastery was built by Sri Bhava Deva in the first half of the 8th century. The original cruciform plan of the central temple was reduced in scale during subsequent rebuilding. The entire basement wall was heavily embellished with decorative elements such as terracotta plaques and ornamental bricks.

To get here, take a shared auto from Kandirpar Circle to Kotbari (Tk 20), a small village just across the Dhaka–Chittagong Hwy and a couple of kilometres from the ruins. Then either walk or take another shared auto (Tk 10) the rest of the way. Your best bet for shared autos is the road leading south off Kandirpar Circle, as that's the way they go to Kotbari. A private CNG will cost Tk 100 to Tk 200 each way.

### Mainimati Museum                          MUSEUM

(admission local/foreigner Tk 10/100; ⊙9am-5pm Oct-Mar, 10am-6pm Apr-Sep) Just past Salban Vihar, and probably the best place to start your visit, is the Mainimati Museum. The collection includes terracotta plaques, bronze statues, 4th-century silver and gold coins, jewellery, kitchen utensils and votive stupas embossed with Buddhist inscriptions. The marvellous terracotta plaques reveal a rural Buddhist art alive with animation and vivid natural realism.

Also on display is an unusually large bronze bell from one of the Buddhist temples and some 1000-year-old large, well-preserved black-stone carvings of Hindu gods and goddesses, including Vishnu, Ganesh and Parvati.

## 🛏 Sleeping

### Ashik Residential Resthouse            HOTEL $

(☑68781; 186 Nazrul Ave; s/d Tk 575/700, with air-con Tk 1000/1400; ❄) Old-school hotel with huge, well-furnished rooms. Slightly run down, and therefore far from spotless, but the space makes up for the tattiness. No hot-water showers, but hot water can be provided. English spoken.

### Hotel Sonali                          HOTEL $

(☑63188; Kandirpar Circle; s/d Tk 350/600, r with air-con from Tk 1000; ❄) A bit shabbier than Ashik, and rooms aren't quite as big, but you do get hot showers, and it's right in the thick of the action, practically overlooking the cra-

# Comilla

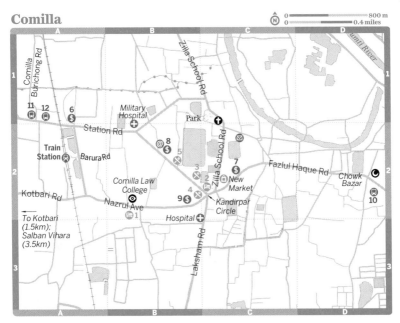

ziness of Kandirpar Circle. Reception is on the 3rd floor. No English sign, but everyone knows this place so just ask.

## ✖ Eating

**Diana Hotel**                           BANGLADESHI **$**
(Kandirpar Circle; mains Tk 70; ☺5am-11pm) Kebab heaven, with charcoal-grilled chicken and mutton *sheekh* topping the list. Also does excellent naan bread. No menu, and limited English, but pointing at the food on other tables tends to do the trick.

**Midpoint Restaurant**                   BANGLADESHI **$**
(Kandirpar Circle; mains Tk 80; ☺7am-11pm) Heaving locals' favourite with spot-on Bengali dishes (curries, biryanis). No English sign or menu, but some English spoken.

**Silver Spoon**                           CHINESE **$$**
(Station Rd; mains Tk 85-250; ☺10.30am-10.30pm) Clean family-friendly restaurant serving Chinese and Thai. English menu.

## ℹ Information

A couple of foreign-friendly ATMs are marked on the map. There are private moneychangers on Nazrul Ave.

**EarthNet-Bd** (internet per hr Tk 20; ☺9.30am-10pm)

## Comilla

## ℹ Getting There & Away

### Bus

It costs Tk 10 in a rickshaw to get from Kandirpar Circle to either bus stand.

The main bus stand serves Sha-ista Ganj (for Srimangal; Tk 200, 4½ hours, 6am to 5pm) and Sylhet (Tk 340, seven hours, 6am to 5pm). Go

## SELECTED TRAINS FROM COMILLA

| DESTINATION | TRAIN NAME | DEPARTS | ARRIVES | FARE (1ST/SHUVON) | OFF DAY |
|---|---|---|---|---|---|
| Akhaura | Samatat Ex | 10.10am | 12.15pm | Tk 40/20 | none |
| Chittagong | Jalalabad Ex | 7.25am | 1.15pm | Tk 140/60 | none |
| Chittagong | Mohanagar Provati | 11.26am | 2.20pm | Tk 140/60 | none |
| Chittagong | Paharika Ex | 3.51pm | 7.25pm | Tk 140/60 | Sat |
| Dhaka | Mohanagar Provati | 9.56am | 2.05pm | Tk 170/75 | Sun |
| Dhaka | Upakul Ex | 4.36pm | 8.30pm | Tk 170/75 | Wed |
| Dhaka | Dhaka Ex | 11.33pm | 5.55am | Tk 409/170/75* | none |
| Sylhet | Paharika Ex | 11.01am | 5pm | Tk 195/120 | Mon |

*Air-con berth/1st seat/shuvon

to the Chittagong bus stand for Chittagong (Tk 140, four hours, 6am to 6pm).

### Coach

Tisha runs comfortable, good-value coaches to Dhaka (Tk 160, two to three hours, 5am to 9pm) and Chittagong (Tk 160, four hours, 6am to 6pm). The Dhaka ones leave from the Tisha office by the main bus stand. The Chittagong ones leave from the office at the Chittagong bus stand.

### Train

See the boxed text for selected train times. Trains to Sylhet all pass through Akhaura (for the Indian border) and Srimangal (1st/shuvon Tk 105/70, four hours). Trains to Dhaka also pass through Akhaura.

# Sylhet Division

## Best Places to Stay

» Nishorgo Eco Cottages (p144)

» Hermitage Guest House (p144)

## Best Places to Eat

» Woondaal (p137)

» Kutum Bari (p143)

» Pritiraj (p137)

## Why Go?

Every corner of Bangladesh is blessed with beautifully green landscape, but none more so, it seems, than Sylhet. From glistening rice paddies and wetland marshes to forested nature reserves and rolling hills blanketed in waist-high tea bushes, Sylhet seems to contain every possible shade of green you can imagine.

With a landscape this diverse it's no surprise to find plenty of off-the-beaten-track adventure for those willing to go that extra mile, but one of the best things about this region is its accessibility. Good transport links mean that Sylhet's famous tea estates, its smattering of Adivasi mud-hut villages and its thick, monkey-filled forests are all just a few hours' drive or train journey from Dhaka.

But rushing Sylhet would be a mistake. The Srimangal area in particular deserves at least a few days of your time, and if you love hiking, cycling or wildlife, even that may not be long enough.

## When to Go
### Sylhet

°C/°F **Temp**　　　　　　　　　　　　　　　　Rainfall inches/mm

| | | | | | | | | | | | |
|J|F|M|A|M|J|J|A|S|O|N|D|

**Mar–Nov**
Tea-picking season. Time for those classic tea-picker photos.

**Oct–Mar**
Dry season; time for hiking, and for bird-watching boat trips.

**Mar–May**
If Dhaka is too hot, Sylhet provides a cooler escape.

# Sylhet Division Highlights

① Cycle through the tea estates of **Srimangal** (p139)

② Keep an eye out for rare hoolock gibbons as you stroll around the walking trails of the forested **Lowacherra National Park** (p141)

③ Get off the beaten track with a daylong hike to remote **Hum Hum Falls** (boxed text p144)

④ Venture north to the hard-to-get-to *haors* (wetlands) around **Sunamganj** (p138)

⑤ Explore the numerous **Adivasi villages** (p142) in the countryside surrounding Srimangal

⑥ Tuck in at some the country's best curry houses in the capital city of **Sylhet** (p135)

⑦ Sample Srimangal's quirkiest brew; the multicoloured **seven-layer tea** (boxed text p145)

# Sylhet

⏱ 0821 / POP 460,000

Friendly Sylhet may be a divisional capital, but it has a small-town feel to it with bustling roadside market stalls, particularly around Bandar Bazar, adding colour to the streets come evening. The majority of British Bangladeshis hail from here and are likely to wax lyrical over the place. Those with stronger ties to the homeland continue to pour money back into the local economy, which has helped create a city that is more modern than others of similar size in Bangladesh. It also means that you'll meet a disproportionately large number of people here who speak excellent English.

Sylhet, of course, is best known for its tea. This is where the country's commercial tea production first began, and there are still more than 150 tea estates in this region, some of which are walking distance from the city centre.

## ◉ Sights

**Shrine of Hazrat Shah Jalal** MAUSOLEUM

The shrine of this revered 14th-century Sufi saint is one of the biggest pilgrimage sites in the country and a fascinating place to visit. The complex contains a mosque (*masjid*) and the main tomb (*mazar*), both of which are accessed via the steps in front of you as you walk through the main entrance (East Darga Gate). Shah Jalal's sword and robes are preserved within the mosque, but aren't on display. His tomb is covered with rich brocade, and at night the space around it is illuminated with candles. The atmosphere is quite magical. You can also walk around the hillside graveyard behind the shrine. Being buried near the saint is considered a great honour.

Non-Muslims are allowed to visit, although be sure to dress conservatively, and remove your shoes before climbing the steps. Women can enter the complex – there is even a special prayer hall for women here – but they are not usually allowed to enter the shrine itself because doing so would mean passing through part of the mosque.

The pond at the northern end of the complex is filled with sacred catfish that are fed by pilgrims and are, according to legend, metamorphosed black magicians of the Hindu raja Gour Govinda, who was defeated by Shah Jalal in 1303.

**Museum of the Rajas** MUSEUM

(Jallarpar Rd; Tk 5; ⏱ 9am-5pm, closed Sat) Mystic, poet and songwriter Dewan Hasan Raja Chowdhury (1854–1922) has become a Bengali folk-music legend, and this two-room museum, housed inside his former family home, contains memorabilia from his life, including some traditional Bengali musical instruments and a number of old photos and family portraits.

**Kean Bridge** BRIDGE

The more central of the two bridges which span the Surma River, Kean Bridge, repaired after being damaged by Pakistani bombers during the Liberation War, is no architectural wonder, but crossing it is an experience in itself, not only because it's unrelentingly chaotic but also because rickshaw-riders here are aided by rickshaw-pushers, who help push passengers up the bridge's steep gradient in return for a few taka (the passengers are expected to pay). The result is a seething

---

**DON'T MISS**

## TEA ESTATES

Despite being slightly less accessible and arguably less scenic than those around Srimangal, the tea estates near Sylhet are still extremely pleasant places to wander around and, if you track down one of the managers on duty (their offices tend to be just inside the entrances to the estates), you should be able to arrange an informal tour of the tea-production factory.

The closest two are Laakatoorah Tea Estate and Malnicherra Tea Estate, both of which are accessed via Airport Rd, to the north of the city centre. The latter was established in 1854 and was the first commercial tea estate to be opened in Bangladesh.

A rickshaw should only cost around Tk 30 to Laakatoorah and around Tk 40 to Malnicherra. The Bengali for 'tea estate' is *cha bagan*.

You could simply walk to either estate as both tea plantations line the main road and are impossible to miss. In any case, both are well signposted in English.

For more on tea plantations, see the boxed text p145.

mass of humanity, driving, cycling, walking and running its way in and out of the city.

## 🛏 Sleeping

**Hotel Golden City**　　　　　HOTEL **$$**
(☎812 846, 01714 674738; www.hotelgoldencitybd .com; East Zinda Bazar Rd; incl breakfast s/d Tk 460/750, with air-con Tk 750/1100; ❈) Clean tiled rooms with sit-down toilets and hot-water showers, and a great location (sandwiched between our two favourite restaurants in Sylhet) make this an excellent-value mid-range choice. Some staff members speak English.

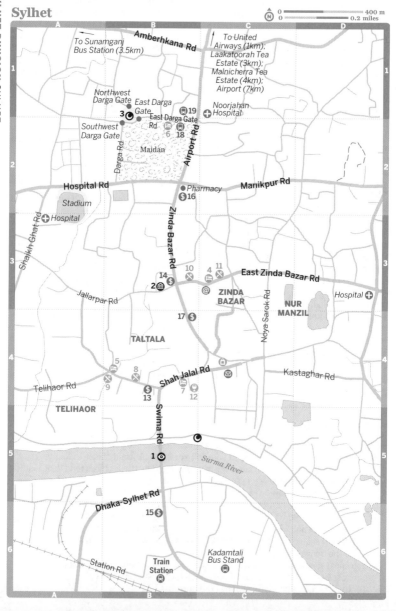

### Sylhet

**Hotel Gulshan**  HOTEL $

(☏717 263; Taltala Rd; s/d Tk 300/500, d with air-con Tk 900;❄) Easily the best-value budget hotel in Sylhet, this long-time travellers' favourite has huge doubles with cavernous bathrooms. Singles are smaller but by no means cramped, and all rooms, despite being somewhat basic, are kept clean and tidy. Hot showers come in the air-con rooms only. If for some unlikely reason Gulshan is full, there are also budget hotels on Telihaor Rd and East Darga Gate Rd.

**Hotel Star Pacific**  HOTEL $$$

(☏283 3091, 01937 776644; www.hotelstarpacific .com; East Darga Gate Rd; s/d incl breakfast from Tk 2800/4200;❄@☎) Central Sylhet's best hotel is sharp, modern and well located, if you want to soak up the atmosphere around the shrine of Hazrat Shah Jalal. Service is excellent, rooms are very comfortable considering this is only a small hotel, and there's a good restaurant plus a small gym. At the time of research this was also the only place

in Sylhet with wi-fi. Discounts of around 20% are common.

**Surma Valley Rest House**  HOTEL $$

(☏712 671; Shah Jalal Rd; r incl breakfast Tk 1450-1650;❄) With more of a guesthouse feel to it than other midrange hotels in Sylhet, Surma Valley comes with sparklingly clean rooms and nice use of space and is full of little homey touches. It's also located beside the only bar in town!

## ✗ Eating

**TOP CHOICE Woondaal**  INDIAN $$

(East Zinda Bazar Rd; mains Tk 100-200; ⊙11am-11pm) If you've ever been to a Bangladeshi-run Indian restaurant on London's Brick Lane – where many of the restaurants are run by expats from Sylhet – then you'll recognise all your curry favourites on the menu here. The service is slick, the decor is modern and the food is simply superb – in fact you'll probably end up having all your evening meals here while you're in Sylhet.

**Pritiraj**  BENGALI $$

(East Zinda Bazar Rd; mains from Tk 100; ⊙7am-11pm) Drag yourself away from Woondaal for at least one meal at this excellent and very friendly locals' restaurant. You'll find filling biryanis, tasty grilled chicken and fish dishes as well as a range of mouth-watering kebabs.

**New Green Restaurant**  BENGALI $

(Taltala Rd; mains Tk 50-100; ⊙5am-10pm) A great place for a Bengali breakfast of dhal, *shobji* (mixed vegetable curry, pronounced 'sabzee'), roti and fried egg, this place does dependable local food – biryanis, curries – and has friendly staff. No English menu. Limited English spoken.

**Nabanna**  BENGALI $

(Taltala Rd; mains from Tk 75; ⊙7am-11pm) Modern-looking and very clean restaurant serving some decent chicken dishes as well as excellent *halim* (slow-cooked mutton curry). Set back slightly from the road. No English sign or menu, but some English spoken.

## ♟ Drinking

**Station Club**  BAR

(Shah Jalal Rd; ⊙7-11pm) Established in the 1880s, this colonial-era club stocks imported beers (from Tk 300) and whiskys and has a strict dress code – no sandals, no shorts, no collarless shirts. Down a lane beside Surma Valley Rest House.

## SELECTED TRAINS FROM SYLHET

| DESTINATION | TRAIN NAME | DEPARTS | ARRIVES | FARE (1ST/SHUVON) | OFF DAY |
|---|---|---|---|---|---|
| Chittagong | Paharika Ex | 10.15am | 7.25pm | Tk 490/320/190* | Sat |
| Chittagong | Udayan Ex | 9.10pm | 5.35am | Tk 490/320/190* | Sun |
| Chittagong | Jalalabad Ex | 10.30pm | 1.15pm | Tk 490/320/190* | none |
| Dhaka | Joyantika Ex | 7.30am | 2.35pm | Tk 270/150 | Thu |
| Dhaka | Parabat Ex | 3pm | 9.45pm | Tk 270/150 | Tue |
| Dhaka | Surma Mail | 8pm | 9.55am | Tk 270/150 | none |
| Dhaka | Upaban Ex | 10pm | 5.15am | Tk 270/150 | none |

*1st berth/1st seat/*shuvon*

## ℹ Information

**Ahana Net & Cyber Café** (East Zinda Bazar Rd; internet per hr Tk 30; ☉10am-9pm)

**HSBC** (Zinda Bazar Rd; ☉10am-4pm Sun-Thu) The best place to change money or use an ATM. Other foreign card–friendly ATMs are marked on the map.

**Sonali Bank** (Zinda Bazar Rd; ☉10am-4pm Sun-Thu) You can pay your Tk 300 'travel tax' here before heading to the Indian border at Tamabil.

## ℹ Getting There & Away

### Air

**United Airways** (☑city 283 0596, airport 283 0612; Airport Rd; ☉8am-8pm) has flights to Dhaka (from Tk 3000) daily except Saturday.

### Bus

Sylhet's main bus stand is Kadamtali bus stand. It's a sprawling collection of roadside bus stands with buses to pretty much anywhere. Most run from around 6am up until around 7pm.

**Dhaka** From Tk 300, five hours.

**Srimangal** Tk 130, two hours.

**Tamabil** For the Indian border. Tk 50, two hours.

Sunamganj bus stand, also known as Kumargaon bus terminal, is a few kilometres northwest of town, along Amberhkana Rd (which intersects Airport Rd) with buses running to Sunamganj (Tk 90, two hours, every 30 minutes 6am to 8.30pm). A CNG to this bus stand costs Tk 100 to Tk 150.

**Green Line** (☑0197 0060034; East Darga Gate Rd) has air-con coaches to Dhaka (Tk 800, five daily 6.45am–5.30pm), and **Unique** (☑0119 162112222; East Darga Gate Rd) is one of a number of companies on this road with non-air-con coaches to Dhaka (from Tk 440, all day).

### Train

See the boxed text for trains to Dhaka and Chittagong. All the trains listed stop at Srimangal (1st class/*shuvon* Tk 90/50, about two hours).

The Chittagong trains also stop at Comilla (Tk 195/120, about six hours).

## ℹ Getting Around

Expect to pay around Tk 100 for the 30-minute CNG ride to the airport. Taxis cost around Tk 300.

## Sunamganj

☑0871/ POP 50,000

Approximately 70km west of Sylhet, this small town acts as a gateway to the *haors* (wetlands) of this region, which are rife with bird life. From midwinter through to the end of March and sometimes April, migrants, winter birds and residents all get together for a big bird party. Varieties of rails, raptors, ducks, sandpipers and others congregate.

## 🏃 Activities

### Bird-watching

Baer's pochard is the rarest bird you're likely to see. Other pochards include the white-eyed and red-crested varieties. The Baikal teal and the falcated teal are both impressive winterers, along with an assortment of crakes, including the ruddy crake and the little crake. You'll also see the spotted redshank and the blue-bearded bee-eater, plus various sandpipers and lapwings. A number of raptors are here as well, including several fishing eagles, such as the grey-headed and spotted Pallas's eagles.

The three *haors* that seem to be the best for bird-watching – Aila Haor, Pasua Haor and Tanguar Haor – are several hours upstream from Sunamganj. Visiting all of them is a four-day affair, which, except for true bird enthusiasts, is probably more than most travellers want. However, a simple overnight trip onboard a riverboat – or even just a day trip, with the help of a motorcycle taxi – will get you into some of the most fascinating and remote rural areas in Bangladesh.

## 🛏 Sleeping & Eating

You can find decent rooms in Sunamganj at **Hotel Nurani** (☎55346, 0119 6142939; Old Station Rd; s/d Tk 550/700, with air-con Tk 700/950;❄), near the old bus stand. Stock up on food and water in Sunamganj as there's little opportunity to buy things on a trip to the *haors*.

## ⓘ Getting There & Away

Buses to Sunamganj leave regularly from Sylhet. If they stop at Sunamganj's old bus stand, it's then a five-minute walk to Gudara Ghat, from where you can hire boats. If your bus stops at the new bus stand, you'll have to first take a shared auto-rickshaw (per person Tk 5) to the old bus terminal. Local guides will probably find you. Otherwise, ask around at Gudara Ghat.

It is possible to hire boats from Gudara Ghat for an overnight trip to Tanguar Hoar, but most travellers go for the quicker option of travelling part of the way by road and then hiring a boat from Solemanpur Bazar, a fishing-boat ghat 10 minutes before the village of Tahirpur. This makes a day trip from Sunamganj possible.

To do this, first cross the Surma River at Gudara Ghat (Tk 5). The other side is called Olir Bazar Gudara Ghat. From here you can hire a motorcycle taxi (Tk 200, 90 minutes, can take two passengers) or a tempo (Tk 70, 2½ hours) to Solemanpur Bazar, from where you can hire boats (Tk 1000) for a four-hour round trip around Tanguar Haor, before coming back the way you came.

# Srimangal & Around

☎08626/ POP 20,000

Sylhet may be the area's major city, but Srimangal is the undoubted star of this region and a few days spent cycling around its tea estates and exploring nearby villages and forests will almost certainly rank among your most treasured experiences in Bangladesh. The town itself is small, friendly and easy to manage, but it's the surrounding countryside that's the real draw, with cycling, hiking, wildlife-watching and, of course, tea-drinking all high on the agenda.

## ⊙ Sights & Activities

### Cycling                                                   CYCLING

The area around Srimangal is one of the best in Bangladesh for cycling. Despite the rolling terrain, the roads are reasonably level and well maintained. And the scenery, of course, is beautiful.

There's an intricate network of lanes connecting all the tea estates and villages to the main roads. Only the major routes are tarred or bricked, but the dirt roads tend to be in decent condition too.

It can be difficult to determine where one estate stops and another starts. Bear in mind that you might inadvertently pedal onto private property. Though you will find that most people are more likely to treat you like a guest than a trespasser, it is polite to seek management's permission to be there.

Most hotels and local guides can help arrange bike hire. At the time of research, the going rate was Tk 200 per day. We rented our bikes from **Anam Cycle Store** (Railway Station Rd; ☺8am-10pm) for the same price; a

**SYLHET DIVISION** SRIMANGAL & AROUND

---

### SRIMANGAL TOUR GUIDES

A number of English-speaking local guides offer informal tours of Srimangal and its leafy surrounds. They tend to be a bit hit-and-miss so it's worth trying to meet a couple of them beforehand so you can decide who you might prefer. Prices tend to be about the same: Tk 800 for a guide for the day, plus about the same again for a CNG to cart you round the sights. Prices are per group (as many as you're willing to squeeze into a CNG!) rather than per person, and are, of course, negotiable.

Below are some guides you may wish to contact. You could also make arrangements through the **Nishorgo Network** (www.nishorgo.org), a government-managed conservation scheme, which also runs the excellent Nishorgo Eco Cottages (p141).

**Tapas Dash** (☎0172 3292994) Excellent English. Good tour-guiding experience.

**Rashed Husan** (☎0171 1078362) Also contactable through Tea Town Rest House.

**Liton Deb** (☎0171 0994099) Enthusiastic and friendly.

**Santosh Kol** (☎0119 9366121) Friendly, but more limited English skills.

# Srimangal

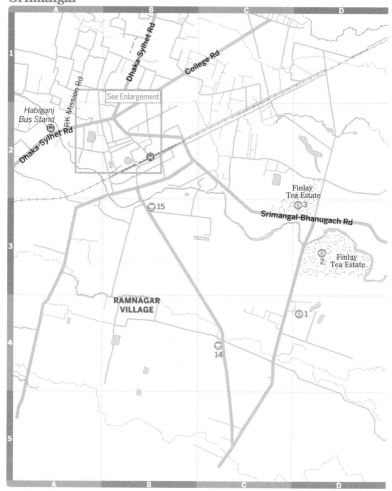

bargain considering the bikes they gave us were brand new, straight off the shelf!

## Tea Estates                                    TEA ESTATES
This region is covered with tea estates, but the closest ones of significance are Zareen and the British-owned Finlays, both of which you can cycle to. In fact, you can walk to Finlays. They are both very informal affairs, and many people just wander into the fields from the side of the road, but it's considered polite to go to the main entrance (follow the signposts) and knock on the door of the manager's office to ask if it's OK to

look round. They will always say yes, and will sometimes throw in a free tour of the tea factory if you ask sweetly.

**Zareen Tea Estate** is home to the renowned Ispahani tea and has tea bushes that seem to bounce across the tops of the rolling hills that so typify this area. It's about 1.5km beyond Radhanagar village and well signposted. The cycle here passes some beautiful farmland.

The sprawling **Finlay Tea Estate**, just on the edge of Srimangal, seems less used to visitors, but it's not normally a problem to wander a short way into the bushes and talk

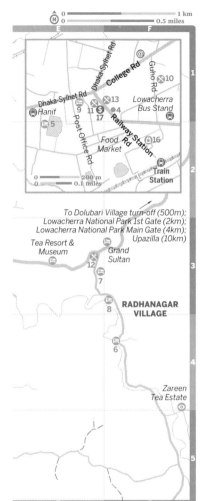

# Srimangal

### ◎ Sights

### ◌ Activities, Courses & Tours

### ◌ Sleeping

### ◌ Eating

### ◌ Drinking

### ◌ Shopping

### ⓘ Information

into. They're not used to having walk-in visitors, so phone ahead if you can.

**Lowacherra National Park**    WILDLIFE RESERVE
(Srimangal-Bhanugach Rd; foreigner/local Tk 350/20; ⊘9am-5pm) This wonderful patch of tropical semi-evergreen forest, around 8km east of Srimangal, provides not only some lovely forest walks but also your best chance of seeing the endangered hoolock gibbons in the wild. These are the only apes found in Bangladesh and there are only around 200 left in the country, 60 of which make their home here.

Protected as part of the government-run Nishorgo Network (www.nishorgo.org), the park now has visitor walking trails as well as eco-guides (albeit at the prohibitively high rate of Tk 300 per hour!). If he's around, **Tapas Dash** (☑01723 292994) comes recommended as a guide.

As well as the hoolocks, a further 19 mammal species have been identified here including capped langur, macaques, the delightful slow loris, orange-bellied Himalayan squirrel and barking deer. There are

to the tea-pickers. Walk or cycle out of town on Srimangal–Bhanugach Rd and you'll soon see the tea gardens stretching out beside you in both directions.

The **Bangladesh Tea Research Institute** (☑71225, 01711 867485), or BTRI, isn't a commercial estate as such but rather the scientific headquarters of Bangladeshi tea production. New strains of tea and new growing techniques are tried out here, and the staff are knowledgeable. There is also a production factory, which with a bit of luck you might be allowed to visit, and a tea-tasting room which you may be ushered

## SRIMANGAL BIKE TRIPS

Cycling aimlessly around the tea estates is fun in itself, but if you need a focus for your forays, you could try some of the following:

» **Finlay Tea Estate Loop** (3km total) Wheel your bike across the railway line just to the east of the train station, then start cycling south away from the station. Pass the first Nilkantha Tea Cabin on your left, then when you see the new, tiger-striped Nilkantha Tea Cabin (on your right at the small crossroads), turn left. Continue to the village crossroads and turn left again before passing the Bangladesh Tea Research Institute (BTRI). Soon after this, you'll have to dismount to cross a small stream. You're now in the middle of Finlay's Tea Estate. Continue to the end of the track then turn left to head back to Srimangal on the Srimangal–Bhanugach Rd.

» **Zareen Tea Estate** (4km one way) Cycle south along Srimangal–Bhanugach Rd then turn right at the still-under-construction Grand Sultan Hotel. Continue along this road, past Nigorsho Eco Cottages and through Radhanagar village before turning left at a signpost for the tea estate.

» **Dolubari Village** (5km one way) Cycle south along Srimangal–Bhanugach Rd then take the first right after the Grand Sultan Hotel, along a road signposted for Nurjahan and Lemon Garden Resort. Then take the first left (after about 1km) to reach this friendly Tripura village.

» **Lowacherra National Park** (7km one way) Cycle south along Srimangal–Bhanugach Rd.

» **Madhapur Lake** (12km one way) Cycle as if heading to Dolubari village, but instead of turning left down the village lane, keep heading straight, for about 5km, before turning right at a crossroads. Continue south for about 2km then turn right at a T-junction a few hundred metres from the lake.

also some 246 bird species and 20 varieties of orchid.

Remember this is dense forest so chances are you'll get nothing more than a fleeting glimpse of anything. One thing you won't miss, though, are the enormous orb spiders; black, red and yellow monsters that hang from Spiderman-sized webs between trees but are, we are told, completely harmless.

There are three walking trails (30 minutes, one hour and three hours), with maps on wooden signboards marking the way. A guide, though, will be able to take you off-piste without getting lost. There's a tea-and-snack stall by the visitor centre.

You can get here from Srimangal by bus (Tk 10), CNG (Tk 100) or bicycle (about 45 minutes; ride straight along the Srimangal-Bhanugach Rd). You could even jump off a moving train from Sylhet as they pass right through the park! (Don't actually do that.)

Note there are two gates to the park. The first one you reach as you come from Srimangal is on the right-hand side of the road and had only just opened at the time of research. A visitor centre and walking trails were being planned, but had yet to be constructed. The main gate is about 2km be-

yond this (on the left-hand side of the road). Both are well marked. The same park fees apply at both gates.

### Adivasi Villages VILLAGES

There are several Khasia villages (called *punji*), Monipuri villages (called *para*) and Tripura villages scattered among the tea plantations in the Srimangal area. Khasia villages are often on hilltops surrounded by betel-nut trees, which is their cash crop. When visiting a Khasia village you should first call in on the local chief, as the community will not extend full hospitality without his permission. The easiest way of visiting one of the Khasia communities is to ask one of the guides at Lowacherra National Park to lead you to one of the villages situated around the park fringes.

The closest Monipuri village to Srimangal is Ramnagar. Local tours will usually include a trip here, but you can walk here yourself. Of all the ethnic groups of this region, the Monipuri are the most integrated into mainstream Bangladeshi society, making villages like this one relatively accessible. Villagers have even opened shops here so tourists can buy the beautiful fabrics that you'll see being woven on handlooms in back yards. Those not involved in weaving tend to work in agriculture so you'll also see fruit trees galore (mango, lemon, jackfruit, banana) as well as the small rice paddies on the edge of the village. Most Monipuri are Hindu, and small temples and shrines dot the village. You may also notice the flame-like Hindu-temple symbol of the Monipuri, which is often woven into the fabrics they sell.

The best known Tripura village near Srimangal is **Dolubari**. It's a half-hour cycle from town, through some gorgeous countryside, and you'll find villagers are friendly and welcoming, even though they speak little English. Dolubari predates Srimangal itself and is set among some beautiful fruit-tree orchards; lemons and pineapples are the order of the day. The village has a much more rural feel to it than Ramnagar, with most villagers – there are around 600 – managing small plots of land beside their mud-hut homes, where they keep farmyard animals and grow vegetables. Tripura are also mostly Hindu, although a handful of families are Christian, hence the small church on the approach into the village.

It's about Tk 100 to get here in a CNG. For cycling directions, see the boxed text p145.

**Satchari National Park**   WILDLIFE RESERVE
About 60km southwest of Srimangal, **Satchari National Park** (foreigner/local Tk 350/20; ⊙9am-5pm) is also part of the Nishorgo Network and has the same set-up as Lowacherra, but is much less visited. Another superb slab of tropical forest, Satchari is also home to a small population of hoolock gibbons as well as fishing cats, Phayre's langur, jungle fowl, pygmy woodpeckers and oriental pied hornbills.

Getting here without your own transport is a bit of a mission, but doable. Take a bus from Srimangal to the crossroads junction known as Sha-ista Ganj (Tk 35, 35 minutes, from 9am). Then take a bus to Sunarghat (Tk 10, 20 minutes) from where you can pick up a shared jeep to Satchari (Tk 15, 25 minutes). Don't leave it too late coming back. Buses in Sunarghat start to thin out at around 5pm, although buses pass through Sha-ista Ganj all evening.

## 🛏 Sleeping

### In Srimangal

**Tea Town Rest House**   HOTEL $
(☑71065; Dhaka-Sylhet Rd; s/d/t Tk 300/600/1000, d with air-con Tk 1000;❄@) A long-time favourite for budget travellers, Tea Town has friendly staff and clean and tidy rooms, although bathrooms are a bit cramped. The large triple room is lovely and bright. Others lack natural light, but are still good value. There's one computer terminal in reception with a stuttering internet connection (per hour Tk 20).

**Green View Rest House**   HOTEL $$
(☑01719 896788, 01711 447757; Sagar Digi Rd; s/d from Tk 500/800) Newly opened in 2012,

---

## BANGLADESH TEA: FAST FACTS

» Bangladesh makes just over 50 million kg of tea a year, making it the world's 10th-largest tea producer.

» Commercial tea production in Bangladesh dates from 1854, when Malnicherra Tea Estate, just north of Sylhet, was set up by the British.

» 163 tea estates are still in operation in Bangladesh, 156 of which are in Sylhet division. Only 27 are still British-owned.

» Most tea-estate workers are descendents of Indian labourers brought in by the British from the then more established tea-growing regions of Bihar, Orissa and West Bengal. As such, you will sometimes see Hindu shrines among the tea bushes.

» The working and social conditions of workers has been called into question by nonprofit organisations such as the Society for Environment and Human Development (www.sehd.org).

» It is usually only women who pick tea leaves, apparently because they have smaller and more delicate hands.

» At just 75m above sea level, Srimangal is one of the world's lowest tea-growing areas. This gives the tea grown here a distinct flavour.

» The picking season here is during the wetter months, from early March to early December. This is also when the factories are in full operation. Tea estates are eerily quiet during winter.

## HUM HUM FALLS

For a proper off-the-beaten-track adventure, set aside a full day and try hiking your way from Srimangal to Hum Hum Falls.

Hidden in the depths of the Rajkandi Forest Reserve, this tall waterfall is only a truly impressive sight during and just after the rainy season; a time when it's very difficult to trek to. During the rest of the year, though, it still makes an excellent focus for your hike; first through farmland and villages, then through the tea gardens of Champarai Tea Estate and finally through the beautiful forests of Rajkandi. Like Lowacherra National Park, the forests here are also home to macaques and even some hoolock gibbons – we were very lucky to see a family of hoolocks on our last visit here. Sadly, parts of the forest are still being logged, particularly for bamboo.

The walk is steep at times, and part of it involves wading through a river, sometimes knee deep in water, but it all adds to the adventure. Take plenty of water and a packed lunch.

You'll never find the falls on your own so pick up a local guide (Tk 200) in Kulmaghat, the last stop on the bus before your hiking begins. One will probably find you as you step off the bus. Otherwise, ask around in the village. None of the guides speaks English, but they will understand where you want to go if you just say 'Hum Hum'. You can buy provisions in Kulmaghat and even have lunch here. The last place you'll be able to buy snacks and water is Kolobagan, a beautiful mud-hut village on the outskirts of the forest.

The walk from Kulmaghat to the falls takes around three hours one way, so try to leave Srimangal as early as possible to avoid having to walk back in the dark. Note, there are two routes to the falls so don't be alarmed if your guide walks back a different way from the way you came.

To get to Kulmaghat, take a bus from the Lowacherra bus stand in Srimangal to Upazilla (Tk 18, 45 minutes, 8am to 6pm) then change buses for Kulmaghat (Tk 20, 45 minutes). The last bus back to Upazilla is at 4.50pm. The last bus from there to Srimangal is at 6pm. If you get stranded, CNGs will come to the rescue. A shared CNG from Upazilla to Srimangal costs Tk 25 per person.

A private CNG from Srimangal to Kulmaghat and back will cost at least Tk 600. You may be able to get your CNG driver to drive all the way to Kolobagan Village, saving you about an hour of walking time each way.

Green View has the cleanest rooms in town, with tiled floors and wood furniture. Some rooms have loads of natural light. Others are windowless, so check first. Squat loos and cold-water showers only, but hot water available on request.

### Around Srimangal

TOP CHOICE **Nishorgo Eco Cottages** BUNGALOW **$$**
(☎0171 6939540, 0171 5041207; www.nishorgo.org; Radhanagar village; concrete huts Tk 1000, bamboo huts Tk 1500) Spread across two locations – one in Radhanagar Village, the other a short walk away – Nishorgo has around half a dozen cottages set in wonderfully idyllic surrounds – some back onto a forest, others onto a trickling stream. All are simple but well looked after, and offer a reasonable level of comfort while blending in perfectly with their surroundings. Booking ahead is highly recommended. If you get the choice, ask for the cottages in the village itself. They're the ones that back onto the trickling stream. Trust us: you'll never want to leave! Meals (breakfast Tk 60, lunch/dinner Tk 220) are available, as are guides and bike hire (sometimes). Only some of the cottages have hot-water showers, but buckets of hot water can be provided. A rickshaw from the train station to Radhanagar village is about Tk 50. To cycle here, head south along Srimangal-Bhanugach Rd then turn right at the Grand Sultan, a six-star hotel complex that was under construction at the time of research.

**Hermitage Guest House** HOMESTAY **$$**
(☎0171 1595265; www.hermitagesrimangal.com; Radhanagar village; r without/with air-con Tk 2500/3000; ❄@📶) This extremely comfortable homestay, run by the affable Sultana and located at the other end of Radhanagar village from Nishorgo Eco Cottages, has a handful of beautifully decorated rooms with modern, hot-water bathrooms and access to a garden terrace that overlooks a forest stream. Internet and laundry are included in the price.

Meals are available on request. Rooms go for as little as Tk 1500 when it's quiet. At other times booking ahead is recommended.

## 🍴 Eating
### In Srimangal

**TOP CHOICE** **Kutum Bari** INDIAN $$
(Railway Station Rd; mains Tk 75-150; ⏱11.30am-11.30pm) Split-level seating with high windows and funky bamboo seating make this the coolest place to eat in town. It also serves up Srimangal's best food; delicious Indian curries and naan bread share the menu with simple Bengali classics. Excellent value.

**Shah Hotel & Restaurant** BANGLADESHI $
(Railway Station Rd; mains from Tk 60; ⏱5am-midnight) Comfortably the most popular place in town for breakfast, this no-nonsense locals' favourite knocks up superb dhal and steaming-hot rotis to have with your *shobji* and fried egg. Later on in the day the dhal gets replaced by biryanis and chicken and mutton curries. No English menu, and limited English spoken.

**Agra** CHINESE $$$
(Guho Rd; mains Tk 150-300; ⏱11am-11pm; ❄) Decent-quality Chinese and Thai food served up in a clean, air-con-cooled restaurant in the plusher, tree-shaded end of town. Popular with families, but has definitely been ousted by Kutum Bari from its previous position as the best restaurant in town.

### Around Srimangal

**Sath Rong Restaurant** BENGALI $$
(Srimangal-Bhanugach Rd; mains Tk 150-200, tea Tk 10 per layer; ⏱6am-9pm) Opposite the Grand Sultan – a monstrous six-star hotel, due to open in 2013 – Sath Rong (seven colours) is a cute roadside cafe-restaurant that serves its own version of the seven-layer tea made famous by Romesh at Nilkantha Tea Cabin. It also does a few Chinese dishes and, at the time of research, was the only restaurant of sorts within walking distance of Nishorgo Eco Cottages or Hermitage Guest House.

## 🛍 Shopping

**M/S Ahmed Tea House** TEA
(Railway Station Rd; ⏱9am-10pm) One of a number of small shops on this stretch of the train station approach road that sells tea from the surrounding tea estates. It's mostly Ispahani tea from the Zareen tea estate, although you'll also see Finlay teas. Expect to pay around Tk 120 per kilo for black tea leaves; more for green. You can buy tea bags as well as loose tea, although the quality of the loose tea is always superior.

## ℹ Information

**AB Bank ATM** (Railway Station Rd) Foreign card–friendly ATM.

**E-Zone Cyber Café** (internet per hr Tk 20; ⏱10.30am-9pm) Fastest connection in town.

## ℹ Getting There & Away
### Bus

**Hanif** (☎72224; Dhaka-Sylhet Rd) Has regular coach services to Dhaka (Tk 350, 3½ hours) between 6am and midnight.

Departures from Habiganj bus stand include Sylhet (Tk 100, two hours, 7am to 8pm) and Sha-ista Ganj (for Satchari National Park; Tk 35, 35 minutes, from 9am)

---

**DON'T MISS**

## SEVEN LAYER TEA

Stony-faced tea-maker extraordinaire Romesh Ram Gour is the man behind the Srimangal institution that is the Nilkantha Tea Cabin (www.nilkantha.blog.com; Ramnagar village; ⏱9am-5.30pm) and the creator of one of the most famous types of tea in Bangladesh. His Willy Wonka–esque seven-colour tea (Tk 70) is known throughout the country and has even appeared in some foreign press articles. Yes, it really does have seven distinct layers of colour and seven equally differing tastes, and it's so popular Romesh has opened up a second tea cabin about 1km further south. You can order any number of layers, from two up to seven. Each layer costs Tk 10, as do the other, more orthodox tea flavours on offer.

It's an easy 10-minute walk from town; cross the railway line at the train station and keep going. The second tea cabin is further along the same road, on the right of the small crossroads. Romesh tends to flit between the two.

Note that other multilayer tea pretenders have opened up in and around Srimangal, but their tea layers tend to merge into a cloudy mess. Nilkantha is the original and, for now at least, still the best.

## SELECTED TRAINS FROM SRIMANGAL

| DESTINATION | TRAIN NAME | DEPARTS | ARRIVES | FARE (1ST/SHUVON) | OFF DAY |
|---|---|---|---|---|---|
| Chittagong | Parharika Ex | 12.30pm | 7.25pm | Tk 250/150 | Sat |
| Chittagong | Udayan Ex | 11.15pm | 5.35am | Tk 370/250/150* | Sun |
| Dhaka | Jayantika Ex | 9.34am | 2.35pm | Tk 200/110 | Thu |
| Dhaka | Parabat Ex | 5.03pm | 9.45pm | Tk 200/110 | Tue |
| Dhaka | Surma Mail | 10.46pm | 9.55am | Tk 300/200/110* | none |
| Dhaka | Udayan Ex | 12.11am | 5.15am | Tk 300/200/110* | none |
| Sylhet | Surma Mail | 7.10am | 12pm | Tk 90/65 | none |
| Sylhet | Parabat Ex | 11.03pm | 1.10pm | Tk 90/65 | Tue |
| Sylhet | Parharika Ex | 2.31pm | 5pm | Tk 90/65 | Mon |
| Sylhet | Jayantika Ex | 6.33pm | 9pm | Tk 90/65 | none |

*1st berth/1st seat/*shuvon*

From Lowacherra bus stand buses go to Lowacherra National Park (Tk 10, 20 minutes, 8am to 6pm) and Upazilla (for Hum Hum Falls; Tk 18, 45 minutes, 8am to 5pm).

### Train

See the boxed text for trains to Dhaka, Sylhet and Chittagong. All Dhaka and Chittagong trains stop at Akhaura (about three hours), for the Indian border. All Chittagong trains also stop at Comilla (four to five hours).

# Understand
# Bangladesh

**population per sq km**

BANGLADESH    INDIA    USA

👤 ≈ 30 people

# Bangladesh Today

Two court trials of huge political significance dominated the most recent term of office for Prime Minister Sheikh Hasina. She was installed for her second nonconsecutive term as the country's leader after her Awami League (AL) party won a landslide victory in the December 2008 elections. Less than two months later, she was forced to deal with one of the country's most shocking events of recent times.

## Border Guards Mutiny

Bangladeshis watched in horror in February 2009 when live TV broadcasts reported on a soldier mutiny at Dhaka's headquarters of the Bangladesh Rifles (BDR), a paramilitary force (since renamed Border Guards Bangladesh) primarily engaged in the country's border control.

Rebel soldiers, who were demanding the removal of army officials plus equal rights and pay, went on a 36-hour killing spree that left 74 people dead, including the BDR director-general Shakil Ahmed, 57 BDR officers and seven civilians. Bodies were disposed of in nearby sewers and shallow graves, and similar mutinies spread to regional BDR headquarters across the country, until the rebel soldiers eventually surrendered.

The incident triggered the largest trial in the history of Bangladesh's judicial system. At the time of research, more than 2000 soldiers had been jailed under the BDR Act for their part in the mutiny, with more still awaiting trial. More than 800 core suspects are being tried in a specially appointed civilian court, established under the Bangladesh Criminal Procedure Code, and could face the death penalty.

The trial process itself came under scrutiny when reports emerged that suspects were being subjected to torture and that at least 47 of those on trial had died while in custody. The New York–based Human Rights Watch has made strong calls for the trial in its current form to be aban-

---

» Population: 142,319,000 (9th largest)

» GDP per capita: US$1,700

» GDP growth rate: 6.3%

» Unemployment rate: 5%

» Employed in agriculture: 45%

» Literacy rate: 47.9% (male 54%, female 41.4%)

» Life expectancy: 70 years

» Population below poverty line: 31.5%

---

## Top News Sources

**BD News 24** (www.bdnews24 .com) The country's first online newspaper.

**Daily Star** (www.thedailystar .net) Bangladesh's best English-language daily.

**Thorn Tree** (www.lonelyplanet .com/thorntree) The Bangladesh branch of Lonely Planet's Thorn Tree forum is easily the best place for up-to-date travel-related news on the region.

## Top Nonfiction

**A History of Bangladesh** (Willem van Schendel, 2009)

**Banker to the Poor** (Dr Mohammad Yunus, 2003)

**Rise of Islam and the Bengal Frontier** (Richard Eaton, 1996)

## GDP per capita
($US dollars)

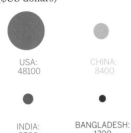

USA:
48100

CHINA:
8400

INDIA:
3700

BANGLADESH:
1700

## if Bangladesh were
## 100 people

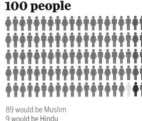

89 would be Muslim
9 would be Hindu
1 would be Buddhist
1 would be Other

doned, stating that mass trials such as this cannot provide justice for victims or real answers about who was responsible for the crimes.

## War Crimes Tribunal

As if one history-defining court case wasn't enough to deal with, Hasina also sanctioned the setting up of a special tribunal in 2010 to try a handful of key suspects charged with crimes against humanity, allegedly committed during the 1971 Liberation War. At least eight men, including Ghulam Azam and Delawar Hossain Sayedee, both high-profile leaders of the country's largest Islamist party, Jamaat-e-Islami, face the charges in a trial which is expected to last for some years.

## Economic Growth

While its recent political scene has been as troubled as ever, Bangladesh's economy continues to grow at about 6%, and some major development projects are in the pipeline. Dhaka's metro system is at an advanced stage of planning, but the chances of its lines being completed during the lifetime of this book are slim. A US$7.5 billion airport is also being planned for Dhaka, while an area off the coast of Cox's Bazar has been earmarked for south Asia's largest deep-water sea port.

## Continued Poverty

There's no escaping the fact that Bangladesh is one of the poorest countries in the world. The economy may be growing at an impressive rate, but in a country that is the most densely populated of any large nation, millions of people are still going hungry. According to the UN, about one-quarter of all Bangladeshis are undernourished, including a staggering 41% of under-fives.

## Top Novels

**The Sacred and the Secular:
Bengal Muslim Discourses**
(Tazeen Murshid, 1996)
**Pakistan: Failure in National
Integration** (Rounaq Jahan,
1996)

**Lajja (Shame)** (Taslima Nasrin,
1993)
**Sultana's Dream** (Rokeya
Sakhawat Hussain, 1905)
**The Good Muslim** (Tahmima
Anam, 2011)
**A Golden Age** (Tahmima Anam,
2007)

**Like a Diamond in the Sky**
(Shazia Omar, 2009)

# History

For much of history, the state that today we call Bangladesh has been a part of a greater India and was known only as Bengal; what happened elsewhere on the subcontinent invariably affected this region too.

Today, around 90% of Bangladesh's massive population is Muslim, but rewind 1000 years and you'd find a Bengal that had been ruled by Buddhist dynasties for more than 1500 years. Hindu armies took hold in the 12th century but were eventually ousted by Muslim powers and soon the might of India's Mughal Empire reigned supreme.

The British later took over and played their part in shaping the future of what was to become Bangladesh by starting in motion the Partition of India, leading to the hugely contentious creation of an East and West Pakistan; a fractious nation connected by the religion of Islam, but split by significant linguistic and cultural divides, as well as some 1600km of Indian territory!

The Bengali-speaking East Pakistan continued to agitate against the politically dominant, Urdu-speaking West Pakistan, and war eventually broke out. 1971 saw nine months of unspeakable events, which the Bangladeshi authorities say led to the deaths of three million people. Eventually India intervened, Pakistan surrendered and the People's Republic of Bangladesh was born.

The exact origin of the word 'Bangla' is unclear, but is thought to derive from the Dravidian-speaking Bang tribe that lived in the region around 1000 BC.

## Buddhist Foundations

Strange though it may now seem in such an overwhelmingly Muslim country, Buddhism has been no small player in the nation's history and culture. Nationwide, less than 1% of people are Buddhists, but in certain areas, such as Chittagong division, Buddhists make up 12% of the population.

The distance from Bodhgaya (in present-day India, where the Buddha reached enlightenment) to Bengal is not far, and the region has played a huge part in the development of Buddhism, including the creation of the mystical Tantric Buddhism.

| TIMELINE | Back in time | 262 BC | 4th century AD |
|---|---|---|---|
| | The earliest mention of the region is in the 9th century BC Hindu epic Mahabharata, which tells of Prince Bhima's conquest of eastern India, including Varendra, an ancient kingdom in what is now Bangladesh. | Chandragupta Maurya creates an empire, then known as Pundravardhana Bhukti. It spreads across northern India under his grandson, Emperor Ashoka, whose conversion to Buddhism has a lasting effect. | In the 4th century AD, northern India comes under the imperial rule of the Guptas; during their reign Buddhism reaches its zenith. |

By the reign of the great Indian Buddhist emperor Ashoka (304–232 BC), Buddhism was firmly entrenched as the number one religion of Bengal and, aside from a few minor skirmishes, it continued to thrive in the region until the 12th century AD, making Bengal the last stronghold of Buddhism in an increasingly Hindu- and Muslim-dominated subcontinent.

Gopala, a Kshatriya tribal chief from Varendra, became the founding figure of the Buddhist Pala dynasty (8th to 11th centuries). He was succeeded by his son Dharmapala, who established the gigantic Somapuri Vihara in Varendra, known today as Paharpur (p92).

In the 12th century, Hindu *senas* (armies) came to rule Bengal, and crushed Buddhism. Surviving Buddhists retreated to the Chittagong area. In less than a century, though, the *senas* were swamped by the tide of Islam.

Though somewhat beaten, Buddhism never totally died out in Bangladesh, and in the Chittagong Hill Tracts there are several monasteries that look to Myanmar (Burma) for religious inspiration, and there are a number of schools in which children learn to read Burmese and Pali (an ancient Buddhist language). As in neighbouring Myanmar, many Buddhist men in this region spend a part of their lives as monks.

## The Muslim Period

They took some time to arrive, but when they did they left a legacy that continues to define the country to this very day. The arrival of the Muslims began with the trickle of a few Sufi (Muslim mystic) missionaries in the 12th century and the construction of the odd mosque on the fringes of Bengal. Then came Mohammed bin Bakhtiar (a Khilji from Turkistan) who, with only 20 men under his command, made short work of capturing Bengal and bringing the area under the rule of the sultanate of Delhi, the centre of Muslim power in India.

Under the Muslims, Bengal entered a new era. Cities developed; palaces, forts, mosques, mausoleums and gardens sprang up; roads and bridges were constructed; and new trade routes brought prosperity and a new cultural life. In 1576 Bengal became a province of the mighty Mughal Empire, which ushered in another golden age in India. Mughal power extended over most of Bengal except the far southeast around Chittagong, and it was during this period that a small town named Dhaka emerged from obscurity to become the Mughal capital of Bengal.

Virtual Bangladesh (www.virtualbangladesh.com/history/overview.html) gives a simple overview of a complicated history.

## British Reign

It was during the reign of Mughal emperor Aurangzeb (1618–1707) that a Bengali nawab (Muslim prince) sold three local villages to the British East India Company. Today one of those villages goes by the name of Kolkata (Calcutta). From here the British gradually extended their influ-

| 1202 | 1342–1487 | 1575 |
|---|---|---|
| Muslims storm into Bengal and convert the region. The Mameluk sultanate is established, until the Tughlaq dynasty overthrows it in 1320. The Tughlaqs are defeated by a wave of Muslim invaders in 1398. | Under the Ilyas Shahi dynasty, a distinct Bengali identity begins to form. The city of Gaud emerges as a cosmopolitan metropolis, remaining the centre of power until the capital is moved to Dhaka in 1608. | Under the command of Akbar, the Mughals defeat Bengali sultan Daud Karrani at the Battle of Tukaroi. His defeat announces the beginning of the Mughal adventure in Bengal. |

TRAVEL INK ©

» Lalbagh Fort (p38)

ence to take in all of Bengal and finally all of the subcontinent, but the going was far from easy.

It has been said that the British Raj ushered Bengal into a period of growth and development, but historians hotly dispute this. The British brought infrastructure, law and government, but they also introduced dictatorial agricultural policies and the establishment of the zamindar (feudal landowner) system, which many people consider responsible for draining Bengal of its wealth.

Most Hindus cooperated with the British, entering British educational institutions and studying the English language. The majority of Muslims, on the other hand, refused to cooperate, preferring to remain landlords and farmers. This religious dichotomy formed a significant basis for future conflict.

Originally a mere clerk for the British East India Company, Robert Clive rose to become local head of the company and, eventually, the effective ruler of Bengal.

## Partition & Pakistan

At the close of WWII it was clear that European colonialism had run its course. The Indian National Congress continued to press for Indian self-rule and the British began to map out a path to independence.

With the Muslim population of India worried about living in an overwhelmingly Hindu-governed nation, the Muslim League was formed. It pushed for two separate Muslim states in South Asia. Lord Mountbatten, viceroy of British India, realising the impossibility of the situation and, quite possibly, looking for a quick British escape, decided to act on these desires and partition the subcontinent.

Though support for the creation of Pakistan was based on Islamic solidarity, the two halves of the new state (East and West Pakistan) had little

### TENSIONS IN THE HILL TRACTS

Since the Liberation War, more and more Bengalis have been migrating into the Chittagong Hill Tracts, a geographically remote part of Bangladesh and traditionally an Adivasi (tribal) stronghold. In 1973 the Adivasi rebel group Shanti Bahini initiated an insurgency over demands for autonomy of the region. To counter it, the government, in 1979, started issuing permits to landless Bengalis to settle there, with titles to Adivasi land. This practice continued for six years and resulted in a mass migration of approximately 400,000 people into the area – almost as many as all the Adivasi groups combined. Countless human-rights abuses occurred as the army tried to put down the revolt.

From 1973 until 1997 the Hill Tracts area was the scene of a guerrilla war between the Bangladeshi army and the Shanti Bahini rebels.

Sheikh Hasina's first government cemented an internationally acclaimed peace accord in December 1997 with Adivasi leader Jyotirindriyo Bodhipriya (Shantu) Larma, but the struggle to have the accord fully honoured continues today.

| 1707 | 1756–57 | 1758–1857 | 1885–1905 |
|---|---|---|---|
| The last great Mughal ruler Aurangzeb dies and the Mughal empire is thrown into disarray. Bengal has long had autonomy, and now breaks away completely from the rest of the empire. | Suraj-ud-Daula, the nawab of Bengal, attacks Calcutta. British inhabitants are packed into a cellar, where most suffocate. To avenge them, Robert Clive kills Suraj-ud-Daula and becomes the de facto ruler of Bengal. | The British East India Company controls Bengal, but their policies do not endear them to the Bengalis. The Sepoy Rebellion inflames local passions. In 1857 the British government takes control of India. | Supported by Hindus and Muslims, the Indian National Congress is founded in 1885. But the division of Bengal in 1905 by Lord Curzon, seen as a religious partition, prompts the formation of the All India Muslim League. |

else in common. Furthermore, the country was administered from West Pakistan, which tended to favour itself in the distribution of revenues.

The Awami League, led by Sheikh Mujibur Rahman, emerged as the national political party in East Pakistan, with the Language Movement as its ideological underpinning. The 1971 national elections saw the Awami League win with a clear majority; in East Pakistan it won all seats but one. Constitutionally, the Awami League should have formed the government of Pakistan, but faced with this unacceptable result, President Khan postponed the opening of the National Assembly.

## The War of Liberation

At the racecourse rally of 7 March 1971 in Dhaka (at what is now Ramna Park), Sheikh Mujibur (Mujib) stopped short of declaring East Pakistan independent. In reality, however, Bangladesh (land of the Bangla speakers) was born that day. Sheikh Mujib was jailed in West Pakistan, igniting smouldering rebellion in East Pakistan.

When the Mukti Bahini (Bangladesh Freedom Fighters) captured the Chittagong radio station on 26 March 1971, Ziaur Rahman, the leader of the Mukti Bahini, announced the birth of the new country and called upon its people to resist the Pakistani army. President Khan sent more troops to quell the rebellion.

General Tikka Khan, known to Bangladeshis as the 'Butcher of Balochistan', began the systematic slaughter of Sheikh Mujib's supporters. Tanks began firing into the halls of Dhaka University. Hindu neighbourhoods were shelled and intellectuals, business people and other 'subversives' were hauled outside the city and shot.

By June the struggle had become a guerrilla war. More and more civilians joined the Mukti Bahini as the Pakistani army's tactics became more brutal. Bangladeshi authorities say that napalm was used against villages, and that rape was both widespread and systematic.

By November 1971 the whole country was suffering the burden of the occupying army. During the nine months from the end of March 1971, 10 million people fled to refugee camps in India.

With border clashes between Pakistan and India becoming more frequent, the Pakistani air force made a pre-emptive attack on Indian forces on 3 December 1971, precipitating a quick end. Indian troops crossed the border, liberated Jessore on 7 December and prepared to take Dhaka. The Pakistani army was attacked from the west by the Indian army, from the north and east by the Mukti Bahini, and from all quarters by the civilian population.

By 14 December the Indian victory was complete and West Pakistan had been defeated. But at what cost? According to Bangladeshi authorities, around three million people were killed in the nine-month war,

In his book *Heroes* (1987) the ever-emotive John Pilger discusses ordinary people in extraordinary situations. The words he dedicates to Bangladesh luridly evoke the fervour of its formation and the passion of the people involved.

The *Bangladesh Newsletter* is a compilation of American newspaper cuttings from the coverage of the Bangladesh Liberation War. You can buy it at Dhaka's Liberation War Museum.

| 1947 | 1952 | 1970 | 1971 |
| --- | --- | --- | --- |
| Pakistan and India come to life. Pakistan is divided into two regions, the Punjab and Bengal. Bengal is known as East Pakistan. A bloody exodus occurs as Hindus move to India and Muslims to East or West Pakistan. | The Pakistani government declares Urdu will be the national language. Riots break out in Dhaka, and on 21 February 12 students are killed by the Pakistani army. Pakistan's democracy gives way to military government. | A catastrophic cyclone kills around 500,000 people in East Pakistan. The Pakistani government is criticised for doing little. War between East and West Pakistan looms large on the horizon. | War between East and West Pakistan. After nine months, the Indian army intervenes. Pakistan's General Niazi surrenders, and on 16 December Sheikh Mujib takes the reins of an independent Bangladesh. |

200,000 women were raped and 10 million people were forced from their homes.

Forty years later, the country would open an internal war-crimes trial, which would see several political leaders face accusations of crimes against humanity.

## The Early Chaos of Independence

The People's Republic of Bangladesh was born into chaos – it was shattered by war, and had a ruined economy and a totally disrupted communications system. Henry Kissinger once described the newly independent Bangladesh as an 'international basket case'. As if to reinforce this point, famine struck between 1973 and 1974 and set the war-ravaged country back even further.

After a couple of years of tumultuous power struggles, General Ziaur Rahman, now the head of the army, took over as martial-law administrator and assumed the presidency in late 1976.

The overwhelming victory of President Zia (as Ziaur Rahman was popularly known) in the 1978 presidential poll was consolidated when his party, the newly formed Bangladesh Nationalist Party (BNP), won two-thirds of the seats in the parliamentary elections of 1979. Martial law was lifted and democracy returned to Bangladesh. Zia proved to be a competent politician and statesman. Assistance began pouring in, and over the next five years the economy went from strength to strength.

Though the country progressed economically during the late 1980s, in early 1990 the economy began to unravel and massive rallies and hartals (strikes) were held. During this period Zia's wife, Begum Khaleda Zia, who had no political experience, became head of the BNP and, in the ensuing election, the Awami League won a majority 33% of the vote. But with more seats, the BNP still won and Begum Khaleda Zia became prime minister in 1991.

My Story of 1971 by university professor Muhammad Anisur Rahman is a personal account of the horrors of the Liberation War. You can buy it at Dhaka's Liberation War Museum.

In July 2002, Pakistani president Musharraf visited Bangladesh and expressed his regret at the excesses carried out by Pakistan during the Liberation War.

### THE SLAUGHTER OF THE INTELLECTUALS

Immediately following Sheikh Mujib's arrest on 26 March 1971, all hell broke out. Blaming the Hindu intellectuals for fomenting the rebellion, the generals immediately sent their tanks to Dhaka University and began firing into the halls, killing students. This was followed by the shelling of Hindu neighbourhoods and a selective search for intellectuals, business people and other alleged subversive elements. One by one they were captured, hauled outside the city and shot in cold blood. Over the ensuing months, the Pakistani soldiers took their search for subversives to every village. By then, if there had ever been a distinction made between intellectuals and Hindus, it was gone. When captured, men were forced to lift their lungis (sarongs) to reveal if they were circumcised; if not, they were slaughtered.

| 1974–6 | 1981 | 2007 | 2009 |
|---|---|---|---|
| A state of emergency is declared in 1974 and Sheikh Mujib proclaims himself president. He is killed in a military coup on 15 August 1975. His surviving daughter Sheikh Hasina becomes prime minister in 1996. | During an attempted military coup in May, President Zia is assassinated. Justice Abdul Sattar is appointed as acting president and, as candidate for the BNP, wins 66% of the vote in the ensuing general election. | Fakhruddin Ahmed's caretaker government declares emergency rule and arrests former prime ministers Begum Khaleda Zia and Sheikh Hasina Wajed before rescheduling elections for late 2008. Cyclone Sidr leaves 3500 dead. | Having won the elections with a landslide victory, the Awami League's Sheikh Hasina becomes prime minister for the second time. |

Never fully accepting the election result, the Awami League, headed by Sheikh Hasina, began to agitate against the BNP. A long and economically ruinous period of hartals eventually brought down the BNP government in June 1996, and the Awami League took power.

## A Brighter Future

The past decade or so has seen little respite in the political twisting and turning. Khaleda Zia's Nationalist Party and its three coalition partners won the 2001 elections. Arguing that the elections were rigged, the Awami League began parliamentary boycotts. In August 2003, two opposition Awami League politicians were murdered, triggering a spate of hartals. In February 2004, the opposition called a series of general strikes in a failed attempt to force the government from power.

The Bangladeshi constitution states that at the end of its tenure the government must hand power over to an unelected, neutral caretaker government which must organise elections within 90 days. In January 2007, with elections due and neither side able to agree on a suitable caretaker government, and street protests over the stalemate becoming increasingly large and violent, a military-backed caretaker government under the leadership of Fakhruddin Ahmed took over. One of its first acts was to declare emergency rule, postpone the elections to late 2008 and ban all political activity. In the meantime they promised to stamp out the corruption that in recent years had seen Bangladesh rate consistently as one of the world's most corrupt nations.

The Awami League's Sheikh Hasina became prime minister for the second time after winning the 2008 elections in a landslide victory, and despite having to deal with the shocking events of the 2009 Border Guards Mutiny (p148), Bangladesh has seen a period of relative stability ever since. Add to that an economy with a growth rate of around 6% and it's easy to see why some analysts are predicting a rosier future for the world's eighth most populous country.

In *Bangladesh: From a Nation to a State* (1997), Craig Baxter discusses the development of national identity. It's a comprehensive and ambitious work that contextualises the nationalistic pride evident in Bangladesh today.

HISTORY A BRIGHTER FUTURE

NATIONAL IDENTITY

**February 2009**

Soldiers from paramilitary group Bangladesh Rifles (BDR) stage a bloody yet unsuccessful mutiny at their Dhaka headquarters, slaughtering 74 people, including 57 of their own officers.

CHRISTOPHER HERWIG / GETTY IMAGES ©

**2011**

Forty years after the atrocities of the Liberation War, an internal war-crimes trial begins, with several former and current political leaders facing accusations of crimes against humanity.

» Political mural

# Environment

## The Land

Famous for being flat and wet, Bangladesh is, largely speaking, one massive piece of gorgeously green farmland criss-crossed by an unfeasibly large network of rivers. It's a rural wonderland, and beautiful to behold. In fact, there's every chance that Bangladesh will be the most gloriously lush country you've ever visited.

There are two exceptions to these flatter-than-flat vistas, although neither is any less green than the rest of the country. First there's Sylhet, in the northeast, with its soft, rolling hills covered in dark-green, waist-high tea bushes. Then there's the Chittagong Hill Tracts, in the far southeast, a forested region punctuated by cliffs, ravines and some small mountains ranges. It's no Himalaya, but the peaks here are comparable in height to those found in the Scottish Highlands, and make for some good hiking.

The great news for travellers is that Bangladesh is very small. With a total area of just 143,998 sq km (roughly the same size as England and Wales combined), it's an easy country to explore, and you can visit much of it in a single trip.

It is surrounded on three sides by India, but also shares a short southeastern border with Myanmar (Burma) for 283km. To the south is the Bay of Bengal, into which flow all those rivers.

The two great Himalayan rivers, the Ganges and Brahmaputra, help divide the land into seven major regions, which correspond to the seven governmental divisions: northwest (Rangpur), west (Rajshahi), southwest (Khulna), south-central (Barisal), central (Dhaka), northeast (Sylhet) and southeast (Chittagong).

Almost all the Bangladesh coastline forms the so-called Mouths of the Ganges, the final destination of the Ganges River, and the largest estuarine delta in the world. The coastal strip from the Sundarbans, in the west, to Chittagong, in the east, is one great patchwork of shifting river courses and silt islands. Across the whole delta, which extends into India, rivers make up 6.5% of the total area.

## Animals

Bangladesh is home to the Royal Bengal tiger and other members of the cat family, including leopards and the smaller jungle cat. Tigers are almost exclusively confined to the Sundarbans, but their smaller relations prey on domestic animals all over the country. There are three varieties of civet, including the large Indian civet, which is now listed as an endangered species. Other large animals include Asiatic elephants (mostly migratory herds from Bihar, although there are still some around Teknaf in the far southeastern tip of Bangladesh), a few black bears in Chittagong division, wild pigs and deer. Monkeys, langurs, gibbons (the only ape on the subcontinent), otters and mongooses are some of the smaller animals.

In all of Bangladesh, the only place that has any stone is a quarry in the far northwestern corner of Sylhet division. It's one reason you'll see bricks being hammered into pieces all over the country: brick fragments are substituted for stones when making concrete.

*Ganges*, the 2007 BBC TV series and DVD, is a sumptuously filmed exploration of the Ganges River, its people and its wildlife. The last program in the series focuses largely on the Sundarbans.

## THE CYCLONE ZONE

Every few years it seems Bangladesh is hit by another disaster. While there are periodic floods and droughts, the most catastrophic disasters in terms of human life are cyclones.

Bangladesh is in the world's worst area for cyclones, averaging one major storm every three years. The worst months are May and June, and October and November, and the area where damage tends to most frequently occur is in the east around Chittagong and Cox's Bazar.

People still talk about the 1970 cyclone when between 300,000 and 500,000 people died. The 1991 cyclone, which occurred during big spring tides, was stronger, affected over twice as many people and destroyed four times as many houses. However, the death toll of between 140,000 and 200,000 was less than half that of the 1970 disaster.

Most recently, in 2007, Cyclone Sidr became the strongest storm to hit the country in 15 years. It struck the southwest coast and left 3500 people dead, but it's generally acknowledged that the death toll would have been far higher were it not for the early warning system that was installed after the 1991 storm.

Reptiles include various ocean turtles, mud turtles, river tortoise, pythons, crocodiles and a variety of venomous snakes. The voluble gecko, named for the sound it makes, is known here as *tik-tiki*.

## Endangered Species

The Royal Bengal tiger is endangered and although the government has set aside three areas within the Sundarbans as tiger reserves, numbers are low. For more information on the environment and the wildlife of the Sundarbans, see p71.

Other rare or threatened species include the Indian elephant, the hoolock gibbon, the black bear and the Ganges River dolphin. Reptiles under threat include the Indian python, the crocodile and various turtles.

Many of the diverse bird species are prolific, but some are vulnerable, including Pallas' fishing eagle and Baer's pochard.

## Birds

Sitting like a cushion between the plains of India and the hills of Myanmar (Burma), the waterways of Bangladesh are a bird-watcher's dream. The country contains more than 650 species of birds – almost half of those found on the entire subcontinent.

The country's positioning means that Bangladesh attracts both Indian species in the west and north of the country, and Malayan species in the east and southeast. It is also conveniently located for migrants heading south towards Malaysia and Indonesia, and those moving southwest to India and Sri Lanka. In addition, a number of Himalayan and Burmese hill species move into the lowlands during the winter.

Madhupur National Park, in Dhaka division, is an important habitat for a variety of owls, including the rare brown wood owl, wintering thrushes and a number of raptors, although sadly it also the victim of ongoing logging. The Jamuna River floods regularly, and from December to February provides winter habitats for waterfowl, waders and the occasional black stork.

The low-lying basin of Sylhet division has extensive natural wetlands, or *haors* (p138), and during winter it is home to huge flocks of wild fowl, including Baer's pochard and Pallas' fishing eagle, along with a great number of ducks and skulkers. The remaining fragments of evergreen and teak forests are also important habitats, especially along the Indian border near the Srimangal area, where the blue-bearded bee-eater, redbreasted trogon and a variety of forest birds are regularly seen.

The Sundarbans Tiger Project (www.sundarbanstigerproject.info) tells you all you ever wanted to know about tigers, the Sundarbans and the ongoing conservation projects taking place there.

Wild buffaloes and rhinoceroses once inhabited the Sundarbans, but became extinct last century.

## WATER WORLD

Floods are almost the first thing that people think of when talk turns to Bangladesh, but even so, if you arrive by air during the monsoon season you'll be astounded at how much of the country appears to be under water. Many first-time visitors to Bangladesh assume that the flooding is due to heavy rainfall during that time of year. In fact, local rainfall is only partly responsible – most of the water comes pouring down the Padma (known as the Ganges upstream in India), the Meghna and the Jamuna (Brahmaputra) Rivers.

For Bangladeshis, annual flooding is a fact of life and one that, with an ever-increasing population, bad land management and global climate change, is only likely to get to worse. However, much of the flooding (which affects about a third of the country) is regarded by farmers as beneficial, as worn soils are replenished with nutrients. It's when the rivers rise above their normal limits that problems emerge.

Major flooding struck northwest Bangladesh and Chittagong in 2007, but in 2004 really heavy flooding over much of the country resulted in the deaths of around 800 people, while in 1998 all three of the country's major rivers reached flood levels at the same time and 16 million people were left homeless. In Dhaka, even houses on fairly high ground were inundated, and the airport was covered with water and had to be shut down.

One of two important coastal zones is the Noakhali region, particularly the islands near Hatiya, where migratory species and a variety of wintering waders (including large numbers of the rare spoon-billed sandpiper, Nordman's greenshank and flocks of Indian skimmers) find suitable refuge.

The Sundarbans (p71), with its miles of marshy shorelines and brackish creeks, supports a number of wetland and forest species, along with large populations of gulls and terns along the south coast. Eight varieties of kingfisher have been recorded here, including the brown-winged, the white-collared, the black-capped and the rare ruddy kingfisher.

The most exciting time of year for bird-watching is during winter, from November to March.

## Plants

About 10% of Bangladesh is still forested. Half of the forest is in the Chittagong Hill Tracts and a quarter in the Sundarbans, with the rest scattered in small pockets throughout the country.

The forests fall into three distinct regional varieties: the tidal zones along the coast, often mangrove but sometimes hardwood, in much of the Sundarbans; the sal trees around Dhaka, Tangail and Mymensingh; and the upland forests of tropical and subtropical evergreens in the Chittagong Hill Tracts and parts of Sylhet.

Away from the forests, Bangladesh is still a land of trees. Lining the old trunk road in the west are huge rain trees, and every village is an arboreal oasis, often with spectacular *oshot* (banyan) trees. The red silk-cotton (kapok) tree is easily spotted throughout the countryside in February and March, when it loses its leaves and sprouts myriad red blossoms. Teak was introduced into the Hill Tracts in the 19th century and the quality approaches that of Myanmar.

Flowering plants are an integral part of the beauty of Bangladesh. Each season produces its special variety of flowers. Among them is the prolific water hyacinth, its carpet of thick green leaves and blue flowers giving the impression that solid ground lies underneath. Other decorative plants that grow easily are jasmine, water lily, rose, hibiscus, bougainvillea, magnolia and an incredible diversity of wild orchids in the forested areas.

SOLITARY PALM

What is thought to be the world's single surviving wild *Corypha taliera* palm tree grows in the grounds of Dhaka University.

# Environmental Issues

Bangladesh faces huge environmental problems, many of which boil down to overpopulation. Farmland soils are being damaged by overuse, rivers are being polluted by chemical pesticides and forests are being chopped down at an alarming rate. The water table is under threat as deep tube-wells extract clean water for drinking.

Annual flooding during the monsoon season is part of life in Bangladesh. Some experts are questioning whether the flooding is getting worse and, if so, whether deforestation in India and especially Nepal (which causes increased runoff) is the reason. Another theory holds that the river beds have become choked with silt from once-forested land, making flooding more severe. Regardless, there has been increased pressure to 'do something' and find a 'permanent solution'. Part of the problem of doing anything, however, is that the country depends on regular flooding for its soil fertility, and simply building massive dykes along river banks could be disastrous for agricultural output.

With the continuance of global warming, Bangladesh, as one of the 10 countries most vulnerable to a rise in sea level, will be drastically affected. If predications are correct, a 1m rise in the Bay of Bengal would result in a loss of 12% to 18% of the country's land.

Loss of land is just one consequence – severe flooding and reduced agricultural potential are almost inevitable. This is indeed a cruel twist of fate, since Bangladesh, as a poor, agricultural society, has contributed very little to global warming. Even with assistance from the Dutch, who are helping to devise a strategy to cope with rising water levels, the question remains whether Bangladesh will have the capacity to develop and apply the appropriate technology.

However, there is some good news. Bangladesh is now taking environmental issues very seriously and has implemented some highly commendable policies.

Responding to the high levels of litter, much of which was plastic, Bangladesh became one of the first countries to almost completely ban plastic bags. In many places, especially Dhaka, goods you buy are now packaged in paper or jute bags (so you also support the local jute industry), and although you will still see plastic bags being used and discarded, especially in smaller towns, the amount is noticeably less than in other parts of south Asia.

The government has also taken steps to reduce the horrendous pollution levels in Dhaka by banning petrol and diesel vehicles from certain central areas of the capital and replacing them with cleaner, greener (and cheaper to run) CNG (compressed natural gas) vehicles. Almost all auto-rickshaws in Bangladesh now are CNG-run. In fact, they are now known colloquially as CNGs.

The government's recent work at improving and protecting national parks should also be lauded, as it attempts to step up environmental education for the public.

Bangladesh's rivers contain unusually high levels of arsenic. When you buy bottled water, always check that it reads 'arsenic free' and that the seal is unbroken.

Bird-watchers will enjoy A Photographic Guide to the Birds of India & the Indian Subcontinent by Bikram Grewal and Bill Harvey. It has useful maps and pictures, and is compact enough to take with you.

> 

# Arts & Literature

The art, music and literature of Bengal is among the strongest of the Indian subcontinent. The people of the Bengal region, whether they're from Bangladesh or India, share a similarity of language, dress, music and literature that crosses the national boundaries.

From the poetry of Nobel laureate Rabindranath Tagore to the unmistakeable sound of the folk music of the Bauls, Bengali culture is steeped in tradition and loved by millions.

## Literature

Best known in the literature of Bangladesh are the works of the great Bengali poets Rabindranath Tagore (1861–1941) and Kazi Nazrul Islam (1899–1976), whose photos are displayed in restaurants and shops countrywide. Tagore received international acclaim in 1913 when he was awarded the Nobel Prize for Literature for his book *Gitanjali (Song Offerings)*. Despite his Hindu upbringing, Tagore wrote from a strong cultural perspective that transcended any particular religion. He celebrated 'humble lives and their miseries' and supported the concept of Hindu–Muslim unity. His love for the land of Bengal is reflected in many of his works, and one of his songs, *Amar Shonar Bangla,* was adopted as the national anthem. Interestingly, Tagore also wrote and composed *Jana Gana Mana,* India's national anthem. Travellers can soak up inspiration from the great man by visiting his former home in a small village just outside Kushtia (p81).

The 'rebel poet' and composer Kazi Nazrul Islam is considered the national poet. When the country was suffering under colonial rule, Islam employed poetry to challenge intellectual complacency and spark feelings of nationalism.

Of modern writers, the most famous is the exiled feminist writer Taslima Nasrin, whose controversial book *Lajja* (Shame; 1993) was not only banned in Bangladesh but also earned her a *fatwa* (death sentence for blasphemy), and forced her to flee the country. It recounts the history surrounding the contentious destruction of the Babri Mosque in Ayodhya, in India, but depicts it through the eyes of a Hindu family in Bangladesh.

Tahmina Anam's acclaimed debut novel, *A Golden Age* (2007), is a story of love, betrayal and family loyalties, set against the backdrop of the Liberation War. The second of her planned trilogy, *The Good Muslim* (2011), follows a war-scarred family as it faces the challenges of peace.

One of the world's first examples of feminist science fiction, *Sultana's Dream* (Rokeya Sakhawat Hussain, 1905) is a groundbreaking novel that depicts a feminist utopia in which women run everything and men are secluded – a mirror image of the traditional Islamic practice of purdah.

*Like a Diamond in the Sky* (Shazia Omar, 2009) is a brave attempt to raise awareness of drug addiction among Dhaka's young middle class.

Non-Bangladeshi authors who have written about the country include Katy Gardner, whose *Songs at the Rivers Edge* (1991) is a wonderful memoir of her year spent living in a small village in Sylhet; and James Novak,

For current news on the arts scene in Bangladesh, as well as what's-on listings in Dhaka, go to the Arts & Entertainment section of the *Daily Star* website (www.thedaily star.net).

## BEST FILMS

**The Clay Bird** (Matir Moina; Tareque Masud, 2002) Celebrated feature-film debut of the late Tareque Masud, which won the International Critic's Award at the 2002 Cannes Film Festival. Simply beautiful.

**Homecoming** (Ontarjatra; Tareque Masud, 2006) Also called *The Journey*, this was Masud's follow-up film; a touching story of a woman and her son returning to Bangladesh from their London home.

**Runaway** (Amit Ashraf, 2010) Edgy, feature-length drama by an American-Bangladeshi director, which exposes the suffering involved when Bangladeshi men leave their families in search of a better life.

**Agami** (Morshedul Islam, 1984) The short film is generally regarded as the film that kick-started Bangladesh's Alternative Film Movement.

**Songs of Freedom** (Muktir Gaan; Tareque Masud, 1995) A documentary of Liberation War footage shot by American filmmaker Lear Levin.

**Bostrobalikara: The Garment Girls of Bangladesh** (Tanvir Mokammel, 2007) A candid look at the workers behind Bangladesh's ever-growing clothes industry.

**Teardrops of Karnaphuli** (Tanvir Mokammel, 2005) This film documents the local tensions that have plagued the Chittagong Hill Tracts since the controversial construction of the Kaptai Dam in Rangamati.

ARTS & LITERATURE MUSIC

whose *Reflections on the Water* (1993) is a passionate account of the birth of Bangladesh from a journalist who worked there in the mid-1980s.

## Music

The distinctive folk music of the Bauls (mystic minstrels), dating from around the 17th century, can be heard across Bengal, as well as in some films about the region. Bauls most commonly play the one-stringed plucked instrument known as the *ektara,* accompanied by other musicians playing lutes, flutes and cymbals. You can see people performing Baul music if you travel to Kushtia, the resting place of the legendary Baul musician Lalon Shah, and the location of a twice-annual folk music festival (boxed text p83).

The poet Rabindranath Tagore was also a prolific song writer and undoubtedly influenced much of the Bangla music that's composed today.

Western influence helped spawn the new phenomenon of Bangla Bands, the name given to any band that plays modern music – from pop and rock to grunge and heavy metal – performed in Bengali.

You can tune your ears to sound of Bangla music before you leave home these days. BBC Radio's **Asian Network** (www.bbc.co.uk/asiannetwork) has a regular Bengali slot, and **Radio Dhaka** (www.radiodhaka.net) has a live online feed.

From popular music to the latest movies, www.banglamusic.com provides news, commentary and events listings from Bangladesh's entertainment industry.

## Cinema

The 1984 short film *Agami,* directed by Morshedul Islam, is widely regarded as the catalyst for the birth of the Alternative Film Movement, the name given to Bangladesh's independent film industry. It provides an alternative to the largely musical-based blockbusters that are churned out each year by Dhaka's mainstream film industry, 'Dhallywood', and has spawned creative talents such as the late Tareque Masud, whose award-winning 2002 film *The Clay Bird* is arguably the best independent film to have come out of Bangladesh.

The Art of Kantha Embroidery, by Naiz Zaman, uses drawings and photographs to explain the technique of nakshi *kantha* and give a face to the women involved in its production.

## Folk Art

Weaving has always held a special place in the artistic expression of the country. In the 7th century, the textiles of Dhaka weavers found their way to Europe, where they were regarded as *textiles ventalis* (fabrics woven of air).

## RICKSHAW ART

One of your first, and perhaps strongest, impressions of Bangladesh is likely to be the rainbow colours of a cycle-rickshaw. More than just a cheap and environmentally sound form of transport, the humble rickshaw is a work of art in Bangladesh and a fleet of rickshaws is the finest art galley any country could conjure up. Art passing by on wheels needs to be bold and eye-catching, and able to be taken in quickly. Rickshaw artists aim to decorate the vehicles with as much drama and colour as possible, and paint images that are both simple and memorable. This is street art for the ordinary man or woman, and it is unashamedly commercial.

*Maliks*, the owners of rickshaw fleets, commission *mistris* (rickshaw makers) to build and decorate the machines to their specification. The artists working in the *mistri's* workshop learn on the job, sometimes starting out as young as 10, when they work decorating the upholstery and smaller sections of the vehicle.

The main 'canvas' is recycled tin, from a drum of cooking oil for example. This forms the backboard of the rickshaw. Enamel paints are used. The artist may also decorate the seat, handlebars, the curved back of the seat, the chassis, the hood and just about every other surface. The handlebar decorations in particular can be wildly elaborate, with intricate coloured plastic tassels 20cm long.

All the dreams of the working man appear on rickshaws. Common themes include idealised rural scenes; wealthy cities crammed with cars, aeroplanes and high-rise buildings; unsullied natural environments; and dream homes with sports cars parked outside. Images of Bangladeshi and Indian film and pop stars are by far the most popular designs. The portraits often make the actors plumper than in real life – a slim figure isn't a fantasy when so many go hungry. The images of women with heart-stopping stares are a great contrast to the real women on the street, who by custom avoid eye contact with unfamiliar men.

The most artistic and expensive ornamental fabric is the *jamdani* (loom-embroidered muslin or silk), which was exclusively woven for the imperial household centuries ago and evolved as an art form under the influence of Persian design.

Needlework has become a cottage industry. Best known are *nakshi kantha,* embroidered and quilted patchwork cloths that hold an important place in village life, with the embroidery recording local history and myth.

Once found only among a woman's private possessions, *nakshi kanthas* can be seen in Bangladesh hanging on the walls of upmarket hotels, offices and in museums, an artistic symbol not just of Bangladeshi women but the nation as well.

Traditionally, *nakshi kanthas* were mostly made in the central and western divisions of Bangladesh. They are made from worn-out clothing, particularly saris, and six or so layers of material are stitched together in a way that leaves a rippled surface. They are often given as wedding gifts to a daughter leaving home, or to a grown son as a reminder of his mother. Besides the usefulness of recycling old material, there is also a folk belief that a *nakshi kantha* made from old material brings good luck. The jealous gods won't harm someone dressed in rags – infants are often dressed in *nakshi kantha* nappies for this reason.

There are women's cooperatives that produce *nakshi kantha* commercially; one good place to look is Aarong in Dhaka (p51).

## Modern Art

Arguably the most pervasive form of popular culture in Bangladesh is the paintings found on rickshaws and other vehicles (see the boxed text p162).

The turbulence of life in Bangladesh has given artists much to express, which they do with wondrous diversity. See the boxed text p43 for galleries in Dhaka.

# Bangladesh Cuisine

The fiery curries and delicately flavoured biryanis that make up so much of Bangladeshi cuisine will keep you drooling throughout your adventures in this country. Bengalis (both in Bangladesh and India's West Bengal) consider their food to be the most refined in the subcontinent and though this causes debate, everyone is in agreement that Bengali sweets truly are the finest you can dip your sticky fingers into.

## Main Meals

A typical Bangladeshi meal includes a curry made with vegetables and either beef, mutton, chicken, fish or egg, cooked in a hot spicy sauce with mustard oil and served with dhal (cooked yellow lentils) and plain rice. Rice is considered a higher-status food than bread – therefore, at people's homes you will generally be served rice.

### Curries

Many menus refer to *bhuna* (or *bhoona*), which is the delicious process of cooking spices in hot oil and is the basis for many Bangladeshi dishes. It also refers to a specific type of dry curry cooked in coconut milk (more common in India than Bangladesh). Another common dish is *dopiaza* (literally 'double onions'), which, as the name suggests, contains large amounts of onion added to the curry in two separate stages. Finding purely vegetarian dishes can be quite difficult because in Bangladesh meat is highly prized. Ask for *bhaji* which, as well as being a ball of fried vegetables (such as the onion *bhaji*) is also a general term for a simple vegetable curry. A mixed vegetable dish would be *shobji bhaji,* although it is sometimes just called *shobji* (pronounced 'sabzee'). At fancy dinners an all-vegetarian meal would not be well received.

### Rice

The three main forms of rice dishes that you're likely to encounter are biryani, *pula* (also known as *polao),* which is similar to biryani but without the meat, and *bhat* (plain rice). Rice and lentils mixed together and cooked is called *khichuri* and is perfect for upset tummies.

### Fish

Fish is every Bangladeshi's favourite meal. The fish you are most likely to eat – boiled, smoked or fried – are *hilsa* and *bhetki.* These are virtually the national dishes of Bangladesh and it's said they can be prepared in around 50 different ways. Smoked *hilsa* is very good, but be prepared to pay five-star prices for it. *Bhetki* is a variety of sea bass with lots of flesh and few bones. It's one of the best fish you'll eat and is served in mid-range restaurants along with prawn and crab dishes.

As in India, *cha* (tea) is sold on practically every street corner in Bangladesh. Unlike in India, though, each cup is made individually (rather than stewing all day), which means that you can order it without sugar (*chini na* or *chini sera*) or without milk (*lal ch;* literally 'red tea').

## HABITS & CUSTOMS

Traditionally, Bengali meals are served on the floor and eaten with fingers rather than cutlery. Each person sits on a *pati* (a small piece of straw carpet). In front of the *pati* is a large platter or banana leaf, around which bowls are placed.

For the uninitiated, eating with your hands feels odd, but it's a strangely liberating experience and we recommend you try it. Bangladeshis say that it allows for an appreciation of textures before they are enjoyed by the tongue.

### Dos & Don'ts

» It is courteous to use only the right hand to receive or give things. This is especially important when it comes to food. The left hand is considered unclean, given its use in the bathroom.

» You may break bread with both hands, but *never* put food into your mouth with the left.

» Water may be drunk from a glass with the left hand because it is not being directly touched.

» Always wash your hands before you eat – for the sake of courtesy as well as of hygiene.

## Kebabs

Kebabs will be some of the most delicious food you'll eat in Bangladesh, and they come in a wide variety including *shami kebab,* made with fried minced meat, and *sheekh kebab,* which is prepared with less spice and usually with mutton or beef. You'll also find tandoori chicken grilled on spits. Chicken tikka is also common and usually served with Indian-style naan (slightly puffed wholewheat bread cooked in a tandoori oven).

*The Book of Indian Sweets,* by Satarupa Banerjee, is a godsend for those who develop a craving for *roshogullas* (a syrupy dessert) and other teeth-rotting Bengali treats.

## Breakfast

A Bengali breakfast is usually *shobji bhaji* and dhal, with a few roti (chapati), sometimes eaten with a spicy omelette, and nearly always washed down with a cup of *cha* (tea). It's fresh, filling and delicious.

## Sweets

The Bangladeshis have a sweet tooth. You'll find sweet shops all over the country, selling all manner of sticky-finger delights. A popular dessert is *misti doi* (sweetened yogurt); another is jaggery, a fudgelike sweet made from sugarcane or date palm. Also look out for *chom chom,* a syrupcoated cake made from paneer, and *monda,* a sweetened yogurt cake.

SYRUPY DESSERTS

# Vegetarians & Vegans

The key phrase to learn here is *'ami mangso khaina'* (I don't eat meat), followed closely by *'ami mash khaina'* (I don't eat fish). Bengali cuisine is filled with fruit and vegetables, but getting restaurants to grasp the fact that you really do only eat vegetables can be tough.

In Dhaka, your choices of restaurants with good vegetarian food will be pretty decent. Don't forget to also try the Western-style cafes. Elsewhere, and particularly in small towns and villages, you'll be mostly eating dhal and *shobji.* There's also a good range of freshly baked flat breads – naan and roti being the most common. Eggs, often in the form of delicious spicy omelettes, are also widely available, while the explosion of Chinese restaurants offers other vegetarian options, such as noodles.

Your on-the-road saviour will be Bangladesh's wonderful array of fresh fruit. Oranges, apples and bananas are everywhere, while the mango orchards in western Rajshahi grow some of the world's best mangoes. Mango season is May to June.

# Survival Guide

# Directory A–Z

## Accommodation

Generally speaking, the quality of accommodation in Bangladesh is poor, although this is reflected in extremely affordable prices. It's probably wise to lower your expectations of comfort and cleanliness before you come, to avoid being too disappointed. Only in Dhaka, and at a handful of other exceptional places around the country, could we find accommodation that was genuinely very good. We have marked these with our TOP CHOICE icon.

### Top End

There are a few international-standard top-end hotels in Dhaka, but apart from these, the top-end hotels we list in this book are, generally speaking, comfortable business-class hotels, rather than luxurious places to stay.

### Midrange

Midrange hotels will be clean, and will come with air-con, TV and an attached bathroom that will usually have a hot-water shower. Rooms in this bracket tend to be rather spartan, though.

### Budget

Places we list as budget really are no-frills. If you're used to roughing it as a budget backpacker around places like India, then they will be clean enough, although they are often far from spotless. In the very cheap places you may want to use your own sleeping sheet or sleeping bag rather than the sometimes grubby bed sheets provided. Budget rooms will come with a small attached bathroom (unless we state otherwise), although budget hotel showers are often cold-water only and the toilets are often squat jobs.

## BOOK YOUR STAY ONLINE

For more accommodation reviews by Lonely Planet authors, check out http://hotels.lonelyplanet.com. You'll find independent reviews, as well as recommendations on the best places to stay. Best of all, you can book online.

## PRICE RANGE FOR HOTELS

$$$ over Tk 2000 a night
$$ Tk 750-2000 a night
$ under Tk 750 a night

### Hotel Facilities

Pretty much every hotel room in every price bracket in Bangladesh comes with a TV, and the good news for sports and movie fans is that TV is almost always multi-channel cable TV, with plenty of English-language options.

Very few hotels outside Dhaka have wi-fi, or an internet connection of any sort, but we've indicated those that do.

Almost all midrange and top-end hotels have their own restaurant. Many budget ones do too.

Budget hotels without hot-water showers will provide a bucket of hot water if you ask.

## Activities

**Cycling** Bangladesh's lush but lazy terrain makes it a wonderful place for cycling, and this country is a magnificent place to cycle tour around. The best place for casual cycling is Srimangal (boxed text p142).

**Hiking** There are some lovely walking and hiking to be done in forest reserves and national parks, particularly in Sylhet and Chittagong divisions, but undoubtedly the best place for hiking is the Chittagong Hill Tracts. See the boxed text p122.

**River Trips** Travelling by riverboat is a way of life in Bangladesh, and river trips are a highlight for most travellers. See p26 for more details.

## Business Hours

Banking hours tend to be 10am to 4pm Sunday to

Thursday. Some banks in bigger cities will also open from 6pm to 8pm. And often, but not always, banks open for a couple of hours on a Saturday afternoon, typically 2pm to 4pm. Banks, like internet cafes and most offices, are never open on a Friday.

Other business hours vary from restaurant to restaurant and from shop to shop, so we've listed them with every review.

# Children

Travelling with young children in Bangladesh is tough because of low levels of hygiene and general health and safety issues, but that doesn't mean it can't be done. Bangladeshis, who are among the most welcoming people you'll ever meet, are fascinated by foreign children and everyone will go out of their way to help you if you have kids in tow.

From a food standpoint, dishes of boiled rice and unspiced dhal (yellow lentils), scrambled or boiled eggs, oatmeal and the huge variety of fruits and vegetables should be enough to keep kids happy. Snacks like biscuits and crisps are also widely available.

You'll be hard pressed coming across highchairs and nappy-changing facilities, but formula milk and disposable nappies can be found at some supermarkets in towns and cities.

## Courses

**HEED** (Health, Education, Economic Development; Map p46; ☑881 2390, 989 6028; hlc@agni. com; House 104, Rd 12, Block

E, Banani, Dhaka) A well-run, friendly language school offering Bengali classes (per hour/month Tk 500/8000) for varying ability levels.

# Customs Regulations

The usual '200 cigarettes, 1L of alcohol' rule applies, though a relatively casual approach is employed at border crossings. Foreigners are permitted to bring in US$5000 without declaring it and Bangladeshis can bring in US$2500.

On departure, tourists are allowed to reconvert 25% of the total foreign currency encashed in the country. This is only possible at the airport in Dhaka, and you will need to have your encashment slips with you as proof.

# Electricity

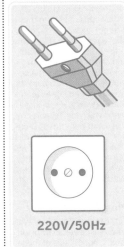

220V/50Hz

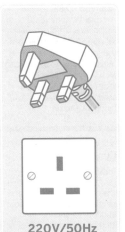

220V/50Hz

# Embassies & Consulates

The following selected embassies and consulates are all in Dhaka and can all be found on Map p46.

**Australia** (☑881 3101-5; www.bangladesh.embassy.gov.au; 184 Gulshan Ave, Gulshan II, Dhaka)

**Canada** (☑988 7091-7; www.canadainternational.gc.ca/bangladesh; Madani Ave, Baridhara, Dhaka)

**France** (☑881 3811-4; www.ambafrance-bd.org; House 18, Rd 108, Gulshan, Dhaka)

**Germany** (☑985 3521; www.dhaka.diplo.de; 178 Gulshan Ave, Gulshan II, Dhaka)

**India** (☑988 9339; www.hcidhaka.org; House 2, Rd 142, Gulshan I, Dhaka)

**Italy** (☑882 2781-3; www.ambdhaka.esteri.it; Plot 2/3, cnr Rds 74 & 79, Gulshan II, Dhaka)

**Myanmar** (☑988 8903; www.mofa.gov.mm/myanmar missions/bangladesh.html; House 3, Rd 84, Gulshan II, Dhaka)

**Netherlands** (☑882 2715-8; bangladesh.nlembassy.org; House 49, Rd 90, Gulshan II, Dhaka)

---

**TRAVEL WITH CHILDREN**

Lonely Planet's *Travel with Children* is a collection of tips and experiences from our team of parent-authors, and includes practical advice on how to avoid hassles, keep boredom at bay and have rewarding travel experiences with kids. Also has a special section on staying healthy.

Thailand (☑881 2795-6; www.thaidac.com; 18-20 Madani Ave, Baridhara, Dhaka)
UK (☑882 2705-9; ukinban gladesh.fco.gov.uk; cnr 13 United Nations Rd & Dutabash Rd, Baridhara, Dhaka)
USA (☑885 5500; dhaka .usembassy.gov; Madani Ave, Baridhara, Dhaka)

## Gay & Lesbian Travellers

Homosexuality is illegal in Bangladesh, and homosexual acts are punishable under Bangladesh law with deportation, fines and/or prison. Such harsh laws are rarely enforced, however. Nevertheless, gay travellers would be wise to be discreet in Bangladesh.

**Boys of Bangladesh** (www.boysofbangladesh.org) is the oldest and largest organization of self-identified Bangladeshi gay men.

**Sakhiyani** (groups.yahoo .com/group/sakhiyani) is Bangladesh's first online group for lesbian and bisexual women.

## Insurance

Any policy you get should cover medical expenses and an emergency flight home. Always check the fine print. Some policies exclude coverage of 'dangerous activities', which can include motorcycling and trekking.

For theft and loss you will require documentation from the Bangladeshi police; getting it can be a hassle and often requires a 'fee'.

Worldwide travel insurance is available at www.lonelyplanet.com/ travel_services. You can buy, extend and claim online any time – even if you're already on the road.

See also p181 for health insurance details.

## Internet Access

### Internet Cafes

Internet cafes are found in every town and city, although they are surprisingly rare in Dhaka. Connections are generally pretty slow, although we've tried to list the fastest ones. Note that internet cafes are always closed on Fridays.

### Wi-fi

Wi-fi is still rare in Bangladesh, although it's increasingly common in Dhaka, where wi-fi coffee shops (boxed text p51) are growing in popularity. Most top-end and some midrange hotels provide free wi-fi and/or internet connection through a cable for laptop users. Some do still charge a fee, though.

### Remote Modems

If you're staying for a few weeks or more it's worth considering buying a remote modem for your laptop so you can connect to the internet anywhere you have phone reception. They come in the form of a USB stick and can be bought from any of Bangladesh's major mobile telephone providers. We recommend **Grameenphone** (www.grameenphone. com), which has reliable coverage and well-run retail outlets. We've listed one in North Dhaka (Map p46) where you can get connected, but they are all over the country. One month's unlimited use costs around Tk 1000.

### Plug Adaptors

Some top-end hotels provide universal power adaptors in rooms, but outside of those rare cases you'll need to bring your own. If you are travelling with a laptop or some other electronic device, remember to bring a 220V, 50 Hz AC adaptor. If you forget to bring one, you may be able to track one down in Dhaka. Stadium Market (Map p40) would be a good bet.

## Legal Matters

Drug offences are taken seriously in Bangladesh and can result in the death penalty if considerable quantities are seized. Anyone, including foreigners, caught smuggling virtually any amount of drugs or gold can end up with a prison sentence for life. As a matter of practice, courts permit those charged to have access to a lawyer.

Under the Vienna Convention on Consular Relations, to which Bangladesh is a signatory, any foreign national under detention has a right to request that their embassy be notified of their situation.

## Maps

The best map publisher, **Mappa** (www.mappa.com.bd), produces English-language maps for Bangladesh, Dhaka, Chittagong, Sylhet and Cox's Bazar. You can find them in some bookshops and the better handicrafts shops in Dhaka.

## Money

The local currency of Bangladesh is the taka (Tk), which is further divided into 100 paisas. The largest note is Tk 1000.

Torn notes may sometimes be refused, although most banks will exchange them for you.

### ATMs

A growing number of ATMs accept foreign bank cards, particularly Visa. At the time of research, the most reliable ATMs were AB Bank, Standard Chartered Bank, Trust Bank and HSBC, which had branches in Dhaka, Chittagong and Sylhet. We've marked foreign-friendly ATMs on our maps.

It's worth stocking up on taka when you can, though, because there are still a lot of places, particularly in more remote areas, where you can't change or withdraw money.

## Cash

It's always a good idea to bring a small amount of cash, in American dollars, for emergencies.

## Credit Cards

Visa, MasterCard and American Express are usually accepted by major hotels and restaurants in Dhaka and Chittagong.

Cash advances on credit cards can be made at Standard Chartered and HSBC banks.

## Moneychangers

There are private moneychangers at border towns.

## Tipping

In expensive restaurants in Dhaka that are mostly frequented by foreigners, waiters often expect a small tip, typically about 5%. In any other type of restaurant it is not necessary to tip.

Most hotels add a service charge, as well as VAT, onto their advertised rates, although this is often negated by the discounts on offer.

## Travellers Cheques

Put simply, don't bother! Only the biggest international banks are likely to accept them and even then it will be with great reluctance.

## Post

Bangladesh's postal system is slow and unreliable, although you should be ok if you use Dhaka's main post office (Map p40), which is also the poste restante.

If you want to be certain of the item you are sending actually reaching its destination, we suggest you use a courier company. DHL and FedEx both have branches in Dhaka.

## Safe Travel

### Road Safety

The most real danger when travelling around Bangladesh is road safety, which is extremely poor, especially on intercity highways. Bus travel is, quite frankly, scary, and road deaths are all too common. Travel by train when you can.

Within larges towns and cities, take extra care when walking as a pedestrian because city-centre roads – and pathways – can best be described as hectic, and are often downright dangerous.

### Crime

Bangladesh is generally pretty safe and few tourists experience crime. Pickpocketing on crowded buses and at busy markets is not as endemic as in some other

Asian countries, but it does happen.

Some foreigners have been mugged, some at gunpoint, in upmarket areas of Dhaka, such as Gulshan – be careful after dark.

There have also been reports of theft committed by both touts and officials at Dhaka and Sylhet airports. Keep a very close eye on your passport and other papers.

Rickshaws present theft and mugging opportunities (keep your handbags out of sight), and women especially should be extremely careful of any taxi containing a driver and his 'friend'.

We have had some rare reports of harassment of foreigners in the form of pushing, stone throwing and spitting, but such incidents are very uncommon.

There are ripples of terrorist activity, targeted assassinations, politically motivated attacks and, sometimes, violent religious rivalry. But major incidents are infrequent. The most recent significant attack was in May 2007, when bombs exploded at train stations in Dhaka, Sylhet and Chittagong, though there were no fatalities. Foreigners have never been targeted in such incidents, but some travel advisories warn foreign nationals to stay away from large gatherings to cut down on the 'wrong place, wrong time' possibility.

You're more likely to get tangled up in a hartal (strike). These can turn violent and it's not unusual for locals who are involved in them to be killed or seriously injured as a result.

The Chittagong Hill Tracts (boxed text p120) is the only part of the country where there is an ongoing security concern, but even here the problem areas are usually out of bounds to foreign tourists.

## Pollution & Illness

Pollution levels are very high in Dhaka and Chittagong and may affect people prone to allergies.

---

### BAKSHEESH

Baksheesh (*bohk*-sheesh), in the sense of a tip or gift rather than a bribe (an admittedly fine line), is part of life in Bangladesh. It's not really seen as begging here; it's part of Islamic morality that rich people give some of their income to those less fortunate. There are some peculiarities to this system, though; if you're going to be repeatedly using a service, an initial tip ensures that decent standards will be kept up.

Don't feel persecuted – well-to-do locals also pay baksheesh on a regular basis. Always be conscious of the expectations that will be placed on the next foreigner in light of the amount you give and don't feel embarrassed about not giving baksheesh to someone who rendered absolutely no service at all.

## STARING & HARASSMENT

Foreigners are still extremely rare in Bangladesh (although less so in Dhaka) and, as such, are a source of fascination for many locals. This usually manifests itself in people being extremely friendly, but it can become overly intrusive at times, particularly for female travellers. People taking photos and videos of you is something you will just have to accept, and on occasion you may find yourself being stared at by large groups of people, all eager to see what you're doing (even if you're actually doing very little). Sharing your food around, particularly if you're being stared at on buses and trains, is always a good ice-breaker, but other than that you will just have to arm yourself with a great deal of patience. Getting angry will only focus attention on you even more.

Stomach upsets are common for visitors to Bangladesh, and malaria is a serious risk in the Chittagong Hill Tracts region. See the Health chapter (p181) for more details.

### Scams

Tourism has not really established itself in Bangladesh, and neither have tourist-related scams. Generally speaking, people are incredibly honest. The most common problem is being over-charged, but in a non-fixed-priced market this can hardly be called a scam.

There are the usual hassles with cycle-rickshaw, CNG (auto-rickshaw) and taxi drivers, though even here the level of harassment is minimal compared to some nearby countries, and in many towns it's possible to just hop on a rickshaw without pre-negotiating a price and not suffer the consequences!

## Shopping

You don't get hassled to buy things here, mainly because there isn't very much produced with the tourist market in mind. Even quality postcards are hard to come by.

Things not to buy are products made from wild animals, reptiles, seashells and coral, all of which are under pressure to survive in this crowded country. There is also a trade in the country's artistic treasures, which are often plundered from Hindu temples.

### Handicrafts

Souvenirs include jewellery, garments, brasswork, leatherwork, ceramics, jute products, artwork, woodcarvings and clay or metal sculptural work. Unique items include *jamdani* (loom-embroidered muslin or silk) saris, jute doormats, wall pieces, glass bangles and reed mats. Quality is generally high and the prices generally low.

Jute carpets, if you have the room, are a real deal. The better ones are similar to Oriental wool carpets, although they don't last as long; perhaps five or more years.

The best place to buy handicrafts is Dhaka – see p51 for details – where you can get almost anything that's sold elsewhere, though you may be able to find more unusual Adivasi handicrafts in the Chittagong Hill Tracts (p122) and in the villages around Srimangal (p142).

### Clothing

The Bangladeshi garment industry is one of the biggest producers of Western clothing, which you can either buy from high-street fashion-label stores around Gulshan or at the enormous Banga Bazar (Map p36) in the form of cheap seconds and overruns. There's also a good range at New Market (Map p40).

Many visitors choose to buy traditional Bangladeshi clothing, either to wear here (it's much more suited to the hot conditions) or to take home as a gift or souvenir. Again, Dhaka is the best place to look. See p51.

## Solo Travellers

Those who are travelling alone on the assumption that they will meet other travellers on the road should think again. You may, but you'll probably be able to count them on one hand. To increase your chances, the best thing to do is join a short tour (to the Sundarbans would be perfect) to suss out candidates. Or, better still, get onto the Bangladesh branch of the Lonely Planet forum Thorn Tree (www.lonelyplanet.com/thorntree) to see if anyone will be in the same places at the same time.

Having said that, travelling alone through Bangladesh can be an extremely rewarding experience, and won't cost you much more money than travelling with company – most hotels offer single-rate rooms.

## Telephone

### Mobile Phones/ Smart Phones

Mobile coverage is good, and hooking up to the local network is both easy and cheap. Make sure your phone has been unlocked before you come, so that you can use it on a foreign network, then just buy a local SIM card (Tk 70 to Tk 150) when you arrive. You'll need a passport photo and a photocopy of your passport to do this.

**Grameenphone** (www.grameenphone.com), which has the best coverage nationwide, has a counter selling SIM cards as you exit customs at the airport (even at 3am!). It also has branches across the country. We've listed one in North Dhaka (p53).

If you haven't brought your phone from home, or it's locked, then just buy a cheap mobile phone in Dhaka for use on the road here. They cost from around Tk 1600.

Local calls and text messages from a local SIM cost next to nothing. International rates depend on the country, but can be as cheap as Tk 7 per minute, or Tk 2 per text.

You can go to almost any phone shop to top up (you don't have to go to the provider whose network you're using), and some corner shops also do top-ups. The phrase used here for topping-up your phone is 'flexi-load'.

Bangladesh still didn't have a 3G network at the time of research, but you could buy a local SIM card for your smart phone, then add a chosen amount of gigabytes' worth of internet usage. 1GB costs around Tk 350.

### Internet Calls

Internet cafes generally don't have headphones or cameras available to allow you to use free-call services such as Skype, but it's worth asking the manager who might at least have headphones to lend you.

### Landlines

Only top-end hotels, and small business centres, which are dotted around the country, will have international lines, but using them will be much more expensive than using your mobile

phone with a local SIM. Rates, though, are 25% lower all day on Friday and on other days from 11pm to 8am.

The numbers for long-distance information are ☑103 (domestic) and ☑162 (international). International operators speak English; others usually don't.

### Phone Codes

To call a number in Bangladesh from outside the country, dial country code ☑880, followed by the city or mobile code without the leading 0, and then the number.

To call a different city from within Bangladesh, dial the city code including the leading zero, followed by the number.

To call another country from Bangladesh, dial ☑00 followed by the country code and city code.

We've listed city codes under the city headings in each regional chapter.

## Time

Bangladesh is six hours ahead of GMT.

## Toilets

In midrange and top-end establishments you'll find sit-down toilets. Otherwise it's squat loos the whole way.

The ritual in toilets is to use your left hand and water, rather than toilet paper. A strategically placed tap and jug are usually at hand. If you can't master the local method or don't even want to try,

toilet paper is widely available to buy, although not available in public bathrooms themselves. Sometimes a basket is provided where paper and tampons can be discarded.

There are very few facilities at bus stations and other public places, and what facilities exist are pretty horrific. It pays to do your thing back at your hotel. Hotel rooms usually have a roll of toilet paper in the bathroom.

By and large you will find that Bangladeshi hospitality extends to letting you use a toilet, if you ask nicely enough.

In rural areas, it can be difficult to find both toilets and privacy. For women in a desperate situation, a long skirt will make this awkward position a little less so.

## Tourist Information

The national tourist office is the **Bangladesh Parjatan Corporation** (www.parjatan. gov.bd), although it has more of a presence in terms of nationwide hotels than useful information. Its hotels are overpriced, but they do offer reliable levels of comfort and cleanliness, and in smaller towns they are often the best place to sleep in terms of quality.

In general, though, for anything other than the most basic tourist-related questions, it's better to consult a private tour company.

### Recommended Tour Companies

**The Guide Tours** (www. guidetours.com)

**Bengal Tours** (www.bengal tours.com)

**Bangladesh Ecotours** (www.bangladeshecotours .com)

**Sundarban Tours & Resort** (www.bangladeshsun darbantours.com)

---

### RICKSHAW ART

One distinctly Bangladeshi souvenir is a piece of authentic rickshaw art. These colourful back flaps of rickshaws are lightweight and easy to pack in the flat of your bag or backpack. Rickshaw art is not a tourist industry, so you'll have to shop where the rickshaw-wallahs shop. The few centrally located shops are on Bangshal Rd (aka Bicycle St) in Dhaka; the area where most bicycle parts and are sold. See the boxed text p162 for more information.

## YOUR GUARDIAN ANGEL

Special mention must be made to Thorn Tree legend **Mahmud Hasan Khan** (☎0171 4044498; mahmud.ban gladesh@gmail.com). Mahmud is essentially the guardian angel of travellers in Bangladesh and can be found dispensing invaluable advice on the Bangladesh branch of Lonely Planet's Thorn Tree forum (www.lonelyplanet .com/thorntree). He doesn't work for the tourist industry, although if he can wrangle some time off work he'll happily accompany you as your guide for a fee. Instead, in the classic manner of many Bangladeshis, he helps travellers only to ensure that they leave Bangladesh with good impressions.

## Travellers with Disabilities

Outside Dhaka's five-star hotels (boxed text p45), facilities for disabled travellers are almost nonexistent in Bangladesh, and conditions in general make travelling extremely challenging. Some footpaths are difficult for even the able-bodied to traverse. In fact, with its squat toilets, overcrowded buses and absence of elevators in all but the finest buildings in Dhaka, it would seem that the country has contrived to keep out everyone except the most fit and able.

On the other hand, hiring private transport and guides, and enlisting the services of a tour company to help you get around, is much cheaper than in other countries.

There are no Bangladesh-based travel companies which specialise in travel for disabled people, but **Able Travel** (www.able-travel.com) has excellent general tips and information on travelling with disabilities to more challenging destinations.

## Visas

With some obscure exceptions, visas are required for citizens of all countries, but note that Israeli passport-holders are forbidden from entering Bangladesh.

Visa validity and the granted length of stay seems to vary from embassy to embassy, but typically you will be issued with a visa, which is valid for three months from the date of issue, and good for stays of one to two months. Visa fees vary according to nationality, whether you are seeking single or multiple entry, and which embassy you are applying through.

### Visa Extensions

To apply for visa extensions you will need to visit the **Immigration and Passport Office** (Map p40; ☎889 750; Agargaon Rd, Dhaka; ◷Sat-Thu) in Dhaka. This is also the office where long-term visitors are required to register.

Extending a tourist visa is relatively painless: fill in the relevant form, pay the fee (this should be the same as the fee for a one-month visa), and pick up a receipt, which will tell you when to return (usually three or four days later – you can keep hold of your passport during this time).

If you just want an extension of a few days, it may be worth simply paying the penalty fee at the airport for overstaying your visa: it's Tk 200 per day, for up to 15 days. After 15 days, though, it's Tk 500 per day, from day one.

## Change of Route Permits

Officially, if you exit Bangladesh by means other than that by which you entered (ie you flew in, but are leaving by land), you will need a change of route permit, also sometimes referred to as a road permit. Change of route permits are also acquired at the Immigration and Passport Office in Dhaka, are free and shouldn't take more than 24 hours to process. You will need a couple of passport photos.

However, it's worth noting that in recent years very few travellers have been asked to show this permit, so in practise there's no need to obtain it. To be absolutely sure, though, check the Thorn Tree forum (www.lonelyplanet. com/thorntree) to see what other travellers have had to do recently.

## Volunteering

NGOs and other charitable organisations have a big presence in Bangladesh and many welcome help from foreign visitors. Listed is a selection of organisations that welcome interns and/or shorter-term volunteers:

**Banchte Shekha** (☎0171 8940644; www.banchteshekha .org; in Jessore, Khulna Division) Fights to improve the quality of life for poor women and children of the region. Contact Shouruve Ansari (education.bs@gmail. com) for possible internships and/or volunteering.

**BRAC** (Bangladesh Rural Advancement Committee; ☎02 988 1265; www.brac.net; in Dhaka) One of the world's largest NGOs; has a range of internship programmes.

**BRIF** (Bangladesh Rural Improvement Foundation; www. brif.org, vbp@brif.org; Goaldihi Village, Dinajpur, Rajshahi Division) Works to raise the socio-economic conditions of poor people across the area. Has volunteer opportunities for skilled workers in fields such as agriculture, business, IT, teaching and childcare.

**CRP** (Centre for the Rehabilitation of the Paralysed; ☏02 774 5464; www.crp-bangladesh.org; in Savar, Dhaka Division) The only organisation of its kind in Bangladesh; focuses on a holistic approach to rehabilitation. Has short-term volunteer opportunities as well as longer-term positions for medically trained professionals such as physiotherapists.

**The Dhaka Project** (☏0171 2620316, 02 891 7550; www.thedhakaproject.org; in Dhaka) Provides food, shelter, clothing, education and medical care for children from the slums of Dhaka. Very well established. Has a number of volunteering opportunities.

**RDRS** (Rangpur-Dinajpur Rural Service; ☏0171 3200185, 0521 66490; www.rdrsbangla.net; in Rangpur, Rajshahi Division) Works on health, education and agricultural projects in Bangladesh's far northwest. Has a formal internship program as well as some shorter-term volunteering opportunities.

# Women Travellers

By and large the default response to the unusual sight of a Western woman travelling in Bangladesh is respect; try not to do anything that would make you less than worthy of it. Bangladesh is safer than a lot of Muslim countries, but it's wise to be careful. How you carry yourself subtly determines how you are treated. A woman who is politely assertive can ask for space and usually gets it. The other side of the harassment coin, and almost as much of a nuisance, is that people are constantly making elaborate arrangements to protect you from harassment.

Keep in mind that in this society women are not touched by men, but because you're a foreigner, it might happen. A clear yet tactful objection should end the matter.

Tampons are available from some upmarket supermarkets (like Agora). Sanitary napkins and panty liners are widely available, but be sure to carry adequate supplies if you're travelling away from major cities.

# What to Wear

Dressing like a local is not obligatory, or even expected, but it will certainly impact on the way you are treated. You will still get attention, but the attention you get will be more respectful and appreciative of the fact that you have made the effort. Many foreigners invest in a *salwar kameez* (a long dresslike tunic worn over baggy trousers). A dupatta (long scarf) to cover your head also increases the appearance of modesty and is a handy accessory in the Bangladesh heat. You can get away with wearing baggy trousers and a long loose-fitting shirt in most parts of the country. Long, loose skirts are also acceptable and provide the added advantage of a modicum of privacy in the absence of a public toilet. Make sure you wear a headscarf at places of worship. Most mosques don't allow women inside, although some have a special women's gallery. If in doubt, ask.

# Eating

In a Bangladeshi middle-class home you would most likely be expected to eat first with the men while the women of the household tuck themselves away in another part of the house or dutifully serve the meal. In rural areas you might not eat with either; instead you would be served first and separately, as a gesture of respect. Accept either graciously. Protest would cause great embarrassment on the part of your host.

In restaurants you may be shown to the curtained women's rooms. This is a courteous offer that you can decline, though you may find that the curtain provides something of a respite from the eyes that will be on you if you sit elsewhere.

# Getting Around

On buses, unaccompanied women are expected to sit at the front. If you are travelling with your 'husband' you are expected to sit on the window side, away from the aisle. Avoid travelling alone at night; Bangladeshi women avoid going out alone at night as much as possible.

## Where to Stay

Women, with or without men, are sometimes unwelcome in budget hotels, usually because the manager thinks the hotel is not suitable. This knee-jerk reaction can sometimes be overcome if you hang around long enough. On the other hand, staying in one of these cheaper establishments, especially if you are going solo, can be more trouble than it is worth. Midrange hotels that are accustomed to foreigners are the best bet. Unmarried couples are better off simply saying they're married.

# Transport

## GETTING THERE & AWAY

### Entering the Country

To enter Bangladesh you will need a passport that's valid for at least six months beyond the duration of your stay. An onward/return ticket is preferred, although not always essential.

Rules and procedures for entering and exiting Bangladesh seem to be in a constant state of flux. In 2011, Bangladesh reintroduced visas on arrival (see the boxed text p173 for details on this and on visas in general), but this could change again.

Note that Bangladesh currently refuses entry to Israeli passport holders.

### Air

#### Airports & Airlines

There are three international airports in Bangladesh:

**Dhaka** Hazrat Shahjalal International Airport (DAC)

**Chittagong** Shah Amanat International Airport (CGP)

**Sylhet** Osmani International (ZYL)

Dhaka's **Hazrat Shahjalal International Airport** (☎02 819 4350; www.caab.gov.bd) is easily the busiest of the three. It's pretty basic for a capital-city airport but it has money-changing facilities, including ATMs that accept foreign cards, some duty-free shops and a couple of restaurants.

There's an official taxi rank, although it's cheaper to try your luck with taxis and CNGs (auto-rickshaws) outside. At some stage in the future, the proposed Dhaka Metro will link the airport to the city, but that's still a long way off.

See p53 for information on airlines.

The unofficial website for the airport (www.shahjalalairport.com) has a useful flight-status feed.

#### Asia

There are direct flights to/from all nearby Asian countries, and the newly agreed route between Dhaka and Rangoon in Myanmar may be operational by the time you read this. Most connections are through Dhaka, although it is possible to use Chittagong airport for India and Thailand. At the time of research, Sylhet's airport only operated occasional international flights, such as those to Mecca during the Hajj pilgrimage.

From Dhaka, you can get particularly cheap flights to Thailand, Malaysia, India, China and the Middle East. Singapore's budget airline, Tiger Airways, had just started flights to Dhaka at the time of research.

#### Australia

There were still no direct flights to and from Australia at the time of research, although steps were being

---

## CLIMATE CHANGE & TRAVEL

Every form of transport that relies on carbon-based fuel generates $CO_2$, the main cause of human-induced climate change. Modern travel is dependent on aeroplanes, which might use less fuel per kilometre per person than most cars but travel much greater distances. The altitude at which aircraft emit gases (including $CO_2$) and particles also contributes to their climate change impact. Many websites offer 'carbon calculators' that allow people to estimate the carbon emissions generated by their journey and, for those who wish to do so, to offset the impact of the greenhouse gases emitted with contributions to portfolios of climate-friendly initiatives throughout the world. Lonely Planet offsets the carbon footprint of all staff and author travel.

made to introduce them. Until that happens, it's easiest to fly via Bangkok, Singapore or Kuala Lumpur.

### Continental Europe

There are plenty of flights linking Dhaka with European countries such as Germany, Italy and the Netherlands, although flights usually go via somewhere like Kuala Lumpur or Kolkata. Turkish Airlines now runs direct flights to Dhaka from Istanbul.

### UK & Ireland

You should get some well-priced fares to and from London, often via the Middle East. Pricier direct flights are also available.

### USA

There are basically two ways to get to Bangladesh from the USA. From the west coast virtually everyone flies to Dhaka via Bangkok or Singapore. You can also fly direct to India and connect from there, but it may cost more.

From the east coast most people fly via Europe.

## Land

### Border Crossings

For all the details on how to travel overland in and out of Bangladesh, see our feature on p22.

### Train

See p55 for details on the twice-weekly train from Dhaka to Kolkata.

# GETTING AROUND

Travelling around Bangladesh is extremely cheap, although in many cases it's pretty uncomfortable. Buses are dirt cheap if you don't mind squashing into the ordinary local ones. More comfortable, more expensive coaches are usually available.

Road safety is a real issue in Bangladesh. The country has some of the worst road-

---

### GETTING A BIKE IN DHAKA

It's best to bring your own bicycle and all other safety and technical gear with you, though a couple of decent-quality bicycle shops do exist in Dhaka.

Head to **Bangshal Rd** (Map p36), an area of Old Dhaka that specialises in making and repairing bikes and rickshaws. Most places sell ordinary, single-gear town bicycles, but a couple of places sell decent-quality bikes and equipment. Try **Lion Cycle Store** (☏0194 7431260; www.facebook.com/LionCycle; 28/1 Bangshal Rd, Old Dhaka).

You may also find OK bike shops in Chittagong, but in other places you'll struggle. However, bike repair shops, catering to all those cycle-rickshaws, are two-a-penny almost everywhere in Bangladesh, so finding basic spare parts shouldn't be a problem unless your bike is unusual.

---

accident figures in the world, and the Dhaka–Chittagong Hwy is notoriously bad.

Trains are a much safer option, although the network is far from extensive, and tickets can be hard to nab. Still, if you can travel by train, you'd be wise to do so.

There are also a handful of domestic flight routes, which are worth considering if you're in a hurry.

Within cities, you'll either be taking rickshaws (cycle-rickshaws) or CNGs (auto-rickshaws), although taxis are also available. Tempos (larger, shared auto-rickshaws) are also common, although tricky to negotiate if you don't speak Bengali.

Of course, the king of travel in Bangladesh is the riverboat. Water travel is an essential part of everyday life for Bangladeshis, and for the foreign traveller a long ferry ride, especially on the smaller rivers where you can watch life along the banks, is one of the undisputed highlights of a trip to Bangladesh. Try to travel by boat whenever you can.

---

## Air

### Airlines in Bangladesh

Bangladesh currently has four domestic airlines. Most travellers say United is the

---

best, although all are distinctly no-frills. All domestic routes are either to or from Dhaka. Destinations include Chittagong, Cox's Bazar, Sylhet, Rajshahi and Jessore. See regional chapters for specific details.

**Biman** (www.biman-airlines .com)

**GMG Airlines** (www.gmgairlines.com)

**Regent Airlines** (www.flyregent.com)

**United Airways** (www.uabdl.com)

---

## Bicycle

### Day Trips

If you hadn't planned a big cycle tour of Bangladesh, but just fancy going on a couple of fun bike rides, then Srimangal in Sylhet division is your best bet. The scenery is lovely, it's easy to rent bikes for the day, and there are plenty of places within easy cycling distance of the town. See the boxed text p142 for more details.

### Touring

With the exception of the city centres of Dhaka and Chittagong, Bangladesh is a wonderful place for cycling and a self-guided cycle tour is a fascinating way to see the country. Most airlines allow you to transport your bike, either for free or for a small fee. Alternatively, you could buy a bike when you arrive in Dhaka before setting off to explore the rest of the country.

With the exception of the tea-estate regions in Sylhet division, the Chittagong Hill Tracts (CHT) and the road between Chittagong and Teknaf, Bangladesh is perfectly flat – you can pedal around very easily with a single-gear bike. In fact, only in the CHT would you definitely need a mountain bike, although given the state of some of the roads you may want a mountain bike in any case, for its sturdiness.

Cities, particularly Dhaka and Chittagong, are not easy or safe places to ride, given manic traffic and pollution, although if you leave early, say 5.30am, you should be able to get out of the city without incident. Alternatively, you can put your bike on the roof of a CNG or a bus. Some travellers have reported not being allowed to take their bikes on board trains.

The trick to cycling in Bangladesh is to avoid major highways as much as possible; look instead for quieter streets that will get you to the same destination. Unfortunately, maps of Bangladesh aren't detailed enough to be of much use – Mappa (p168) is your best bet – so be prepared for some interesting, unintentional detours.

Most paths are bricked and in good condition, and even if it's just a dirt path, bikes will be able to pass during the dry season. A river won't hinder your travel, since there's invariably a boat of some sort to take you and your bike across.

The ideal time to go cycling is in the dry season from mid-October to late March; during the monsoon many tracks become impassable.

Though cycling can by and large be a relaxing way to explore Bangladesh, don't get complacent about your belongings; snatches from saddlebags are not unheard of.

## Boat

See our special feature on boat travel in Bangladesh; p26.

## Bus

Local bus travel is cheap and extremely convenient. Buses to main towns leave frequently, and tickets don't need to be booked in advance, so you can just turn up at a bus station and wait for the next one.

The downside, though, is the often extreme lack of comfort and worryingly poor safety.

For something more comfortable – but no safer – try a private coach instead, although these are less frequent and more expensive.

The country has an extensive system of passable roads. When your bus encounters a river crossing, it generally comes on the ferry with you; the queues of buses waiting to be loaded onto ferries is one of the more frustrating aspects of travel here.

It's illegal to ride on top of a bus, like many locals do, but the police won't stop you. If you do ride on top, though, remember that low trees do kill people each year.

Most bus stations are located on the outskirts of towns, often with different stations for different destinations.

If you're unsure of which bus station to use, just hop in a rickshaw and say the name of the destination you want to travel to followed by the words 'bus stand'. The rickshaw rider will know which bus stand is the best one for your destination. Note, bus stations are nearly always

called bus stands, although some larger ones are known as bus terminals.

Coach companies often have their ticket offices in the town centre rather than at the bus stands, and you sometimes need to book tickets in advance.

### Coaches

The most comfortable bus options are private coaches, which are distinguished by their adjustable seats and extra leg room. Some also have air-con.

Departure hours are fixed and less frequent than local buses, especially for long journeys. Seats should be reserved in advance, although just turning up at the ticket office half an hour before the coach leaves sometimes suffices.

Some coach services travelling between Dhaka and cities on the western side of the country operate at night, typically departing sometime between 5pm and 9pm and arriving in Dhaka at or before dawn. While you'll save on a night's accommodation, you probably won't get a decent night's sleep as there are no proper sleeper buses; you'll just be sleeping in a reclinable seat.

Prices vary from company to company, but there are basically two types of coach – those with air-con and those without. Those with air-con cost about twice as much as those without. Unlike local buses, coaches will often make a lunch stop at a roadside restaurant if you're travelling through the middle of the day.

## POPULAR COACH COMPANIES

Green Line (www.greenlineparibahan.com)
Soudia (☎0119 7015636)
Hanif (☎02 912 0116)
Shohagh Paribahan (www.shohagh.biz)

## RICKSHAW!

To hail a rickshaw, stick your arm straight out and wave your hand downwards. The usual way of waving your arm upwards used in the West appears to a Bangladeshi as 'Go away! To hell with you!'

## Local Buses

Among the ordinary buses there are express buses and local ones, which stop en route. The latter charge about 25% less but can be very slow. In more remote areas local buses may be your only option. Most buses are large, but there are a few minivans (coasters).

The buses run by private companies tend to be in better condition than those of the state-run BRTC.

If you're tall, you're in for a shock; leg room hardly allows for short people to sit with their knees forward, let alone 6ft-tall Westerners. On long trips this can be exceedingly uncomfortable, so try to get an aisle seat if you can.

Women travelling alone sit together up the front, separate from the men. If there is an accident, this is the most dangerous part of the bus to be on. Women travelling with their husbands sometimes sit in the main section, usually on the window side. On long-distance bus trips *cha* (tea) stops can be agonisingly infrequent and a real hassle for women travellers – toilet facilities are rare indeed and sometimes hard to find when they do exist.

One of the most underappreciated professions would have to be the buswallah. These are the men who hang out the door helping people on and off, load oversized luggage onto the roof, bang on the side of the bus telling the driver to stop and go, and uncannily

keep track of who needs how much change. They are usually extremely helpful – they often rearrange things so you are comfortably seated and rarely fail to let you know when the bus has arrived at your destination.

## Car

Travelling by private car has some obvious advantages and disadvantages. On the plus side, it gives you the freedom to quickly and easily go where you please, when you please, and allows for all manner of unexpected pit stops and adventures. On the minus side, it does insulate you somewhat from Bangladesh and it is far more expensive than public transport,

There are two possibilities: either you'll be driving your own vehicle or you'll be the passenger in a rental car, which comes complete with its own driver.

### Hire

Self-drive rental cars are not available in Bangladesh, and that's probably a good thing. However, renting cars with drivers is easy, at least in the big towns.

In Dhaka there are innumerable companies in the rental business. For the best cars and the safest drivers, try one of the more reputable tour operators (p55). Expect to pay at least Tk 4000 a day for a car, plus fuel and driver expenses; when you stay out of town overnight, you must pay for the driver's food and lodging, but this won't cost much. Make sure you determine beforehand what all those extra rates will be, to avoid any misunderstandings. Insurance isn't required because you aren't the driver.

Outside Dhaka, the cost of renting vehicles is often marginally less, but actually finding an available car and driver is much harder and virtually impossible if you want an air-con vehicle. Asking at

the town's top hotel normally produces results.

### Owner-Drivers

Driving in Bangladesh takes nerves of steel and a lot of patience. On the major highways, you'll be pushed onto the curb every few minutes by large buses hurtling down the road. Dhaka presents its own unique driving perils because of the vast number of rickshaws and CNGs. It's a far better – and safer – option to hire a car and driver.

It's sad to say, but if you're in a serious or fatal traffic accident, the local custom is to flee, if you can. Few have much faith in the justice system, so there is an element of self-law in the form of an angry crowd.

## Hitching

Hitching is never entirely safe in any country in the world, and we don't recommend it. Travellers who decide to hitch should understand that they are taking a small but potentially serious risk. People who choose to hitch will be safer if they travel in pairs, and let someone know where they are planning to go. Solo women are particularly unwise to hitchhike. Generally speaking, you will be expected to pay for any ride, as the locals do.

## Local Transport

Bangladesh has an amazing range of vehicles – on any highway you can see buses, cars, rickshaws, CNGs, tempos, tractors with trays laden with people, motorbikes, scooters, bicycles carrying four people, bullock and water-buffalo carts, and bizarre home-made vehicles all competing for space. One local favourite in Rajshahi and Khulna divisions is a sort of minitractor, known as a *nazaman*, which is powered by incredibly noisy irrigation-pump motors.

In Dhaka and Chittagong motorised transport has increased tremendously over the past decade, and traffic jams in Central Dhaka are a nightmare. In Old Dhaka it's not unusual to get caught up in a snarling hour-long traffic jam consisting entirely of cycle-rickshaws. In fact, in Old Dhaka, it's almost always quicker to walk.

What freaks out new arrivals the most is the total chaos that seems to pervade the streets, with drivers doing anything they please and pedestrians being the least of anybody's worries. Accidents do happen and sometimes people are killed, but the odds of you being involved are still fairly slim.

## Boat

Given that there are some 8433km of navigable inland waterways, boats are a common means of getting around. Even if you're not on a long-distance trip, you may find yourself having to cross rivers by boat. Usually you pay a couple of taka for a place on a small wooden ferry. You can also hire private boats, known as *reserve* boats, to get from one town to another. Public ferries, known as a launch, are always worth inquiring about if you're at a town with a river ghat. They may be slow, but they're cheap and are certainly the most pleasant way to get from A to B.

## ONLINE TRAIN TIMETABLES

For a full list of routes, times, journey durations and prices of tickets of all the trains in Bangladesh, go to the official website of **Bangladesh Railway** (www.railway.gov.bd). You can't book tickets here, but it's very useful for planning your journey.

For more on boat travel see p26.

## Bus

If you thought long-distance buses were crowded, wait till you try a local city-centre bus. Just getting on one is a challenge in itself. It can be something of a death-defying process. Firstly, assess whether the bus will get you to your desired destination by screaming the name of the destination to the man hanging out the door. If he responds in the affirmative, run towards him, grab firmly onto a handle, if there is one, or him if there isn't, and jump aboard, remembering to check for oncoming traffic. The chances are you won't be able to squeeze any further inside than the doorway, so just hang on.

## CNG

In Bangladesh three-wheeled auto-rickshaws are called CNGs because most of them these days run on Compressed Natural Gas. As with the rickshaw-wallahs, CNG drivers almost never own their vehicles. They're owned by powerful fleet-owners called *mohajons*, who rent them out on an eight-hour basis. Also like rickshaws, they're designed to take two or three people, but entire families can and do fit.

In Dhaka and Chittagong CNGs are everywhere – most people use them instead of regular taxis. Faster and more comfortable than rickshaws on most trips, CNGs cost about twice as much.

See p55 for more details.

## Rickshaw

In Bangladesh all rickshaws are bicycle driven; there are none of the human-puller variety. Rickshaw-wallahs usually do not speak English, although you may find some English-speaking wallahs hanging around outside top-end hotels; this is certainly the case in Dhaka.

Fares vary a lot, and you must bargain if you care

about paying twice as much as locals, although even that still won't be very expensive. In any case, it is probably unrealistic to expect to pay exactly what Bangladeshis do. As a very rough guide, Tk 10 per kilometre is about right.

## Taxi

Taxis are less abundant than you'd think, even in Dhaka; most people use CNGs. You might be able to hail one from the side of the road if they are on their way to their usual hang-out, but if they're all occupied you are better off heading straight to an intersection or top-end hotel, where you will find a fleet of them waiting. Taxis are all metered, though as with CNGs, drivers are hardly ever willing use them, so you should negotiate the fare before boarding.

Outside Dhaka there are precious few taxis. In Chittagong you'll find a few at the airport or at large hotels and around GEC Circle. In Sylhet, Khulna, Saidpur and possibly Rajshahi you'll see no taxis except for a few at the airport. They are not marked, so you'll have to ask someone to point them out to you.

## Tempo

This is a larger, shared auto-rickshaw, with a cabin in the back. Tempos run set routes, like buses, and while they cost far less than CNGs, they're more uncomfortable because of the small space into which the dozen or so passengers are squeezed. On the other hand, they're a lot faster than rickshaws and as cheap as local buses. You will find tempos in most towns, even relatively small ones.

## Train

Trains are a lot easier on the nerves, knees and backside than buses, and those plying the major routes aren't too bad, while in 1st class they are positively luxurious. However, travel is slowed down by unbridged rivers requiring ferry crossings, circuitous routing and different gauges. This means that a train ride usually takes longer than a bus ride.

## Classes

Intercity (IC) trains are frequent, relatively fast, clean and reasonably punctual, especially in the eastern zone. Fares in 1st class are fairly high (about a third more than an air-con coach), but in *shuvon* chair (2nd class with reserved seating, and better carriages than ordinary *shuvon*) the fare is comparable to that in a non-air-con coach, and the trip is a lot more pleasant and safe.

The carriages in 1st class, which have three seats across, facing each other and separated by a small table, initially seem little different from those in *shuvon*, which have four seats across without tables. However, the difference is that there's always room for just one more passenger in *shuvon*, whereas in 1st class what you see is what you get. Some IC trains also have an air-con 1st class, which is well worth the extra money. Seats here are of the soft and comfortable variety and are similar to those found on trains in the West. This class is always very popular but seats are limited – it's a good idea to reserve as far in advance as you can to get a seat or berth in air-con 1st class, though a quiet word to the station

master can sometimes work wonders.

There are generally no buffet cars, but sandwiches, snacks and drinks are available from attendants. If you're lucky, these attendants will be sharply dressed waiters handing out dainty china cups of tea.

Second-class cars with unreserved seating are always an overcrowded mess and on mail trains (which do allow for some passenger cargo) your trip will be even slower than on an IC train. However, you may come out of the experience with a few good stories.

The only sleeper berths are on night trains, and the fare is about 40% more than a 1st-class seat.

## Reservations

The relatively recent introduction of computerised ticketing has made the purchase of train tickets from major stations far less of a headache than it used to be. A fully automated e-ticketing system, allowing passengers to buy tickets online, may well be in operation by the time you read this. Otherwise, you'll have to buy tickets in the old-school way; from a ticket counter at a train station.

Note, in 2012 the ticket-reservation system was changed to only allow passengers to buy tickets three days in advance of their journey (previously it had been 10 days in advance). Check that this is still the case when you arrive, as it's wise to try to book your tickets as soon as they become available to buy.

Ticket clerks will often assume that you want the most expensive seats, unless you make it clear otherwise. Buying tickets on local short-distance trains is a drag because they don't go on sale until the train is about to arrive, which means that while you're battling the ticket queue all the seats are being filled by hordes of locals.

# Health

Travellers tend to worry about contracting infectious diseases in this part of the world, but infections are a rare cause of serious illness or death in travellers. Pre-existing medical conditions such as heart disease, and accidental injury (especially traffic accidents) account for most life-threatening problems. Becoming ill in some way, however, is very common.

Environmental issues such as heat and pollution can cause health problems. Hygiene is generally poor throughout the region so food- and water-borne illnesses are common. Many insect-borne diseases are present, particularly in tropical areas. Fortunately most travellers' illnesses can either be prevented with some commonsense behaviour or be treated easily with a well-stocked traveller's medical kit. Medical care remains basic so it is important to be well prepared before travelling to Bangladesh.

The following advice is a general guide only and does not replace the advice of a doctor trained in travel medicine.

## BEFORE YOU GO

Pack medications in their original, clearly labelled, containers. A signed and dated letter from your physician describing your medical conditions and medications, including generic names, is very useful. If carrying syringes or needles, be sure to have a physician's letter documenting their medical necessity. If you have a heart condition, bring a copy of your ECG taken just prior to travelling.

If you take any regular medication, bring double your needs in case of loss or theft. In most South Asian countries, including Bangladesh, you can buy many medications over the counter without a doctor's prescription, but it can be difficult to find some of the newer drugs, particularly the latest antidepressant drugs, blood-pressure medications and contraceptive pills, in particular outside Dhaka.

## Insurance

Even if you are fit and healthy, don't travel without health insurance – accidents do happen. Declare any existing medical conditions you have – the insurance company *will* check if your problem is pre-existing and will not cover you if it is undeclared. You may require extra cover for adventure activities such as scuba diving. If your health insurance doesn't cover you for medical expenses abroad, consider getting extra insurance. If you're uninsured, emergency evacuation is expensive.

Find out in advance if your insurance plan will make payments directly to providers, or whether the company will reimburse you later for your overseas health expenditures. (In Bangladesh, doctors expect payment in cash.)

## Vaccinations

Specialised travel-medicine clinics are your best source of information; they stock all available vaccines and will be able to give specific recommendations for you and your trip.

Most vaccines don't produce immunity until at least two weeks after they're given, so visit a doctor four to eight weeks before your planned departure. Ask your doctor for an International Certificate of Vaccination (otherwise known as 'the yellow booklet'), which will list all the vaccinations you've received.

### Recommended Vaccinations

The World Health Organisation (WHO) recommends the following vaccinations for travellers to South Asia:

**Adult diphtheria and tetanus** Single booster recommended if none in the past 10 years. Side effects include sore arm and fever.

**Hepatitis A** Provides almost 100% protection for up to a year; a booster after 12 months provides at least another 20 years' protection. Mild side effects such as headache and sore arm occur in 5% to 10% of people.

**Hepatitis B** Now considered routine for most travellers. Given as three shots over six months. A rapid schedule is also available, as is a combined vaccination with Hepatitis A. Side effects are mild and uncommon, usually headache and sore arm. In 95% of people, lifetime protection results.

**Measles, mumps and rubella** Two doses of MMR are required unless you've had the diseases. Occasionally a rash and flulike illness can develop a week after receiving the vaccine. Many young adults require a booster.

**Polio** In 2003 polio was still present in Nepal, India and Pakistan, but it has been eradicated in Bangladesh. Only one booster is required for an adult for lifetime protection. Inactivated polio vaccine is safe during pregnancy.

**Typhoid** Recommended for all travellers to Bangladesh, even if you only visit urban areas. The vaccine offers around 70% protection, lasts for two to three years and comes as a single shot. Tablets are also available, however the injection is usually recommended as it has fewer side effects. Sore arm and fever may occur.

**Varicella** If you haven't had chickenpox, discuss this vaccination with your doctor.

These are recommended for long-term travellers (more than one month) or those at special risk:

**Japanese B Encephalitis** Three injections in all. Booster recommended after two years. Sore arm and headache are the most common side effects. Rarely, an allergic reaction comprising hives and swelling can occur up to 10 days after any of the three doses.

**Meningitis** Single injection. There are two types of vaccination: the quadravalent vaccine gives two to three years' protection; meningitis group C vaccine gives

around 10 years' protection. Recommended for long-term backpackers aged under 25.

**Rabies** Three injections in all. A booster after one year will then provide 10 years' protection. Side effects are rare – occasionally headache and sore arm.

**Tuberculosis** A complex issue. Long-term adult travellers are usually recommended to have a TB skin test before and after travel, rather than vaccination. Only one vaccine given in a lifetime.

## Required Vaccinations

The only vaccine required by international regulations is yellow fever. Proof of vaccination will only be required if you have visited a country in the yellow-fever zone within the six days prior to entering Bangladesh. If you are travelling to Bangladesh from Africa or South America, you should check to see if you will require proof of vaccination.

## Internet Resources

**World Health Organization** (WHO; www.who.int/ith) Publishes the superb *International Travel and Health*, which is revised annually and available for free online.

**MD Travel Health** (www.mdtravelhealth.com) Provides complete travel-health recommendations for every country and is updated daily.

**Centers for Disease Control and Prevention** (CDC; www.cdc.gov) Good general information.

## Further Reading

**Healthy Travel – Asia & India** (Lonely Planet) Handy pocket-sized book.

**Travelling Well** (Dr Deborah Mills) Also has its own website (www.travellingwell.com.au) and smart-phone app.

**Traveller's Health** (Dr Richard Dawood)

# IN BANGLADESH

## Availability of Health Care

In general, medical facilities are not up to international standards and serious cases are likely to be evacuated. Facilities are severely limited outside Dhaka and, as a result, it can be difficult to find reliable medical care in rural areas. Your embassy and insurance company can be good contacts.

See p52 for recommended clinics and hospitals in Dhaka.

Self-treatment may be appropriate if your problem is minor (eg traveller's diarrhoea), you are carrying the relevant medication and you cannot attend a recommended clinic. If you think you may have a serious disease, especially malaria (see p184), do not waste time – travel to the nearest quality facility to receive attention.

Buying medication over the counter is easy, but not generally recommended, as fake medications and drugs that have been poorly stored or are out of date are common.

## Infectious Diseases

### Anthrax

Several hundred cases of the coetaneous form of anthrax were reported in Bangladesh in 2010, in people who consumed beef or had contact with diseased animals. This disease shows up as a boil-like skin lesion that forms an ulcer. Further outbreaks could occur, and the World Health Organisation (WHO) advises travellers to buy beef and beef products from reliable sources and ensure they are well cooked.

### Coughs, Colds & Chest Infections

Respiratory infections are common in Bangladesh. This

## MEDICAL TRAVEL KIT

The following items could be considered for your personal medical kit:

☐ antibacterial cream eg Mupirocin

☐ antibiotics for skin infections eg Amoxicillin/Clavulanate or Cephalexin

☐ antibiotics for diarrhoea eg Norfloxacin or Ciprofloxacin; for bacterial diarrhoea, Azithromycin; for giardia or amoebic dysentery, Tinidazole

☐ antifungal cream eg Clotrimazole

☐ antihistamine: there are many options, eg Cetrizine for daytime and Promethazine for night

☐ antiseptic eg Betadine

☐ antispasmodic for stomach cramps, eg Buscopan

☐ contraceptive method

☐ decongestant eg Pseudoephedrine

☐ DEET-based insect repellent

☐ diarrhoea treatment: consider an oral rehydration solution (eg Gastrolyte), diarrhoea 'stopper' (eg Loperamide) and antinausea medication (eg Prochlorperazine)

☐ first-aid items such as scissors, elastoplasts, bandages, gauze, thermometer (but not mercury), sterile needles and syringes, safety pins and tweezers

☐ Ibuprofen or another anti-inflammatory

☐ indigestion tablets such as Quick Eze or Mylanta

☐ iodine tablets to purify water (unless you are pregnant or have a thyroid problem)

☐ laxative eg Coloxyl

☐ migraine medicine: take your personal medicine

☐ paracetamol

☐ permethrin to impregnate clothing and mosquito nets

☐ steroid cream for allergic/itchy rashes, eg 1% to 2% hydrocortisone

☐ sunscreen and hat

☐ throat lozenges

☐ thrush (vaginal yeast infection) treatment eg Clotrimazole pessaries or Diflucan tablet

☐ Ural or equivalent, if you're prone to urine infections.

usually starts as a virus and is exacerbated by environmental conditions such as pollution in the cities. Commonly a secondary bacterial infection will intervene – marked by fever, chest pain and coughing up discoloured or blood-tinged sputum. If you have the symptoms of an infection, seek medical advice or commence a general antibiotic.

### Dengue Fever

This mosquito-borne disease is becoming increasingly problematic in the tropical world, especially in the cities. As there is no vaccine avail-

able it can only be prevented by avoiding mosquito bites. The mosquito that carries dengue bites day and night, so use insect avoidance measures at all times. Symptoms include high fever, severe headache and body ache (dengue was previously known as 'breakbone fever'). Some people develop a rash and experience diarrhoea. There is no specific treatment, just rest and paracetamol – do not take aspirin as it increases the likelihood of haemorrhaging. See a doctor to be diagnosed and monitored.

### Hepatitis A

A problem throughout the region, this food- and waterborne virus infects the liver, causing jaundice (yellow skin and eyes), nausea and lethargy. There is no specific treatment for hepatitis A; you just need to allow time for the liver to heal. All travellers heading to South Asia should be vaccinated against hepatitis A.

### Hepatitis B

The only sexually transmitted disease that can be prevented by vaccination, hepatitis B is spread by body fluids, including sexual contact. In some parts of South Asia up to 20%

of the population are carriers of hepatitis B, and usually are unaware of this. In Bangladesh the number of carriers is just below 10%. The long-term consequences can include liver cancer and cirrhosis.

## Hepatitis E

Transmitted through contaminated food and water, hepatitis E has similar symptoms to hepatitis A, but is far less common. It is a severe problem in pregnant women and can result in the death of both mother and baby. There is currently no vaccine, and prevention is by following safe eating and drinking guidelines.

## HIV

HIV is spread via contaminated body fluids. Avoid unsafe sex, unsterile needles (including those in medical facilities) and procedures such as tattoos. The rate of HIV infection in South Asia is growing rapidly, although Bangladesh itself is a low HIV-prevalence country, with less than 0.1% of the population estimated to be HIV-positive.

## Influenza

Present year-round in the tropics, influenza (flu) symptoms include high fever, muscle aches, runny nose, cough and sore throat. It can be very severe in people over the age of 65 or in those with underlying medical conditions such as heart disease or diabetes – vaccination is recommended for these individuals. There is no specific treatment, just rest and paracetamol.

Avian influenza has been confirmed in Bangladesh; short-term travellers are not considered to be at high risk.

## Japanese B Encephalitis

This viral disease is transmitted by mosquitoes and is rare in travellers. Like most mosquito-borne diseases it is becoming a more common problem in affected countries. Most cases occur in rural areas and vaccination is recommended for travel-

---

## HELP PREVENT MOSQUITO BITES

» Use a DEET-containing insect repellent on exposed skin. Wash this off at night, as long as you are sleeping under a mosquito net. Natural repellents such as citronella can be effective, but must be applied more frequently than products containing DEET.

» Sleep under a mosquito net impregnated with permethrin.

» Choose accommodation with screens and fans (if not air-conditioned).

» Impregnate clothing with permethrin in high-risk areas.

» Wear long sleeves and trousers in light colours.

» Use mosquito coils.

» Spray your room with insect repellent before going out for your evening meal.

---

lers spending more than one month outside of cities. There is no treatment, and a third of infected people will die, while another third will suffer permanent brain damage.

## Malaria

For such a serious and potentially deadly disease, there is an enormous amount of misinformation concerning malaria. You must get expert advice as to whether your trip puts you at risk. In the Chittagong Hill Tracts region in particular, the risk of contracting malaria far outweighs the risk of any tablet side effects. Remember that malaria can be fatal. Before you travel, seek medical advice on the right medication and dosage for you. Malaria in South Asia, including Bangladesh, is chloroquine resistant.

Malaria is caused by a parasite, transmitted through the bite of an infected mosquito. The most important symptom of malaria is fever, but general symptoms such as headache, diarrhoea, cough or chills may also occur. A diagnosis can only be made by taking a blood sample.

Two strategies should be combined to prevent malaria: mosquito avoidance and antimalarial medications. Most people who catch ma-

laria are taking inadequate or no antimalarial medication. There is a variety of antimalarial medications:

**Doxycycline** This daily tablet is a broad-spectrum antibiotic that has the added benefit of helping to prevent a variety of tropical diseases including leptospirosis, tick-borne diseases and typhus. The potential side effects include photosensitivity (a tendency to sunburn), thrush in women, indigestion, heartburn, nausea and interference with the contraceptive pill. More serious side effects include ulceration of the oesophagus – you can help prevent this by taking your tablet with a meal and a large glass of water, and never lying down within half an hour of taking it. It must be taken for four weeks after leaving the risk area. Note: while we advise you bring any antimalarial medication with you from home, Doxycycline is available to buy at Lazz Pharma (p53), a 24-hour pharmacy in Dhaka.

**Lariam** (Mefloquine) Lariam has received much bad press, some of it justified, some not. This weekly tablet suits many people. Serious side effects are rare but include depression, anxiety, psychosis and having fits. Anyone with a history of depression, anxiety, other psychological disorders or epilepsy should not take Lariam. It is considered safe in the second and third trimesters of pregnancy. Tablets must be taken for four weeks after leaving the risk area.

**Malarone** This drug is a combination of Atovaquone and Proguanil. Side effects are uncommon and mild, most commonly nausea and headache. It is the best tablet for scuba divers and for those on short trips to high-risk areas. It must be taken for one week after leaving the risk area.

A final option is to take no preventive medication but to have a supply of emergency medication should you develop the symptoms of malaria. This is less than ideal, and you'll need to get to a good medical facility within 24 hours of developing a fever. If you choose this option, the most effective and safest treatment is Malarone (four tablets once daily for three days). Other options include Mefloquine and Quinine but the side effects of these drugs at treatment doses make them less desirable. Fansidar is no longer recommended.

## Measles

Measles remains a significant problem in Bangladesh. This highly contagious bacterial infection is spread via coughing and sneezing. Most people born before 1966 are immune as they had the disease in childhood. Measles starts with a high fever and rash, and can be complicated by pneumonia and brain disease. There is no specific treatment.

## Rabies

This is a common problem in South Asia. Around 30,000 people die from rabies in India alone each year, and there are more than 2000 deaths annually in Bangladesh. This uniformly fatal disease is spread by the bite or lick of an infected animal – most

commonly a dog or monkey. You should seek medical advice immediately after any animal bite and commence postexposure treatment. Having pretravel vaccination means the postbite treatment is greatly simplified. If an animal bites you, gently wash the wound with soap and water, and apply iodine-based antiseptic. If you are not prevaccinated, you will need to receive rabies immunoglobulin as soon as possible. This is very difficult to obtain outside of Dhaka.

## STDs

Sexually transmitted diseases most common in Bangladesh include herpes, warts, syphilis, gonorrhoea and chlamydia. People carrying these diseases often have no signs of infection. Condoms will prevent gonorrhoea and chlamydia but not warts or herpes. If, after a sexual encounter, you develop any rash, lumps, discharge or pain when passing urine, seek immediate medical attention. If you have been sexually active during your travels, have an STD check on your return home.

## Tuberculosis

While TB is rare in travellers, those who have significant contact with the local population, such as medical and aid workers, and long-term travellers, should take precautions. Vaccination is usually only given to children under the age of five, but adults at risk are recommended to have pre- and post-travel TB testing. The main symptoms are fever, cough, weight loss, night sweats and tiredness.

## Typhoid

This serious bacterial infection is spread via food and water. It gives a high and slowly progressive fever and headache, and may be accompanied by a dry cough and stomach pain. It is diagnosed by blood tests and treated with antibiotics. Vaccination is recommended for all travellers spending more

than a week in South Asia. In Bangladesh the risk is medium level but the infection is also antibiotic resistant. Be aware that vaccination is not 100% effective, so you must still be careful with what you eat and drink.

## Traveller's Diarrhoea

Traveller's diarrhoea is by far the most common problem affecting travellers; between 30% and 70% of people will suffer from it within two weeks of starting their trip. In over 80% of cases, traveller's diarrhoea is caused by bacteria, and therefore responds promptly to treatment with antibiotics. Treatment with antibiotics will depend on your situation – how sick you are, how quickly you need to get better and where you are etc.

Traveller's diarrhoea is defined as the passage of more than three watery bowel actions within 24 hours, plus at least one other symptom such as fever, cramps, nausea, vomiting or generally feeling unwell.

Treatment consists of staying well hydrated; rehydration solutions such as Gastrolyte are the best for this. Antibiotics such as Norfloxacin, Ciprofloxacin or Azithromycin will kill the bacteria quickly.

Loperamide is just a 'stopper' and doesn't get to the cause of the problem. It can be helpful, for example, if you have to go on a long bus ride. Don't take Loperamide if you have a fever, or blood in your stools. Seek medical attention quickly if you do not respond to an appropriate antibiotic.

### Amoebic Dysentery

Amoebic dysentery is rare in travellers but is often misdiagnosed by poor-quality labs in South Asia. Symptoms are similar to bacterial diarrhoea: fever, bloody diarrhoea and generally feeling unwell. You should always seek reliable medical care if you have blood in your diarrhoea. Treatment involves two drugs: Tinidazole or Metronidazole to kill the parasite in your gut, and then a second drug to kill the cysts. If left untreated, complications such as liver or gut abscesses can occur. Bacterial dysentery is more common.

## Giardiasis

Giardia is a parasite that is relatively common in travellers. Symptoms include nausea, bloating, excess gas, fatigue and intermittent diarrhoea. 'Eggy' burps are often attributed solely to giardia, but work in Nepal has shown that they are not specific to giardia. The parasite will eventually go away if left untreated, but this can take months. The treatment of choice is Tinidazole, with Metronidazole being a second-line option.

# Environmental Hazards

## Air Pollution

If you have severe respiratory problems, speak with your doctor before travelling to any heavily polluted urban centres. Dhaka and Chittagong are among the most polluted cities in the world. This pollution also causes minor respiratory problems such as sinusitis, dry throat and irritated eyes. If troubled by the pollution, leave the city for a few days and get some fresh air. There's plenty of it in Bangladesh!

## Food

Eating in unhygienic restaurants can cause traveller's diarrhoea. Ways to avoid it include eating only freshly cooked food, and avoiding shellfish and food that has been sitting around in buffets. Peel all fruit, cook vegetables, and soak salads in iodine water for at least 20 minutes. Eat in busy restaurants with a high turnover of customers.

## Heat

Parts of Bangladesh are hot and humid throughout the year. For most people it takes at least two weeks to adapt to the hot climate. Swelling of the feet and ankles is common, as are muscle cramps caused by excessive sweating. Prevent these by avoiding dehydration and excessive activity in the heat. Take it easy when you first arrive. Don't eat salt tablets (they aggravate the gut), but drinking rehydration solution or eating salty food helps. Treat cramps by stopping activity, resting, rehydrating with double-strength rehydration solution, and gently stretching.

### HEAT EXHAUSTION

Dehydration is the main contributor to heat exhaustion. Symptoms include feeling weak, headache, irritability, nausea or vomiting, sweaty skin, a fast, weak pulse and a slightly elevated body temperature. Treatment involves getting out of the heat and/or sun, fanning the victim and applying cool, wet cloths to the skin, laying the victim flat with their legs raised, and rehydrating with water containing one-quarter of a teaspoon of salt per litre. Recovery is usually rapid, but it is common to feel weak for some days afterwards.

### HEATSTROKE

Heatstroke is a serious medical emergency. Symptoms come on suddenly and include weakness, nausea, a hot, dry body with a temperature of over 41°C, dizziness, confusion, loss of coordination, fits and eventually collapse and loss of consciousness. Seek medical help and commence cooling by getting the person out of the heat, removing their clothes, fanning them, and applying cool, wet cloths or ice to their body, especially to the groin and armpits.

### PRICKLY HEAT

Prickly heat is a common rash in the tropics, caused by sweat being trapped under the skin. The result is an itchy rash of tiny lumps. Treat by moving out of the heat and into an air-conditioned area for a few hours and by having cool showers. Creams and ointments clog the skin, so they should be avoided. Locally bought prickly-heat powder can be helpful.

## Insect Bites and Stings

### BEDBUGS

Bedbugs don't carry disease, but their bites are very itchy. They live in the cracks of furniture and walls, and then

---

### DRINKING WATER

» Never drink tap water, and avoid ice.

» Bottled water is generally safe – check the seal is intact, and that it is labelled 'arsenic free'.

» Avoid fresh juices – they may have been watered down.

» Boiling water is the most efficient method of purifying it.

» The best chemical purifier is iodine. It should not be used by pregnant women or those with thyroid problems.

» Water filters should also filter out viruses. Ensure your filter has a chemical barrier such as iodine and a small pore size, eg less than four microns.

migrate to the bed at night to feed on you. You can treat the itch with an antihistamine.

### TICKS
Ticks are contracted after walking in rural areas. They are commonly found behind the ears, on the belly and in the armpits. If you have had a tick bite and experience symptoms such as a rash at the site of the bite or elsewhere, fever or muscle aches, you should see a doctor. Doxycycline prevents tick-borne diseases.

### LEECHES
Leeches are found in humid rainforest areas. They do not transmit any disease, but their bites are often intensely itchy for weeks afterwards and can easily become infected. Apply an iodine-based antiseptic to any leech bite to help prevent infection.

## Skin Problems

Fungal rashes are common in humid climates. There are two common fungal rashes that affect travellers. The first occurs in moist areas that get less air, such as the groin, armpits and between the toes. It starts as a red patch that slowly spreads and is usually itchy. Treatment involves keeping the skin dry, avoiding chafing and using an antifungal cream such as Clotrimazole or Lamisil. *Tinea versicolor* is also common – this fungus causes small, light-coloured patches, most commonly on the back, chest and shoulders. Consult a doctor.

Cuts and scratches become easily infected in humid climates. Take meticulous care of any cuts and scratches to prevent complications such as abscesses. Immediately wash all wounds in clean water and apply antiseptic. If you develop signs of infection (increasing pain and redness), see a doctor.

## Sunburn

Even on a cloudy day sunburn can occur rapidly. Always use a strong sunscreen (at least factor 30) and always wear a wide-brimmed hat and sunglasses outdoors.

HEALTH ENVIRONMENTAL HAZARDS

# Language

Bengali (বাংলা *bang*·la) is the national language of Bangladesh and the official language of the Indian states of Tripura and West Bengal. It belongs to the Indic group of the Indo-Aryan family of Indo-European languages (with Hindi, Assamese and Oriya among its close relatives), and is spoken by approximately 220 million people. Today's Bengali has two literary forms – *sha*·d'u·b'a·sha সাধুভাষা (lit: elegant language), the traditional literary style of 16th-century Middle Bengali, and *chohl*·ṭi·b'a·sha চলিত ভাষা (lit: running language), a more colloquial form based on the Bengali spoken in Kolkata.

Bengali is written in the Brahmi script. Just read our coloured pronunciation guides as if they were English, and you'll be understood. Most Bengali vowel sounds are very similar to English ones. The length of vowels (like the difference between the sounds a and aa) is important. Note that a is pronounced as in 'run', ạ as in 'tap', aa as in 'rather', ai as in 'aisle', ay as in 'day', e as in 'red', ee as in 'bee', i as in 'bit', o as in 'shot', oh as in 'both', oy as in 'boy', u as in 'put', and ui as in 'quick'. Bengali has 'aspirated' consonants (produced with a puff of air, ie a slight 'h' sound). In this language guide we've used the apostrophe to indicate aspirated consonants (eg b'). Another feature of Bengali is the 'retroflex' consonant (pronounced with the tongue bent backwards). In this language guide the retroflex variants of d, r and t are represented by ḍ, ṛ and ṭ respectively. Stress normally falls on the first syllable; in our pronunciation guides the stressed syllable is indicated in italics.

## WANT MORE?

For in-depth language information and handy phrases, check out Lonely Planet's *Hindi, Urdu & Bengali Phrasebook*. You'll find it at **shop.lonelyplanet.com**, or you can buy Lonely Planet's iPhone phrasebooks at the Apple App Store.

## BASICS

'Please' and 'thank you' are rarely used in Bengali. Their absence shouldn't be misread as rudeness – instead, these sentiments are expressed indirectly in polite conversation.

**Hello.** (Muslim greeting)
আস্সালাম ওয়ালাইকুম। · as·*sa*·lam wa·*lai*·kum

**Hello.** (Muslim response)
ওয়ালাইকুম আস্সালাম। · wa·*lai*·kum as·*sa*·lam

**Hello.** (Hindu greeting and response)
নমস্কার। · no·mohsh·kar

**Goodbye.** (Muslim)
আল্লাহ হাফেজ। · al·laa ha·fez

**Goodbye.** (Hindu)
নমস্কার। · no·mosh·kar

**Yes./No.**
হ্যাঁ/না। · hạng/naa

**Please.**
প্লিজ। · pleez

**Thank you (very much).**
(অনেক) ধন্যবাদ। · (o·nek) d'oh·noh·baad

**Excuse me.** (before a request)
শুনুন। · shu·nun

**Excuse me.** (to get past)
একটু দেখি। · ek·tu de·k'i

**Sorry.**
সরি। · so·ri

**How are you?**
কেমন আছেন? · kạ·mohn aa·ch'en

**Fine, and you?**
ভাল, আপনি? · b'a·loh aap·ni

**What's your name?**
আপনার নাম কি? · aap·nar naam ki

**My name is ...**
আমার নাম ... · aa·mar naam ...

**Do you speak English?**
আপনি কি ইংরেজি বলতে পারেন? · aap·ni ki ing·re·ji bohl·ṭe paa·ren

**I don't understand.**
আমি বুঝতে পারছি না। · aa·mi buj'·ṭe paar·ch'i na

## ACCOMMODATION

| Where's a ...? | ... কোথায়? | ... koh·t'a·e |
|---|---|---|
| guesthouse | গেষ্ট হাউস | gest ha·us |
| hotel | হোটেল | hoh·tel |
| tourist bungalow | টুরিষ্ট বাংলো | tu·rist baang·loh |
| youth hostel | ইউথ হস্টেল | ee·ut' hos·tel |

| Do you have a ... room? | আপনার কি ... রুম আছে? | aap·nar ki ... rum aa·ch'e |
|---|---|---|
| double | ডবল | do·bohl |
| single | সিঙ্গেল | sin·gel |

**Can I see it?**
আমি কি এটা দেখতে পারি?   aa·mi ki e·ta dek't'·te paa·ri

| How much is it per ...? | প্রতি ... কত? | proh·ti ... ko·toh |
|---|---|---|
| night | রাতে | raa·te |
| person | জনে | jo·ne |
| week | সপ্তাহে | shop·ta·he |

| heating | হিটার | hi·tar |
|---|---|---|
| hot water | গরম পানি | go·rohm pa·ni |
| running water | কলের পানি | ko·ler pa·ni |

| The ... doesn't work. | ... কাজ করে না। | ... kaaj koh·re na |
|---|---|---|
| air con | এয়ারকন্ডিশনার | e·aar·kon·di·shoh·nar |
| fan | ফ্যান | fan |
| toilet | টয়লেট | toy·let |

## DIRECTIONS

**Where's the (station)?**
(ষ্টেশন) কোথায়?   (ste·shohn) koh·t'ai

**What's the address?**
ঠিকানা কি?   t'i·kaa·na ki

**How far is it?**
এটা কত দূর?   e·ta ko·toh dur

**How do I get there?**
ওখানে কি ভাবে যাব?   oh·k'a·ne ki b'a·be ja·boh

**Can you show me (on the map)?**
আমাকে (ম্যাপে) দেখতে পারেন?   aa·ma·ke (ma·pe) da·k'a·te paa·ren

| Turn ... | ... টান করবেন | ... taarn kohr·ben |
|---|---|---|
| at the corner | কর্নারে | kor·na·re |
| at the traffic lights | ট্রাফিক লাইটে | tra·fik lai·te |
| left | বামে | baa·me |
| right | ডানে | daa·ne |

## SIGNS

### General

| ভিতর | Enter |
|---|---|
| বাহির | Exit |
| ধুমপান নিষেদ | No Smoking |
| হোটেল | Hotel |
| বাস | Bus |
| শৌচাগার | Toilets |
| মহিলা | Women (also for reserved bus seats) |
| পুরুষ | Men |
| পুলিশ স্টেশন | Police Station |
| হাসপাতাল | Hospital |

### Cities

| ঢাকা | Dhaka |
|---|---|
| খুলনা | Khulna |
| রাজশাহি | Rajshahi |
| সিলেট | Sylhet |
| চট্টগ্রাম | Chittagong |
| বরিশাল | Barisal |

| near ... | ...-এর কাছে | ...er ka·ch'e |
|---|---|---|
| on the corner | কর্নারে | kor·na·re |
| straight ahead | সোজা | shoh·ja |

## EATING & DRINKING

| Can you recommend a ...? | একটা ভাল ... কোথায় হবে বলেন তো? | ak·ta b'a·lo ... koh·t'a·e ho·be boh·len toh |
|---|---|---|
| cafe | ক্যাফেটেরিয়া | ka·fe·te·ri·a |
| restaurant | রেস্তোরা | res·toh·ra |

| Where would you go for (a) ...? | ... জন্য কোথায় যাবো? | ... john·no koh·t'a·e ja·boh |
|---|---|---|
| cheap meal | সস্তা খাবারের | shos·ta·e k'a·ba·rer |
| local specialities | এখানকার বিশেষ খাবার | e·k'an·kar bi·shesh k'a·bar |

| I'd like to reserve a table for ... | আমি ... একটা টেবিল রিজার্ভ করতে চাই। | aa·mi ... ak·ta te·bil ri·zarv kohr·te chai |
|---|---|---|
| (eight) o'clock | (আটার) সময় | (aat·tar) sho·moy |
| (two) people | (দুই) জনের জন্য | (dui) jo·ner john·no |

**What would you recommend?**
আপনি কি খেতে বলেন? *aap·ni ki k'e·ţe boh·len*

**What's in that dish?**
এই খাবারে কি কি আছে? *ei k'a·ba·re ki ki aa·ch'e*

**I'll have that.**
আমি ওটা নিব। *aa·mi oh·ta ni·boh*

**I'm vegan.**
আমি মাছ মাংস ডিম *aa·mi maach mang·shoh*
দুধ খাই না। *dim dud' k'ai na*

**I'm vegetarian.**
আমি ভেজিটেরিয়ান। *aa·mi ve·ji·te·ri·an*

**I don't eat (meat/chicken/fish/eggs).**
আমি (মাংস/মুরগী/মাছ/ডিম) *aa·mi (mang·shoh/mur·gi/*
খাই না। *mach/dim) k'ai na*

**Not too spicy, please.**
মশলা কম, প্লিজ। *mosh·la kom pleez*

**Is this bottled water?**
এটা কি বোতলের পানি? *e·ta ki boh·ţoh·ler pa·ni*

**No more, thank you.**
আর না, ধন্যবাদ। *aar naa d'oh·noh·baad*

**That was delicious.**
খুব মজা ছিল। *k'ub mo·ja ch'i·loh*

**I'm allergic** আমার ...-এ *aa·mar ...·e*
**to ...** এ্যালার্জি আছে। *ą·lar·ji aa·ch'e*

  **nuts** বাদাম *baa·dam*

  **shellfish** চিংড়ি মাছ *ching·ŗi maach'*

**Please bring ...** ... আনেন প্লিজ। *... aa·nen pleez*

  **a fork** একটা কাটা *ąk·ta ka·ta*

  **a glass** একটা গ্লাস *ąk·ta glash*

  **a knife** একটা ছুরি *ąk·ta ch'u·ri*

  **a menu** মেনু *me·nu*

  **a spoon** একটা চামুচ *ąk·ta cha·much*

  **an ashtray** একটা এ্যাসট্রে *ąk·ta ąsh·tre*

  **the bill** বিলটা *bil·ta*

## Key Words

| beer | বিয়ার | *bi·ar* |
|---|---|---|
| bread | রুটি | *ru·ti* |
| breakfast | নাস্তা | *nash·ţa* |
| chilli | মরিচ | *moh·rich* |
| coffee | কফি | *ko·fi* |
| dinner | রাতের খাবার | *ra·ţer k'a·bar* |
| egg | ডিম | *ḑim* |
| fish | মাছ | *maach'* |
| fruit | ফল | *p'ol* |
| lentils | ডাল | *ḑaal* |
| lunch | দুপুরের খাওয়া | *du·pu·rer k'a·wa* |
| meat | মাংস | *mang·shoh* |
| milk | দুধ | *dud'* |

| rice | ভাত | *b'aaţ* |
|---|---|---|
| tea | চা | *cha* |
| vegetable | সবজি | *shohb·ji* |
| water | পানি | *pa·ni* |
| wine | মদ | *mod* |

## EMERGENCIES

**Call ...!** ... ডাকেন! *... da·ken*

  **a doctor** ডাক্তার *ḑak·ţar*

  **the police** পুলিশ *pu·lish*

**Help!**
বাচান! *ba·chan*

**Go away!**
চলে যান! *choh·le jan*

**I'm lost.**
আমি হারিয়ে গেছি। *aa·mi ha·ri·ye gą·ch'i*

**Where are the toilets?**
টয়লেট কোথায়? *toy·let koh·ţ'a·e*

**I'm sick.**
আমি অসুস্থ। *aa·mi o·shush·ţ'oh*

**It hurts here.**
এখানে ব্যাথা করছে। *e·k'a·ne bą·ţ'a kohr·ch'e*

**I'm allergic to (antibiotics).**
আমার (এ্যান্টিবায়োটিক)এ *aa·mar (ąn·ti·bai·o·tik)·e*
এ্যালার্জি আছে। *ą·lar·ji aa·ch'e*

## SHOPPING

**Where's** ... কোথায়? *... koh·ţ'a·e*
**a/the ...?**

  **bank** ব্যাংক *bąnk*

  **department** ডিপার্টমেন্ট *di·part·ment*
  **store** স্টোর *stohr*

  **market** বাজার *baa·jar*

  **tourist** পর্যটন *pohr·joh·tohn*
  **office** কেন্দ্র *ken·droh*

**I'd like to buy (an adaptor plug).**
একটা (এ্যাডাপ্টার প্লাগ) *ąk·ta (ą·ḑap·tar plag)*
কিনতে চাই। *kin·ţe chai*

**I'm just looking.**
আমি দেখছি। *aa·mi dek·ch'i*

**Can I look at it?**
এটা দেখতে পারি? *e·ta dek'·ţe paa·ri*

**How much is it?**
এটার দাম কত? *e·tar dam ko·ţoh*

**Can you write down the price?**
দামটা কি লিখে দিতে *dam·ta ki li·k'e di·ţe*
পারেন? *paa·ren*

**That's too expensive.**
বেশী দাম। *be·shi dam*

**Can you lower the price?**
দাম কমান। *dam ko·man*

## TIME & DATES

Bengalis use the 12-hour clock. There's no such concept as 'am' or 'pm' – the time of day is indicated by adding *sho·kaal* (morning), *du·pur* (afternoon) or *raaṭ* (night) before the time. To tell the time, add the suffix *·ta* to the ordinal number which indicates the hour.

**What time is it?**
কয়টা বাজে? *koy·ta baa·je*

**It's (10) o'clock.**
(দশটা) বাজে। *(dosh·ta) baa·je*

**Quarter past ...**
সোয়া ... *shoh·aa ...*

**Half past ...**
সাড়ে ... *shaa·ṛe ...*

**Quarter to ...**
পৌনে ... *poh·ne ...*

**At what time ...?**
কটার সময় ...? *ko·tar sho·moy ...*

**At (10) in the morning.**
সকাল (দশটা)। *sho·kaal (dosh·ta)*

**today**
আজকে *aaj·ke*

| | | |
|---|---|---|
| **yesterday ...** | গতকাল ... | *go·ṭoh·kaal ...* |
| **tomorrow ...** | আগামিকাল ... | *aa·ga·mi·kaal ...* |
| **morning** | সকাল | *sho·kaal* |
| **afternoon** | দুপুর | *du·pur* |
| **evening** | বিকাল | *bee·kaal* |

| | | |
|---|---|---|
| **Monday** | সোমবার | *shohm·baar* |
| **Tuesday** | মঙ্গলবার | *mohng·gohl·baar* |
| **Wednesday** | বুধবার | *bud'·baar* |
| **Thursday** | বৃহস্পতিবার | *bri·hosh·poh·ṭi·baar* |
| **Friday** | শুক্রবার | *shuk·roh·baar* |
| **Saturday** | শনিবার | *shoh·ni·baar* |
| **Sunday** | রবিবার | *roh·bi·baar* |

| | | |
|---|---|---|
| **January** | জানুয়ারি | *jaa·nu·aa·ri* |
| **February** | ফেব্রুয়ারি | *feb·ru·aa·ri* |
| **March** | মার্চ | *maarch* |
| **April** | এপ্রিল | *ep·reel* |
| **May** | মে | *me* |
| **June** | জুন | *jun* |
| **July** | জুলাই | *ju·lai* |
| **August** | আগস্ট | *aa·gohst* |
| **September** | সেপ্টেম্বার | *sep·tem·baar* |
| **October** | অক্টোবার | *ok·toh·baar* |
| **November** | নভেম্বার | *no·b'em·baar* |
| **December** | ডিসেম্বার | *di·sem·baar* |

## TRANSPORT

### Public Transport

| | | |
|---|---|---|
| **Which ... goes to (Comilla)?** | কোন ... (কুমিল্লা) যায়? | *kohn ... (ku·mil·laa) ja·e* |
| **bus** | বাস | bas |
| **train** | ট্রেন | tren |
| **tram** | ট্রাম | ṭram |
| | | |
| **When's the ... (bus)?** | ... (বাস) কখন? | *... (bas) ko·k'ohn* |
| **first** | প্রথম | *proh·t'ohm* |
| **last** | শেষ | shesh |
| **next** | পরের | *po·rer* |
| | | |
| **... bus** | ... বাস | ... bas |
| **city** | শহর | *sho·hohr* |
| **express** | এক্সপ্রেস | *eks·pres* |
| **intercity** | ইন্টারসিটি | *in·tar·see·ti* |
| **local** | লোকাল | *loh·kaal* |
| **ordinary** | অর্ডিনারি | *o·di·naa·ri* |

| Numbers | | |
|---|---|---|
| 1 | ১ | ạk |
| 2 | ২ | dui |
| 3 | ৩ | ṭeen |
| 4 | ৪ | chaar |
| 5 | ৫ | paach |
| 6 | ৬ | ch'oy |
| 7 | ৭ | shaaṭ |
| 8 | ৮ | aat |
| 9 | ৯ | noy |
| 10 | ১০ | dosh |
| 20 | ২০ | beesh |
| 30 | ৩০ | ṭi·rish |
| 40 | ৪০ | *chohl·lish* |
| 50 | ৫০ | *pon·chaash* |
| 60 | ৬০ | shaat |
| 70 | ৭০ | *shohṭ·ṭur* |
| 80 | ৮০ | *aa·shi* |
| 90 | ৯০ | *nohb·boh·i* |
| 100 | ১০০ | ạk shoh |
| 200 | ২০০ | dui shoh |
| 1000 | ১০০০ | ạk haa·jaar |
| 100,000 | ১০০০০০ | ạk laak' |
| one million | ১০০০০০০ | dosh laak' |

## Question Words

| | | |
|---|---|---|
| how many | কয়টা | koy·ta |
| how much | কত | ko·toh |
| when | কখন | ko·k'ohn |
| where | কোথায় | koh·t'ai |
| who | কে | ke |
| why | কেন | kạ·noh |

| | | |
|---|---|---|
| A ... ticket (to Dhaka). | (ঢাকার) জন্য একটা ... টিকেট। | (d'aa·kaar) john·noh ạk·ta ... ti·ket |
| 1st-class | ফার্স্ট ক্লাস | farst klaas |
| 2nd-class | সেকেন্ড ক্লাস | se·kend klaas |
| one-way | ওয়ানওয়ে | wan·way |
| return | রিটার্ন | ri·tarn |
| student | ছাত্র | ch'aṭ·roh |

### Where's the booking office for foreigners?
বিদেশিদের জন্য
বুকিং অফিস কোথায়?
bi·de·shi·der john·noh
bu·king o·feesh koh·t'a·e

### Where do I buy a ticket?
কোথায় টিকেট কিনবো? koh·t'a·e ti·ket kin·boh

### What time does it leave?
কখন ছাড়বে? ko·k'ohn ch'aaṛ·be

### How long will it be delayed?
কত দেরি হবে? ko·toh de·ri ho·be

### How long does the trip take?
যেতে কতক্ষন লাগবে? je·ṭe ko·tohk·k'ohn laa·ge

### Do I need to change trains?
আমাকে কি চেঞ্জ
করতে হবে ট্রেন?
aa·maa·ke ki chenj
kohr·ṭe ho·be tren

### Is this seat available?
এই সিট কি খালি? ay seet ki k'aa·lee

### What's the next stop?
পরের স্টপ কি? po·rer stop ki

### Please tell me when we get to (Sylhet).
(সিলেট) আসলে আমাকে
বলবেন, প্লিজ।
(si·let) aash·le aa·maa·ke
bohl·ben pleez

### I'd like to get off at (Mongla).
আমি (মঙ্গলাতে)
নামতে চাই।
aa·mi (mong·laa·ṭe)
naam·ṭe chai

### Is this taxi available?
এই ট্যাক্সি খালি? ay tạk·si k'aa·li

---

### How much is it to ...?
... যেতে কত লাগবে? ... je·ṭe ko·toh laag·be

### Please put the meter on.
প্লিজ মিটার লাগান। pleez mee·tar laa·gan

### Please take me to this address.
আমাকে এই ঠিকানায়
নিয়ে যান।
aa·ma·ke ay t'i·kaa·nai
ni·ye jaan

## Driving & Cycling

| | | |
|---|---|---|
| I'd like to hire a/an ... | আমি একটা ... ভাড়া করতে চাই। | aa·mi ạk·ta ... b'a·ṛa kohr·te chai |
| 4WD | ফোর হুইল ড্রাইভ | fohr weel draiv |
| bicycle | সাইকেল | sai·kel |
| car | গাড়ি | gaa·ṛi |
| motorbike | মটরসাইকেল | mo·tohr·sai·kel |
| diesel | ডিজেল | di·zel |
| regular | পেট্রোল | pet·rohl |
| unleaded | অকটেন | ok·ten (octane) |

### Is this the road to (Rangamati)?
এটা কি (রাঙ্গামাটির)
রাস্তা?
e·ta ki (raang·a·maa·tir)
raas·ṭa

### Where's a petrol station?
পেট্রোল স্টেশন কোথায়? pet·rohl ste·shohn koh·t'a·e

### Please fill it up.
ভর্তি করে দেন, প্লিজ। b'ohr·ṭi koh·re dạn pleez

### I'd like (20) litres.
আমার (বিশ) লিটার
লাগবে।
aa·mar (beesh) li·tar
laag·be

### I need a mechanic.
আমার একজন
মেকানিক লাগবে।
aa·mar ạk·john
me·kaa·nik laag·be

### The car/motorbike has broken down at (Sylhet).
গাড়ি/মটরসাইকেল
(সিলেট) নষ্ট হয়ে গেছে।
gaa·ṛi/mo·tohr·sai·kel
(si·let) nosh·toh hoh·e gạ·ch'e

### I have a flat tyre.
আমার গাড়ির একটা চাকা
পাংচার হয়ে গেছে।
aa·mar gaa·ṛir ạk·ta chaa·ka
pank·char hoh·e gạ·ch'e

### I've run out of petrol.
আমার পেট্রোল শেষ
হয়ে গেছে।
aa·mar pet·rohl shesh
hoh·e gạ·ch'e

## GLOSSARY

**Adivasis** – tribal people

**AL** – Awami League; the mainstream centre-left, secular political party in Bangladesh, and the governing party as of the 2008 elections

**baby taxi** – auto-rickshaw, usually called a CNG these days

**baksheesh** – donation, tip or bribe, depending on the context

**Bangla** – the national language of Bangladesh (see *Bengali*);

also the new name for the Indian state of West Bengal

**bangla** – architectural style associated with the Pre-Mauryan and Mauryan period (312–232 BC); exemplified by a bamboo-thatched hut with a distinctively curved roof

**baras** – ancient houseboats

**bawalis** – timber workers in the Sundarbans

**Bengali** – the national language of Bangladesh, where it is also known as *Bangla*, and the official language of the state of Bangla (formerly West Bengal) in India

**BIWTC** – Bangladesh Inland Waterway Transport Corporation

**BNP** – Bangladesh Nationalist Party; the mainstream centre-right political party in Bangladesh, and the largest opposition party as of the 2008 elections

**BRAC** – Bangladesh Rural Advancement Committee

**BRTC** – Bangladesh Road Transport Corporation

**cha** – tea, usually served with milk and sugar

**char** – a river or delta island made of silt; highly fertile but highly susceptible to flooding and erosion

**CNG** – auto-rickshaw run on compressed natural gas

**DC** – District Commissioner

**Eid** – Muslim holiday

**ghat** – steps or landing on a river

**hammam** – bath house

**haors** – wetlands

**hartals** – strikes, ranging from local to national

**jamdani** – ornamental loom-embroidered muslin or silk

**jor bangla** – twin-hut architectural style

**kantha** – traditional indigo-dyed muslin

**khyang** – Buddhist temple

**kuthi** – factory

**launch** – public ferry

**madhu** – honey; also *mau*

**mahavihara** – large monastery

**maidan** – open grassed area in

a town or city, used as a parade ground during the Raj

**mandir** – temple

**masjid** – mosque

**mau** – honey; also *madhu*

**maualis** – honey-gatherers in the Sundarbans

**mazar** – grave/tomb

**mela** – festival

**mihrab** – niche in a mosque positioned to face Mecca; Muslims face in this direction when they pray

**mishuk** – smaller auto-rickshaw with a four-stroke; now banned in Dhaka

**mistris** – rickshaw makers

**mohajons** – rickshaw- or taxi-fleet owners (also known as *maliks*)

**Mughal** – the Muslim dynasty of Indian emperors from Babur to Aurangzeb (16th to 18th century)

**mustan** – Mafia-style bosses who demand, and receive, payment from auto drivers, roadside vendors and people living on public land

**nakshi kantha** – embroided quilt

**nava-ratna** – nine-towered; used to describe certain mosques

**nawab** – Muslim prince

**paisa** – unit of currency; there are 100 paisa in a taka

**Parjatan** – the official Bangladesh-government tourist organisation

**Raj** – also called the British Raj; the period of British government in the Indian subcontinent, roughly from the mid-18th century to the mid-20th century

**raj** – rule or sovereignty

**raja** – ruler, landlord or king

**rajbari** – Raj-era palace or mansion built by a *zamindar*

**Ramzan** – Bengali name for Ramadan

**rekha** – buildings with a square sanctum on a raised platform

**reserve** – privately hired vehicles, including boats

**rest house** – government-owned guesthouse

**rickshaw** – small, three-wheeled bicycle-driven passenger vehicle

**rickshaw-wallah** – rickshaw rider

**Rocket** – paddle steamer

**sadhu** – itinerant holy man

**salwar kameez** – a long, dress-like tunic (kameez) worn by women over a pair of baggy trousers (salwar)

**shankhari** – Hindu artisan

**Shi'ia** – Islamic sect that sees the authority of Mohammed as continuing through Ali, his son-in-law

**Shiva** – Hindu god; the destroyer, the creator

**shuvon** – upper-2nd class on a train

**shulov** – lower-2nd class on a train

**stupa** – moundlike structure or spire containing Buddhist relics, typically the remains of the Buddha

**Sufi** – ascetic Muslim mystic

**Sunni** – school of Islamic thought that sees the authority of Mohammed as continuing through Abu Bakr, the former governor of Syria

**taka** – currency of Bangladesh

**tea estate** – terraced hillside where tea is grown; also tea garden

**tempo** – shared auto-rickshaw

**vihara** – monastery

**zamindar** – landlord; also the name of the feudal-landowner system itself

**zila** – district

# behind the scenes

## SEND US YOUR FEEDBACK

We love to hear from travellers – your comments keep us on our toes and help make our books better. Our well-travelled team reads every word on what you loved or loathed about this book. Although we cannot reply individually to postal submissions, we always guarantee that your feedback goes straight to the appropriate authors, in time for the next edition. Each person who sends us information is thanked in the next edition – the most useful submissions are rewarded with a selection of digital PDF chapters.

Visit **lonelyplanet.com/contact** to submit your updates and suggestions or to ask for help. Our award-winning website also features inspirational travel stories, news and discussions.

Note: We may edit, reproduce and incorporate your comments in Lonely Planet products such as guidebooks, websites and digital products, so let us know if you don't want your comments reproduced or your name acknowledged. For a copy of our privacy policy visit lonelyplanet.com/privacy.

## OUR READERS

**Many thanks to the travellers who used the last edition and wrote to us with helpful hints, useful advice and interesting anecdotes:**

Reinaut Aerts, Renee Ahar, Emmanuelle Ahmed, Mehzabin Ahmed, Monirul Ahsan, Shayne Atkins, Leonie Bartlett, Jenny Boehm, Stacey Bradbury, Mélody Braun, Anna Burnat-Olech, Sam Butler, Nelson Chen, Abu Naser Chowdhury, Jens Conrad, Kelly Dewey, Margot Emart, Karin Fankhauserf, Claas Feye, Jérôme Fontana, Josh Foreman, David French, Jordan Goulding, Pauline Groussaud, Moynul Hasan, Markus Kaim, Maria Jeppesen Knudsen, Rainer Kopp, Simonas Laukaitis, Benjamin Linder, James Mackie, Saki Marais, Nicolas Merky, Brandon Mewhort, Jinsoo Min, Jane Newcombe, Biklane Nilse, Krzysztof Olech, Chloe Pinel, Lars Repp, Syed Salehein, Sandra Schreck, Alice Self, Lucie Sindelkova, Giles Skerry, Jiri Smitak, Mike Stapleton, David Starritt, Martina Turner, Jessica Vabner, Maerle & Sjoerd van Berkel, Judith van den Hoven, Rombout van Kuijk, Stefania Vele, Nicholas Watson, Jonas Wernli, Elizabeth Williams, Stefan F Windberger, Wojciech Wojcik

## AUTHOR THANKS

### Daniel McCrohan

Huge thanks to Mahmud Hasan Khan, not only for his tireless efforts in helping me put together this guidebook but also for being the guardian angel of travellers to Bangladesh. We all appreciate your boundless enthusiasm and generosity. Big thanks too to Fazlay Rabby for his hiking expertise, and to Mahfuz Hossain Khan for his advice on the wetlands.

For help and good company on the road, cheers to Ollie Fitchie (UK), Anisur Noyon (Dhaka), Sumon (Mymensingh), Khalid Hasan (Tangail) and Ismile Hossain Mehedi (Chittagong).

A special thank you goes to my mum – nurse-in-absentia extraordinaire – for being by the phone when it mattered. And love, as always, to my darling Taotao and our two incredible children.

## ACKNOWLEDGMENTS

Climate map data adapted from Peel MC, Finlayson BL & McMahon TA (2007) 'Updated World Map of the Köppen-Geiger Climate Classification', *Hydrology and Earth System Sciences*, 11, 163344.

Cover photograph: A man selling fruit from his boat on the Buriganga River, GMB Akash/Panos.

# THIS BOOK

This guidebook was commissioned in Lonely Planet's Melbourne office. It was written by Daniel McCrohan, with the Health chapter based on text written by Dr Trish Bachelor, and produced by the following:

**Commissioning Editors**
Kate Morgan, Glenn van der Knijff

**Coordinating Editors**
Rebecca Chau, Kate James

**Coordinating Cartographer** Jacqueline Nguyen

**Coordinating Layout Designer** Jacqui Saunders

**Managing Editor** Barbara Delissen

**Senior Editors** Andi Jones, Susan Paterson

**Managing Cartographer** Shahara Ahmed, Adrian Persoglia

**Managing Layout Designer** Jane Hart

**Assisting Editor** Cathryn Game

**Cover Research** Naomi Parker

**Internal Image Research** Rebecca Skinner

**Language Content** Branislava Vladisavljevic

**Thanks to** Piotr Czajkowski, Brigitte Ellemor, Ryan Evans, Larissa Frost, Joshua Geoghegan, Trent Paton, Martine Power, Gerard Walker

NOTES

NOTES

# index

## A

accommodation 166, *see also individual locations*
  eco-resorts 128
  language 189
activities 166, *see also individual activities*
Adivasi people 11, 64, **11**
  in Chittagong Hill Tracts 120
  Ethnological Museum 110
  Tribal Cultural Institute Museum 119
Adivasi villages 115-16, 142-3
Aggameda Khyang 124
Ahsan Manzil 37-8
air travel
  airlines 175, 176
  airports 13, 55, 175
  to/from Bangladesh 175-6
  within Bangladesh 176
Akhaura border crossing 22, 23
amoebic dysentry 185-6
animals, *see* wildlife
area codes 171
Armenian Church of the Holy Resurrection 39
art 161-2
art galleries 43, *see also* museums
arts, *see* literature, music
ATMs 168-9

## B

Bagerhat 76-9, **78**
Baitul Mukarram Mosque 42
baksheesh 169
Bandarban 113-17, **114**
Banga Bazar 51
Bangladesh Tea Research Institute 141
Bangladesh Tiger Action Plan 73
Bangshal Rd (Bicycle St) 39
Bara Katra 38-9

**000** Map pages
**000** Photo pages

Bara Khyang statue 127-8
Barisal 83-5, **84**
Barisal division 31, 83-6, **67**
  climate 66
  highlights 67
  travel seasons 66
bathrooms 171
bazaars, *see* markets & bazaars
beaches 14
  Cox's Bazar 124-7, **126**
  Kuakata 85-6
  St Martin's Island 128-30
bedbugs 186
Benapole border crossing 22, 23
Bicycle St (Bangshal Rd) 39
bicycle travel, *see* cycling
birds 73, 133, 157-8
bird-watching
  field guides 159
  Sunamganj 29, 138-9
Birisiri 64-5
Bishwa Ijtema 16
boat trips 6, 15, 26-9, 166, **6**
  Chittagong division 106, 112
  Dhaka 43
  Fatra Char 86
  Rocket (paddle-wheel steamer) 9, 26-7, 28, 71, **9**
  Sangu River 115-16
Bogra 89-91, **90**
books
  bird-watching field guides 159
  food 164
  nonfiction 148-9, 153, 154, 155
  novels 149
border crossings 22-5
budgeting 12, 166
Buriganga River 28, 37
Burimari border crossing 23-4
bus travel 177-8, 179
business hours 166-7

## C

cabs 179
car travel 178
  language 192
cash 169
cathedrals, *see* churches
cell phones 170-1
*cha, see* tea
Chakma Islands 119
chars (sandbank islands) 91, 95
Chhota Sona Masjid 102
chemists 53
children, travel with 167
China Clay Hills 28, 65
Chittagong 108-13, **108**

Chittagong division 31, 106-32, **107**
  boat trips 106, 112
  climate 106
  highlights 107
  hiking & walking 106
  travel seasons 106
Chittagong Hill Tracts 11, 116, 120-1, **8**
Chota Katra 38-9
Chowdhury, Dewan Hasan Raja 135
churches
  Armenian Church of the Holy Resurrection 39
  St Paul's Catholic Church 74
cinema 161
climate 12, 16-17, *see also individual regions*
CNG (auto-rickshaw) travel 179
coffee shops (Dhaka) 51
Comilla 130-2, **131**
consulates 167-8
costs 12, 166
courses 167
Cox's Bazar 14, 124-7, **126**
credit cards 169
crime 169
currency 168
curries 163
customs regulations 167
cycling 166, 176-7
  around Srimangal 8, 139-40, 142
  language 192

## D

dangers, *see* safety
departure tax 24
Dhaka 30, 34-56, **35**, **40-1**, **46-7**
  accommodation 34, 43-7
  activities 42-3
  climate 34
  coffee shops 51
  cycling 176
  drinking 50
  entertainment 50-1
  food 34, 47-50
  highlights 35
  history 36-7
  Old Dhaka 11, **36**
  orientation 38
  shopping 51-2
  sights 37-42
  tea stalls 49
  tours 43
  travel seasons 34
  travel to/from 53-5
  travel within 55-6
Dhaka division 30, 57-65, **58**
  climate 57
  highlights 58

# how to use this book

These symbols will help you find the listings you want:

| | | | | | |
|---|---|---|---|---|---|
| ⊙ | Sights | ☞ | Tours | ⊻ | Drinking |
| 🏊 | Beaches | 🎎 | Festivals & Events | ☆ | Entertainment |
| 🏃 | Activities | 📒 | Sleeping | 🔒 | Shopping |
| 🤝 | Courses | ✕ | Eating | ❶ | Information/Transport |

**Look out for these icons:**

| | |
|---|---|
| TOP CHOICE | Our author's recommendation |
| FREE | No payment required |
| 🌱 | A green or sustainable option |

*Our authors have nominated these places as demonstrating a strong commitment to sustainability – for example by supporting local communities and producers, operating in an environmentally friendly way, or supporting conservation projects.*

These symbols give you the vital information for each listing:

| | | | | | |
|---|---|---|---|---|---|
| ☑ | Telephone Numbers | ☎ | Wi-Fi Access | 🚌 | Bus |
| ⊙ | Opening Hours | ⊠ | Swimming Pool | ⛴ | Ferry |
| P | Parking | ✎ | Vegetarian Selection | Ⓜ | Metro |
| ⊖ | Nonsmoking | ▣ | English-Language Menu | Ⓢ | Subway |
| ✳ | Air-Conditioning | ✦ | Family-Friendly | ⊖ | London Tube |
| @ | Internet Access | ✿ | Pet-Friendly | 🚋 | Tram |
| | | | | 🚆 | Train |

Reviews are organised by author preference.

## Map Legend

### Sights
- ⊙ Beach
- ⊜ Buddhist
- ⊙ Castle
- ⊙ Christian
- ⊙ Hindu
- ⊙ Islamic
- ⊗ Jewish
- ❶ Monument
- ⊕ Museum/Gallery
- ⊗ Ruin
- ⊛ Winery/Vineyard
- ⊛ Zoo
- ⊙ Other Sight

### Activities, Courses & Tours
- ⊜ Diving/Snorkelling
- ⊛ Canoeing/Kayaking
- ⊙ Skiing
- ⊙ Surfing
- ⊜ Swimming/Pool
- ⊙ Walking
- ⊙ Windsurfing
- ⊙ Other Activity/Course/Tour

### Sleeping
- ⊜ Sleeping
- ⊙ Camping

### Eating
- ⊗ Eating

### Drinking
- ⊜ Drinking
- ⊜ Cafe

### Entertainment
- ⊙ Entertainment

### Shopping
- ⊙ Shopping

### Information
- ⑤ Bank
- ⊙ Embassy/Consulate
- ⊕ Hospital/Medical
- @ Internet
- ⊙ Police
- ⊙ Post Office
- ⊙ Telephone
- ⊙ Toilet
- ❶ Tourist Information
- ● Other Information

### Transport
- ⊙ Airport
- ⊗ Border Crossing
- ⊙ Bus
- ⊹⊙⊹ Cable Car/Funicular
- -⊙- Cycling
- -⊙- Ferry
- ⊙ Monorail
- P Parking
- ⊙ Petrol Station
- ⊙ Taxi
- ⊹⊙⊹ Train/Railway
- ⊹⊙⊹ Tram
- Ⓜ Underground Train Station
- ● Other Transport

### Routes
- Tollway
- Freeway
- Primary
- Secondary
- Tertiary
- Lane
- Unsealed Road
- Plaza/Mall
- Steps
- ⊐ ⊐ Tunnel
- Pedestrian Overpass
- Walking Tour
- Walking Tour Detour
- Path

### Geographic
- ⊙ Hut/Shelter
- ⊙ Lighthouse
- ⊙ Lookout
- ▲ Mountain/Volcano
- ⊙ Oasis
- ⊙ Park
- )( Pass
- ⊙ Picnic Area
- ⊙ Waterfall

### Population
- ⊙ Capital (National)
- ◉ Capital (State/Province)
- ● City/Large Town
- ⊙ Town/Village

### Boundaries
- ––– International
- ––– State/Province
- –– Disputed
- – – Regional/Suburb
- Marine Park
- Cliff
- Wall

### Hydrography
- River, Creek
- Intermittent River
- Swamp/Mangrove
- Reef
- Canal
- Water
- Dry/Salt/Intermittent Lake
- Glacier

### Areas
- Beach/Desert
- + + + Cemetery (Christian)
- × × × Cemetery (Other)
- Park/Forest
- Sportsground
- Sight (Building)
- Top Sight (Building)

# OUR STORY

A beat-up old car, a few dollars in the pocket and a sense of adventure. In 1972 that's all Tony and Maureen Wheeler needed for the trip of a lifetime – across Europe and Asia overland to Australia. It took several months, and at the end – broke but inspired – they sat at their kitchen table writing and stapling together their first travel guide, *Across Asia on the Cheap*. Within a week they'd sold 1500 copies. Lonely Planet was born.

Today, Lonely Planet has offices in Melbourne, London and Oakland, with more than 600 staff and writers. We share Tony's belief that 'a great guidebook should do three things: inform, educate and amuse'.

# OUR WRITER

### Daniel McCrohan

Daniel first fell in love with Bangladesh way back in 1998 and has since made multiple trips here, chalking up many months' worth of Bangla-travel. He has worked extensively throughout Asia (his adopted home since leaving England more than eight years ago), but particularly enjoys this region, one of the few parts of South Asia, he says, that still has yet to be properly discovered by travellers. Daniel has worked on more than a dozen other Lonely Planet guides including *India*, *Tibet* and *China*. He also cohosted the Lonely Planet television series *Best in China*. You can follow his Asia travels on Twitter (@danielmccrohan), or through his website (danielmccrohan.com).

Read more about Daniel at
lonelyplanet.com/members/danielmccrohan

**Published by Lonely Planet Publications Pty Ltd**
ABN 36 005 607 983
7th edition – December 2012
ISBN 978 1 74179 458 8
© Lonely Planet 2012   Photographs © as indicated 2012
10 9 8 7 6 5 4 3 2 1
Printed in Singapore

Although the authors and Lonely Planet have taken all reasonable care in preparing this book, we make no warranty about the accuracy or completeness of its content and, to the maximum extent permitted, disclaim all liability arising from its use.